THE BIG 50

ST. LOUIS CARDINALS

The Men and Moments that Made the St. Louis Cardinals

Benjamin Hochman

TRIUMPH
BOOKS

Library of Congress Cataloging-in-Publication Data

Names: Hochman, Benjamin.
Title: The big 50 St. Louis Cardinals : the men and moments that made the St. Louis Cardinals / Benjamin Hochman.
Description: Chicago, Illinois : Triumph Books, 2018.
Identifiers: LCCN 2017049064 | ISBN 9781629375366 (paperback)
Subjects: LCSH: St. Louis Cardinals (Baseball team)—History. | Baseball players—United States—Biography. | BISAC: SPORTS & RECREATION / Baseball / General. | TRAVEL / United States / Midwest / West North Central (IA, KS, MN, MO, ND, NE, SD).
Classification: LCC GV875.S3 H62 2018 | DDC 796.357/640977866—dc23 LC record available at https://lccn.loc.gov/2017049064

This book is available in quantity at special discounts for your group or organization. For further information, contact:

Triumph Books LLC
814 North Franklin Street
Chicago, Illinois 60610
(312) 337-0747
www.triumphbooks.com

Printed in U.S.A.
ISBN: 978-1-62937-536-6

Design by Andy Hansen
All photos are courtesy of AP Images unless otherwise indicated.

To Angela, Dad, Mom, Emily, and Peggy.

[Contents]

[Foreword]

In *The Big 50: St. Louis Cardinals*, Benjamin Hochman explains the special history of the St. Louis Cardinals through 50 selected story lines that honor, inform, and entertain. His creativity and writing talents come together to make a great read.

I appreciate this opportunity to offer some insights as to why and how the stories described in the chapters became part of the Cardinals history. These insights are based on years of admiring the Cardinals as a player, an American League manager, and as a teammate.

Although my comments about the organization are totally positive, they are in no way meant to imply the Cardinals exclusively own these positive attributes. Too often when someone or something is praised, it comes off as a negative compared to others. Each of Major League Baseball's 30 organizations has its own story to tell about its unique and distinctive features.

When I joined the Cardinals in 1996, right away I was challenged to understand and commit to focusing on their priorities. My first mentors were Jack Buck and Mike Shannon. Jack had a unique teaching point. Over the years I realized that was an example of his brilliance. He explained Cardinals greatness was an equation where by definition both sides had equal weight.

One side of the equation was the Cardinals fans. He acknowledged that many teams had passionate fans, but only ours would support their team "win or lose," while other fans' support was limited to "win or tie." In addition to Jack's sharp description of St. Louis fans, I had attended the World Series in 1982, '85, and '87 and was impressed by their joy and sense of fair play. Over the years, I totally understood how much the fans significantly impacted how hard the team played every day of every season.

Mike was in charge of the other side of the equation—the competitive side. He and I had dinner early on in 1996. Some of the priorities he stressed were: make it all about team (teammates and teamwork), compete with maximum effort to win, concentrate on execution, and be good and tough enough.

The players felt these priorities were beyond talking points and that they defined how they played. They could not get away from these messages and did not want to. The history was powerful and all around them. For example, the Hall of Famers and other Cardinals players were encouraging and were expecting them to carry the torch.

The way the equation came together was classic. One side led by the fans, history, and veteran players made sure that the current team was mentally geared to compete. Then the other side's focus on playing hard and playing the game the right way provided their map to competing. As a result, the expectations and responsibility provided a healthy, positive edge.

From my perspective, this equation is a part of every chapter in this book. It's a term that is helpful to understand how it all comes together. And you will appreciate the real historical significance of this amazing franchise by concentrating on how each chapter contributes to the whole.

I was hooked as soon as I read the table of contents. Right away, each player and situation triggered wonderful memories. I couldn't wait to enjoy reading the stories told in those chapters and I'm sure you'll enjoy it, too.

—Tony La Russa
Cardinals manager, 1996–2011

[Author's Note]

I wanted to write a book I'd want to read. And I wanted to do something fresh—fun essays that capture everything that encompasses the Cardinals from the tradition to the quirks and from the classic moments to the moments and men who became cult classics.

And so this isn't as much of a book as it is a love letter. It's an homage to the city of St. Louis, to the fans of its baseball team, to everyone and everything that makes St. Louis a rich and rarefied baseball community. The book spans Willie to Whitey, "Here Comes The King" to "The Heat Is On," 1.12 to 1120, No. 5 to Channel 5, Tom Lawless' bat flip to toasted ravioli, and Dmitri Young's triple to David Freese's triple.

And I took a new take on old topics, such as a circus expert's analysis of the acrobatic Ozzie Smith or looking at Stan Musial's love affair with St. Louis restaurants—and how that defined The Man's relationship with St. Louis.

As I researched the book, I naturally interviewed the famous names, but I also talked to those who are pieces of the Cardinals' quilt, including the Busch Stadium organist, the team's official scorer, and That One Guy. I interviewed famous fans like Jenna Fischer, Jon Hamm, and Christopher Jackson, the original George Washington in *Hamilton*. And I interviewed everyday fans whose stories are relatable and remarkable.

I poured my heart into each chapter. I hope you enjoy them all!

THE BIG 50
ST. LOUIS CARDINALS

1

THE 2011 WORLD SERIES

The Knights of the Cauliflower Ear invited the Cardinals over for dinner. It was August 24, 2011, and the Cardinals stunk. But the group of esteemed St. Louisans were still honored to honor St. Louis' team. So after yet another loss to the Los Angeles Dodgers, the Cards arrived at the big banquet. The Knights of the Cauliflower Ear were founded in 1935, and the most famous guest to ever attend the dinner was Harry Truman, who also was known for a surprising upset.

That night in '11, the Cards were 10½ games back of the wild-card, 10 back of the National League Central-leading Milwaukee Brewers and their trash-tweeting outfielder Nyjer Morgan. In front of the Knights, an almost apologetic general manager John Mozeliak spoke, and then emcee Tom Ackerman interviewed Adam Wainwright, the injured pitcher and sports' tallest cheerleader. "Right now, it's not easy for anyone because we're not winning. This city deserves us to win, and we want to win," Waino said. "The way I look at it, we play the Brewers six more times. Yeah, we're down 10 games now. But if we beat them all six times, we're down four games. I don't think anybody in their right mind would be comfortable ahead of us, only up four games. So we've got a great chance because no one expects us to come back and win. We have a greater chance to do it because nobody is expecting it. We've proven it before that we can surprise people and we have the people that can do it!"

I lived in Denver at the time. I was born in St. Louis on May 5, 1980 and was 17 hours old when I heard my first Cardinals game.

Nestled in my father's arms in a room at St. John's Hospital, I dozed to the soothing lullaby of Jack Buck's play-by-play.

The first question any St. Louisan ever asks is: "Where'd ya go to high school?" Well, I went to Clayton High School and then studied journalism at the University of Missouri. In 2011 I was at *The Denver Post.* And as the Cards backdoored into the playoffs on the final night of the season, I was higher than anyone in town, and that's saying something.

The Cards won the National League Division Series in the epic Carpenter-Halladay game—something like an old Bob Gibson-Ferguson Jenkins duel, and on my wall is a framed copy of the *St. Louis Post-Dispatch* with Chris Carpenter engulfed by a hugging Yadi Molina. The headline reads: "PHILLIE-BUSTER."

That set up the delicious series against Milwaukee. The last time the two met in the postseason, St. Louis defeated Milwaukee in the '82 World Series. I was soon convinced it would happen again. See, as I got to the airport, heading home for the Cardinals-Brewers postseason rematch, I realized I was on American Airlines Flight 1982.

* * *

David Freese was one of us. It was so cool that a Cardinals player was actually from St. Louis. It's like he was the one, the lottery winner, the predestined Redbird plucked from the stands at some Cards-Expos game in '93 to be on the team when he grows up. He went to Lafayette High School. He was a Cardinal, he was superhuman, but he was about as human as one of the super ones can be.

He'd actually dropped out of Missouri and quit baseball, temporarily, only to go from a community college to a random college to the Major League Baseball Draft. And he battled demons, including a number of drunk-driving incidents. Every 24-year-old in St. Louis had an "I saw David Freese partying" story, and Freese admitted to *USA TODAY* in 2017 that he suffers from depression and drinking problems.

But he found balance, marrying a St. Louis girl. A Pittsburgh Pirate in 2017, Freese still receives raucous ovations at Busch Stadium. He's even still in TV ads for Imo's Pizza, a local St. Louis joint that makes flat-crust pizza lathered in Provel cheese. "He's just a normal, regular good guy," said Joe Buck, Jack's son and the FOX broadcaster for the '11 World Series. "I mean sometimes as childish as it sounds—or unfair as it sounds—when the good guys do well, it makes the moment that much sweeter for even the guy calling it. And he just had the moment of a lifetime."

Well, two. But even before the World Series—and not everyone remembers this—Freese was the best offensive player against the Brewers in the National League Championship Series. He won the MVP of that series, too.

But entering October 27, 2011, the Cardinals trailed the Texas Rangers three games to two. I flew back into town, had bleacher seats. Last row. That day, I went to lunch at Carl's Drive-In located on Route 66—not to be confused with (but often is) Carl's Deli, four miles away. Carl's Drive-In, this cube of goodness, is basically a door, a counter, a middle area to make steakburgers, another counter, and another door. There are 10 stools on each side. I looked across that day of Game 6, and there was Cardinals closer Jason Motte. "It's a good little spot," said Motte, six years later. "We kind of found it by accident, driving around one day. We ended up going there maybe once a homestand, once a month. We're normal people, we've got to eat, too. And it's a good spot. I'd never know if I wanted a small root beer or a large, and Kelly behind the counter would be like: 'Come on.' So I'd end up getting the large and also fries and a triple burger with cheese. Kelly would always give us a hard time and stuff like that. We came in there before Game 6, and she said, 'When you guys win tonight, you're going to have to come back tomorrow.'"

And man, that night, under the toothbrush lights, I was in a vacuum. This was the world, this was all that mattered. Game 6, it took a hold of me. Bottom of the ninth. Cardinals trailed 7–5. The tall Texas closer, Neftali Feliz, flirted with triple-digits.

Two on.

Two outs.

Two strikes.

Freese.

He thwacked the pitch, driving it to right field, where I watched from the last row of the bleachers. It was headed right below us. It all happened so fast, the outfielder racing toward the warning track, leaping in the air with his glove extended. Then? Wait, I couldn't see anything! Did he catch it? Did it go over the fence? The World Series had froze. Then I spotted it, rolling away from the wall. *There's the ball!* And like a superhero or something, Freese soared headfirst into third base. Tie game.

* * *

That night on the set of *Mad Men*, St. Louisan Jon Hamm was enraptured. Draped as Don Draper, Hamm crammed beside other cast members into the tiny trailer of Jay Ferguson (Stan Rizzo on *Mad Men*), who happened to be a fan of the Texas Rangers. "They'd knock on the door and say, 'We need you on set,'" Hamm shared with me. "And we'd all tumble out of the trailer, run back to the set, shoot whatever we needed to shoot, run back to the trailer, and watch the World Series…sprinting, I mean, sprinting in dress shoes and '60s suits. Freese triples, Jay's crestfallen, and I'm running around doing a victory dance. Literally, the trailer is bouncing."

* * *

I felt bad even talking about it with Motte. "It's all part of the story," he said. "Some people remember, some people don't, but I went back out and pitched the 10th inning. And that's when Josh Hamilton hit the two-run home run off me and put them back up again by two. I remember when Hamilton hit it, I literally thought to myself on the mound, *Man, I just lost the World Series.*"

But St. Louis chipped away. A 9–7 score became 9–8 in the bottom of the 10th inning.

And again…Two on, two out, two strikes. Lance Berkman hit an RBI single to tie the game at 9.

Said Buck on the broadcast: "They. Just. Won't. Go. Away."

* * *

That night, on the set of *The Office*, St. Louisan Ellie Kemper was enraptured. "I remember listening to Game 6 of the 2011 World Series on the radio," she shared. "We were shooting the "Pool Party" episode

Local legend David Freese celebrates his 11th inning, walk-off home run during Game 6 of the 2011 World Series.

of *The Office*, and fellow St. Louisan Phyllis Smith and I kept rushing back out to a passenger van to keep up with the game on the van's radio. I'm not sure why we didn't just watch it on our phones. Phyllis and I had our own style of doing things. But listening to it actually made it all the more exciting. Game 6 of that series was one of the most thrilling games ever. Even though I was away in California, I felt so happy to have sweet Phyllis and our St. Louis spirit so close."

* * *

It's a feeling you can't explain, but you don't need to because everyone else in town experienced it, too. Tie game, bottom 11th. Freese's walk-off homer won Game 6.

A celebratory Hamm really was a mad man. Ellie hugged Phyllis. I hugged strangers. "We. Will see you. Tomorrow night!" Buck said on FOX, an indelible moment and also an homage to his late father, who made the very same call on an extra-innings, Game 6, walk-off World Series homer back in 1991 by Kirby Puckett. Freese, the St. Louisan, had just saved St. Louis. "You could author any number of moments, but nothing could ever be like that," said Ackerman, the KMOX Radio sports director and emcee from the Knights of the Cauliflower Ear dinner. "You can't recreate that magic, and I don't know if you'd want to."

Before Game 7, manager Tony La Russa told the team about the 1980 U.S. Olympic hockey team. They beat the Soviet Union, of course. But they still had one more game to play—against Finland—to secure the gold medal. It was the perfect parallel. If you don't win Game 7, Game 6 won't matter.

Motte stuck with the same pregame routine. "We went back to Carl's the next day," he said. "Oh yeah, you got to. We're a little superstitious, us baseball players. It had to have been the Carl's that helped us win. And it ended up being one of the best nights."

The Cards actually trailed 2–0 in the first inning of Game 7. It was Freese who tied it with a two-run double. Of course it was. I watched from the same last row of the right-field bleachers, standing next to Michael Slonim, my best friend from growing up. We were going to experience this thing together. "We were up four in the ninth, when they called down and told me I had it," Motte said. "I remember walking out of the bullpen and taking everything in, more than I had in the past. *Man, this is pretty cool.* After the final out was made, I turned to Yadi and was like, 'Hey, come get some, baby!' He was running out, and I remember going to put my arms around him, as he's jumping in the air, and then next thing you know, I'm getting sideswiped from the rest of the bench! And I completely had blinders on. I hadn't been looking at anyone else, just seeing Yadi. And I know my joy and my emotion in that moment was pretty awesome, but for me, I got to see Yadi's face. He's got that smile, running out at me, and it's one of those things I'll never forget baseball-wise. It's burned into my mind."

Ours, too.

2

THE MAN

He sure loved those crab cakes. Kreis' Steakhouse in St. Louis fittingly opened in 1948, the greatest year of all of Stan Musial's great years. And even into his final years, The Man would order the Jumbo Lump Crab Cakes with that remoulade sauce. And he'd devour the Florida Stone Crabs at Gerard's over at Ballas and Manchester, the old place that seems frozen in 1981. And at The Charcoal House, known for the Chateaubriand, he'd just get the burger and enjoy the heck out of it.

Musial ate up restaurants. He loved the experience of these St. Louis spots, and St. Louis loved the experience of spotting Musial. So many people have an "I saw Stan at dinner" story. My uncle, Lenny Zeid, once saw him at Busch's Grove in Ladue, Missouri. It was someone's birthday, so Stan whipped out his harmonica and played "Happy Birthday." "I was so excited," Lenny said, "I turned to my client and his wife to point him out and I spilled red wine all over my client's jacket." Others saw Stan at Faratto's, dining with his wife of 70 years (not a typo) and then passing out autographed cards to the kids.

He was The Man but carried himself as a regular one. Musial's grandson, Brian Schwarze, was The Man's right-hand man for Musial's final dozen or so years. "To think that he was on the same level of Ted Williams and those guys and then to get to know him and how great of a person he was," Schwarze said, "and he was a lot of fun, the life of the party. I saw a tweet the other day that I really liked. They said, 'I Googled Stan Musial, and every single photo I see of that guy, he's smiling.' He was always having a good time. His joke was, 'You'd always be smiling, too, if you knew you were going to hit .300!' He embodies to me what we love about St. Louis. He's just a genuine, great person. Maybe it's the Midwestern feel to him, as well. People always ask, 'Would he have been different if he had played for the Yankees?' And I say, 'I hope not.' But maybe St. Louis made him who

Just as great off the field as he was on it, Hall of Famer Stan Musial poses in 1958.

he is a little bit. It definitely rubbed off on him. He is what we love most about this town—and what St. Louis can be."

In a turbulent, complex era for St. Louis—and, really, the country as a whole—it's an important reminder that just being a nice person isn't a negative quality or a sign of weakness. After all, the nicest guy we ever had was also our biggest stud and biggest star. He's not just our town's DiMaggio. He was any town's DiMaggio—and maybe better than DiMaggio—just without the pinstripes and Marilyn and song lyric.

Musial played 22 seasons, skipping 1945 to serve in the Navy. His career batting average was .331. His on-base percentage was .417, and his slugging percentage was .559. And so, his OPS (on-base-percentage-plus-slugging-percentage) was .976. That's bonkers. For some modern perspective, Mike Trout's first five seasons were otherworldly. He finished first or second in the MVP voting every year. Trout's OPS for those five seasons was .975.

Musial met numerous commanders-in-chief over the decades, including Bill Clinton, who imitated Stan's peek-a-boo batting stance inside the Oval Office. And the 2011 trip to the White House was for America's version of knighthood, the Presidential Medal of Freedom. Contemporaries such as Hank Aaron, Frank Robinson, Williams, and DiMaggio had previously received the honor. Stan's grandson, of course, was by the slugger's side. "It was surreal and it's surreal to even look back," Schwarze said. "He definitely excelled at a lot in life. And that's one of the things he loved so much about the Presidential Medal of Freedom. He would say, 'This isn't just about baseball. This is about my life and what I've given back.' And it was so cool to see St. Louis just fixated on his honor. It was like St. Louis was there with us in a way."

And today in St. Louis, they give out awards named after him. The annual Musial Awards presentation is one of the cooler things they do in my hometown. The awards honor the virtues of sportsmanship and they can be won by any athlete—from a Little Leaguer to a big leaguer. How amazing was Musial? He was a first-ballot Hall of Famer, but the awards of his name are given to those who embody something even bigger than his greatness on the field. When Musial retired in 1963, Cardinals general manager Bing Devine said of The Man: "He was a man's man, a great ballplayer, a fine gentleman. He's the type of fellow, I think, if you could have everybody just like Stan Musial, we'd have one of those perfect worlds."

Stan loved restaurants so much that he bought one. For decades in St. Louis—until its close in 1986—Stan Musial and Biggie's was a staple over at 6435 Chippewa Avenue. (They opened another location, too, at 5130 Oakland Avenue.) Harmonica in pocket, Musial would hang out at Musial and Biggie's. The latter was the nickname of co-owner Julius "Biggie" Garagnani. Any customer from Stan's hometown of Donora, Pennsylvania, would eat for free.

Stan was friends with Al Hirt, the Grammy-winning trumpeter and celebrity from decades ago. According to the great columnist Bill McClellan, Hirt visited Stan for the 1982 World Series, so they stopped into the restaurant. Dick Balsano played the piano at Musial and Biggie's, and that night Hirt played along on the trumpet. Stan then hopped over and played a little harmonica. As one couple was leaving, the woman said to an employee, "That trio is pretty good. Will they be here tomorrow night?"

Another close friend was Jack Buck, the iconic Cardinals broadcaster. They were legitimate friends, explained Jack's son, FOX broadcaster Joe Buck. "It wasn't a put on, it wasn't fake, it wasn't: *Oh, you're a good broadcaster, you're a great player,*" Joe Buck said. "I was born in '69 so I missed everything. I only knew Stan as my dad's good friend...of all the people that could've visited my dad in the hospital, he wasn't going to be denied visiting my dad in the hospital. They just liked each other's company. They'd play golf on Mondays out at the Missouri Bluffs, and just being around him was great. Everybody would kind of hover around the first tee, my dad would slap something out there, and then Stan would get up, and everybody was quiet. He's like, 'No, everybody make noise, I love hearing noise! Come on, everybody, let's clap.' He just was genuinely a good person. So, I wish I could say something like, 'Oh, man, he wore out the bat between here and here and the sweet spot here and he's the greatest hitter.' I wish I could've seen him, but you didn't need to know how great of a player he was to know how great of a person he was."

In the 2000s after his stint as a college ballplayer and a handful of at-bats in the Appalachian League, Schwarze returned home. He started helping his grandparents around the house and soon Schwarze was with his grandpa almost every day, beginning at 10:00 AM. They'd stop by Musial's office for Grandpa to sign some autographs and then they'd go to lunch with Musial's friend and business manager, Dick Zitzmann. "He called us his 'bookends,'" Schwarze said. "We definitely had a routine. Monday and Thursdays was lunch at the Hilton in Frontenac, the little bar area there. Tuesdays and Fridays were Missouri Athletic Club West. As he got older, we went there more and more. And then Wednesday was Schneithorst's."

They'd have appointments in the afternoon, including Stan's massage twice a week. "He deserved it," Schwarze said. And then they'd take naps before going out to dinner. "At one point, I told Grandpa, 'Hey, if we're going to go out to dinner this much, I mean, I got to date a little bit.' And he said, 'Take them with us!' Most girls, I try not to bring it up at first, but at dinner when people would start to ask for autographs, you had to answer some questions. They would normally first come to the house, actually. I'd meet her once or twice, then they'd come over to Grandpa's house, and then the three of us would ride to dinner. He always, always wanted me to get married, but I think it was more for him than for me because he wanted to be the best man. He said it was the only thing he never did in life was be a best man. These girls' faces would get so red when he would say at dinner, 'Why don't the two of you get married?' And I'd say, 'Grandpa, this is the first date!' And he'd say, 'I don't care, I'll pay for it!' So hopefully when I get married someday, somebody's going to have to step in for Stan as best man. It was a promise I made him."

Musial died in 2013. Age 92. But, man, Stan lives on in St. Louis at the Musial Awards, at The Stan Musial Veterans Memorial Bridge, at the famous Musial statue of him in his batting stance outside the stadium. And he lives on in the restaurants, where St. Louisans snack on the crab cakes and tell stories about the time they saw Stan there and just how nice he was.

3

YADI

George Gobel was the final guest on an episode of *The Tonight Show*. The actor walked out and greeted Johnny Carson, and, sure enough, the guests before him, who were still on the couches, were Dean Martin and Bob Hope. So Gobel sat down, looked around, and said: "You ever get the feeling that the world was a tuxedo—and you're a pair of brown shoes?"

That's how I felt one particular day at Busch Stadium. Inside a room before a game were members of the Cardinals' Hall of Fame each in their resplendent red blazers. There was Bob Gibson! Red and Ozzie, too. I spotted two icons I wanted to chat with, so I politely asked to join a table—with Ted Simmons and Tony La Russa. I was their George Gobel.

We started talking, and I told the two about this book. I wanted to get their thoughts on Yadier Molina. La Russa, of course, was Yadi's first major league manager. And Simmons, an eight-time All-Star, was the greatest retired Cardinals catcher. Suddenly, two revered baseball men became boys, gushing about their favorite player as if they'd just gotten his Topps card in a pack. "I say this," La Russa shared, "with all due respect to guys who are famous and in the Hall of Fame—Fisk and Berra and Bench— there aren't any of them better than No. 4. The way his brain works, the adjustments he makes, the feel he has for what the pitcher and hitter can do, he checks every box in excellence."

"He's the best defender I've ever seen," Simmons chimed in. "Complete and total awareness."

There might not ever be another one like him, a catcher

who makes catching legends gawk. A player so proactive behind the plate, he turns defense into an offense. A man who plays the game with a ferocious glare but then unleashes the happiest, widest grin when they win. A Cardinal who received noticeably louder cheers than every other player at every home game.

"He was the rock. If you mess with the Cardinals, you're messing with Molina," FOX broadcaster and St. Louis native Joe Buck said. "I remember once asking Chris Carpenter in a production meeting about Yadier, and he said, 'He's my left tackle. He's my blind-side protector, and nothing's getting to me as long as he's out there. He will protect me both literally in a physical sense and mentally. He won't let me make mistakes on the mound or with pitch selection. He just won't. He's my blind-side guy.'"

Yadi came to us from Puerto Rico, where his father, a technician at a factory, built catchers as a side job. Benjamin Molina fathered three boys who played in the big leagues. All three became catchers and World Series winners. Born in 1982, Yadier was the youngest.

The Cards drafted him in 2000, and a year later, as the famous story goes, starting catcher Mike Matheny told his wife: "I saw the kid that's going to steal my job."

Word spread each spring. *There's this kid.* Fans and media alike would gather and gossip about this prospect, almost like music fans would for some cool new band still looking for a label. "It wasn't all over the Internet. You had to go see it for yourself," said Tom Ackerman, the sports director for the famed St. Louis radio station KMOX. "I remember spring training, and somebody taking me out to the backfields. *You got to see Bengie and Jose Molina's younger brother.* I remember going out, and he just looked the part. The arm— the snap throw—is what sticks in my head and just how comfortable he looked back there...And now I think when it's all said and done, he will be the greatest catcher of all time, and that's coming from a town where Yogi Berra is from."

In 2004 Yadi was a St. Louis Cardinal, debuting at age 21. Just two Octobers prior, Yadi was at the Anaheim Angels' World Series workout, watching his brothers from the dugout while wearing an Angels sweatshirt.

ST. LOUIS CARDINALS

By October of 2004, he was playing in the World Series. "Matheny catches the first three games. I catch Yadi the fourth game," La Russa said of the rookie backstop. "Second time around the lineup, Manny Ramirez is hitting, David Ortiz is on deck. We're over there just watching. All of a sudden, I see Yadi look toward Ortiz, look toward Ramirez, and he backs up, and Yadi is jawing him. Hmmm. What's going on? So what happened was Ortiz is giving Ramirez pitch location. So this kid at 22 in the World Series says, 'Tell your partner I speak Spanish, and if he keeps this shit up, somebody's going to get hurt.' Ramirez says, 'No, no, no.' And he says, 'Bullshit, I know what you're doing.'"

Today, some players call him *El Marciano*—"The Martian"—because he plays at such a higher level it's as if he's from a different planet. Over the years he makes these throws from his knees to second. Or picks off a runner. Or throws out a guy in the World Baseball Classic at first base as the batter is celebrating a hit but walks slowly back to first after rounding it. You hear these stories how he makes good pitchers great with all these little techniques, and it's taken on an almost mythical status. A perennial Gold Glove winner, he has tattoos of them on his left bicep, and the trophy given to the World Series winner is on his right. He's become an icon in St. Louis because St. Louis knows how much he cares about being a St. Louis Cardinal. He famously got in the face of rival Brandon Phillips of the Cincinnati Reds. And he is fiercely loyal to his team; he'll occasionally even bark to sportswriters about something negative written about a teammate.

And Yadi is steadfast in his ways. He once posted on Instagram: "I train to play 174 games because that's what it takes to be Champion," which adds up to the 162 regular season games, 11 playoff wins (the amount needed for the World Series title), and one other game— presumably a reference to, yup, the All-Star Game.

As of 2017, he'd played in eight of the latter, the same number as Simmons. "What makes him special compared to the average big league catcher?" Adam Wainwright said. "Nothing he does is average. Everything he does is above average. His play-calling is above average. His preparation, his pitch framing has always been, in my opinion, the best I've ever seen. And it's not even close, honestly.

What he can do with a low strike—or a ball that's a little bit low—and bring it up to the bottom of the strike zone to make it look like a strike instead of pushing the ball down. Most people don't understand: when you've got a guy throwing a 97 mile-an-hour sinker or a nasty slider and breaking ball and it's going down sharp and late right at the bottom of the zone, the natural [catching] reaction is to push that ball down. And you don't mean to. It's just that's the way the ball is heading. And so it's really hard *not* to do it. But Yadier has this amazing ability to vacuum or suction cup that thing from the bottom of the zone. And he gets so many strike calls that way. Even if he doesn't get a strike on it the first time, the umpire goes, 'Dang, was that a strike?' It's remarkable."

He steals strikes and keeps base runners from stealing. But for all the analysis of his game and praise for his leadership, perhaps the best way to describe Yadi's greatness comes from a Chicago Cubs fan. "I've hated him thoroughly for like a decade now," said my good friend Nate Kreckman, a Cubs die-hard. "But watching the World Baseball Classic and the way the Latin players all gravitate to him, I'm finding myself starting to kind of like him...and it's annoying me. Winning over a Cubs fan is the greatest compliment."

OZZIE SMITH

École Nationale de Cirque in Montreal is the premiere circus school in North America and opened its tent flaps, if you will, in 1981. That same year in St. Louis, the circus came to town as the Cardinals traded for a new shortstop. And during that same time period, a young boy from St. Louis grew up fascinated by Ozzie Smith. The circus, too. And by his 30s, Duncan Wall was a teacher of circus history and criticism at, yup, École Nationale de Cirque. He even wrote a book: *The Ordinary Acrobat: A Journey Into the Wondrous World of the Circus, Past and Present.*

There's a beautiful symmetry—even if it happened subconsciously—to a circus scholar's childhood featuring the feats and acrobatics of the back-flipping Ozzie Smith. "Most sports operate within a specific kind of physical vocabulary," Wall said, "and then a few of them can interrupt that whole vocabulary. In soccer it was always the bicycle kick—the thing you all aspired to do as kids, and when somebody did it in a game, it was like a whole other thing. And the dive in baseball, it's kind of like that, this rare and extraordinary feat when somebody does it that requires some other kind of ability. They literally have to be able to do something physically that other people can't do. The most physical, capable people in our society are professional athletes. And yet their physical capability is according to some kind of moves. It codifies the life. Yet there are a few dudes who manage to have this other thing."

Ozzie Smith had this other thing. Often with athletes from yesteryear, we have these images in our minds that are almost cartoon-like. Their physical travails become fish tales. And then you see grainy old footage and you're like, "Oh, that was it?" But the defensive plays of Smith hold up over time. He wasn't just ahead of his time. He was ahead of *any* time. "I mean, we called him 'the Wizard,'" Wall said. "We have created a new version of the Wizard. It used to be Merlin or somebody with a sort of spiritual side and now it's a baseball player who can not only hit the ball quite well, but can also do actual physical feats. I think about my own childhood, the number of kids who, around St. Louis playgrounds, were diving around totally because of him. That's kind of a fun scene to think about. I was doing it, you were doing it…It just seemed it became part of our physical lexicon as kids. It's what we would do—the diving and the tumbling—because of him. And it's kind of cool."

Indeed, on Lancaster Drive my father would toss a tennis ball far to my left, and I would scurry, tracking that thing down with my plastic Cardinals glove, a giveaway from a game. And then I would leap and awkwardly throw the ball back in mid air, and the thing would pounce back to Dad a few bounces and a few feet to his side, but damn it, for that brief moment in the air, I felt like I was Ozzie Smith!

"When I would talk about Ozzie and try to describe him to people, I remember some moment where he dove, but the ball took a wrong bounce, and while diving he reached up and grabbed it with his bare hands," Wall said of arguably Ozzie's greatest play, which was actually from his earlier San Diego Padres days. "In my childhood mind, it was beyond. He's gone beyond. It's like he's not even using the equipment anymore. It becomes transcendent. It becomes supernatural. You're not even using the tools you're given. What is the glove? It's an enlarged hand that we allow players to use to do the job because the ball travels fast and hard. And Ozzie didn't need it. It's almost like he's defying the laws of nature…There's also the caricature of Ozzie after he retired…Ozzie in his fur coat, making appearances around town, at the Italian restaurant, or the steak restaurant. This local hero. I never actually saw him, but you'd hear that he was at places in a way that reminds me of these old essays I'd read about DiMaggio or Mickey Mantle in New York after they retired. These seminal figures and you don't quite know what they're doing. They probably have a car dealership or something, and you don't know how they fit in, but they seem to be doing well. And everybody's excited to see them."

* * *

Chad Harbach birthed Henry Skrimshander, the boy obsessed with the position of shortstop. The great novelist Harbach was born in Racine,

Wisconsin, in 1975, which means Harbach was about six or seven during the 1982 World Series. I was seven in 1987, and maybe this happened to you, too, but seven was the age that I first fell for baseball. It was a World Series year for my team, as it was for Harbach in '82. "I can still recite the entire roster and stats of that team," he told me. "My favorite player was Robin Yount, my hometown shortstop, beautiful to watch in his own right with his closed stance and his long strides like a young deer. [He] won MVP that year, and I despised with a child's fiery passion—and still do—the Cardinals, who came back from 3-2 down to beat us in that series and break my heart. And yet there was one Cardinal I could never despise, and that was Ozzie Smith. The ground he covered—from the foul line to the far side of second base and deep into the outfield grass—the leaps and dives and tumbles, the magnetic hands, the acrobatic throws, the backflip. It was actual magic. The Wizard defied all the laws that any child yearns to defy—the law that says you're earthbound, the law that says you can't be in two places at once, the law that says you're doomed to make mistakes. I was entranced by the ease and the grace and the magic. And I could tell, too, how good he was. There was no excess flourish, no flashiness for its own sake. Every move and gesture was purposeful, functional, geared toward winning. Excellence and beauty: that was what I was after."

In 2011 Harbach finally and triumphantly released *The Art of Fielding*, the novel he'd been writing for nearly a decade. It was a masterpiece. The story of Henry Skrimshander and the Harpooners earned the kind of critical praise that is reserved for books that shake up a generation. It was the kind of book you read, and in the middle of a particular sentence, you stop reading and gasp out loud, "Holy shit, that is *good*." Harbach's book reached *The New York Times*' bestseller list. It was nominated for numerous national book awards. It was *The Natural* for this generation.

Henry, the protagonist, yearned to play shortstop with the gall and gusto and glamour of Aparicio Rodriguez, Henry's hero. "As a player *The Art of Fielding*'s Aparicio Rodriguez is entirely modeled on Ozzie: a balletic Cardinals shortstop with a placid demeanor who captures a young boy's imagination," Harbach said. "Off the field, Aparicio took on his own personality. He's Venezuelan, he's written a book of mystical baseball philosophy, he has political ambitions, but his whole character stems from how I perceived Ozzie when I was young. That's why I made Henry a Cardinals fan, whereas I myself can't stand the Cards. It made me wince to have Henry wearing that hat all the time, but what can you do? He and I aren't alike in every way. I got my revenge later on in the novel, when the Westish team, ragtag and dressed in blue, plays its arch rivals in their crisp red uniforms with their smug fans, superior funding, and long history of victory. Westish beats them finally and claims its championship. I didn't realize it at the time—it was mostly subconscious—but that chapter was, among other things, my Brewers' revenge for '82."

* * *

Once a summer the Rotary Club of Cairo, Illinois, would take a trip across the river. They'd pass the Arch and arrive at the bottle-cap stadium with the arch-pattern architecture around the circumference. Their seats were just so high up. "And I remember sitting up there like it was the most magical place in the world to me," Christopher Jackson told me.

It was surreal to hear Jackson's voice. He is forever the George Washington of George Washingtons, being the first person to portray the first president in the Broadway smash *Hamilton*. He's the guy on the soundtrack. I actually got to see Jackson and the original cast perform in New York. It's rare to be able to say you saw them perform together at their peak. They are theater's version of the '85 Cardinals.

Jackson grew up in Cairo, 150 miles from Busch Stadium. "Very much small-town Illinois. Everybody in that area is Cardinal oriented," he said. "Everyone in the 300-mile radius is Cardinal oriented. Making it to St. Louis was like the highlight of the year for me growing up because it was just far enough that it wasn't an easy trip to make. So when you go to St. Louis, you pray you could do the trifecta, or my trifecta. And that was go to a game at Busch Stadium, go to Six Flags, and then hit the Riverboat McDonald's before you had to go back home. That made me the happiest person in the whole world."

As a boy, like so many others, Jackson wanted to be like Ozzie Smith. One day that became literal. He attempted Ozzie's trademark backflip, which the Wizard unleashed on Opening Day and to open a playoff series. "That began and ended on a fateful day in my front yard, when I was about 11," Jackson said. "My buddy, Granger Davis, tried to spot me. It didn't go well. It was a one-off. It made me appreciate Ozzie even more in every way. Fateful day. I think about it often, never attempting it again. I leave that to those who can... The backflip, the smile, there was an element of show business about Ozzie, and he was always in the community. I would look for him on *This Week In Baseball*—any kind of fielding tips. And he looked like my uncles, you know what I mean? He looked like the folks I'd see at family reunions. And you talk about the '80s, this was before the Jordan of it all and the way sports took off. So he felt like someone who would like be at your [Little League] game. But he was just an amazing fielder and an amazing player, and you could tell he was the glue of those Cardinals teams in the '80s."

In 2012, three summers before *Hamilton* debuted, Jackson lived out a dream while in *Dreamgirls*. The show was at The Muny, the halcyon outdoor theatre in St. Louis' Forest Park, which is famous for being larger than New York's Central Park. Jackson was asked to sing the national anthem at a Cardinals game. "All the emotions came flooding back," he said. "Coming to St. Louis and watching Ozzie Smith, that was magical. You often hear folks talk about playing the game the right way. And Ozzie wasn't the biggest, he wasn't the strongest, but he played the game the right way. He exuded sportsmanship and competitiveness. And for an area of the country that's obviously seen its share of social, economic, and racial struggles, Ozzie kind of transcended all of those—not in a way that made you forget about it, but in a way that made you reassured that it could be okay. For that area I know how important that kind of message really is. And he was just being himself. And because of the magic he was able to sort of wield on a baseball field, it just made everything seem okay. And it's that spirit that keeps people coming back to the park, it keeps people coming back to Busch. It's not about buying $20 beers or hot dogs. It's just about what that atmosphere engenders in people. It brings the best out of people, especially in that area."

WAINWRIGHT'S CURVEBALL TO BELTRAN

It was a premature coronation. Adam Wainwright stood atop the Shea Stadium mound in the bottom of the ninth inning. And as the rookie readied to deliver his 0–2 pitch, his head, sure enough, aligned with the lone ad on the wall, the one behind home plate. It was for Budweiser Select, a new brew from St. Louis. And as the pitcher peered toward his peerless catcher, it appeared as if the beer's logo—a red crown—was atop Wainwright's head. Sure enough, moments later, he unleashed this swooping whoosh of a curveball, which froze their potential "Freese." Bases loaded, Game 7, two outs, and down two runs, Carlos Beltran succumbed. The best hitter on the best regular-season team struck out, and Waino earned his Cardinals the National League crown. "That was probably the best curveball I've seen," said Cards reliever Brad Thompson, who watched that 2006 night from the bullpen, "and for sure was the fastest sprint I've ever done in my life."

The Waino curve was a brushstroke, a masterstroke. It was violent, yet beautiful. As the ball reached its highest point—seemingly in line with Beltran's shoulder blades—it suddenly dropped, as if it was rolled down the side of St. Louis' Arch. And there was beautiful symmetry. As Waino's follow-through flung the right-hander's body to the left, the ball popped in the farthest right corner of the strike zone. "It was just one of the damnedest pitches in the history of postseason baseball," said manager Tony La Russa, coincidentally just after returning from a 2017 trip to New York. "Mets fans are still pissing and moaning about Beltran! I said, 'You watch the tape and you see the arc of the top of that curveball. Every major league hitter, when he sees the ball that high, he quits on it.'"

And so, in a way, the 2006 Detroit Tigers became the 2004 Cardinals. Thanks to the Waino curve, the 2006 version of the Cardinals pulled off an improbable win of the National League Championship Series, an instant classic, just like the '04 Boston Red Sox and Dave Roberts and David Ortiz against the New York Yankees.

In the 2004 World Series, the Red Sox came and buzzsawed and conquered the Cards. But the '04 Red Sox are more remembered for, finally and impossibly, knocking off the Yanks. Well, Tony's '06 Cards went on to defeat the Tigers, seemingly easily, if a World Series can be won seemingly easily. Wainwright notched the final out, again. "But I think that [Beltran] moment, even more than the World Series moment, is the moment that people point to," Wainwright shared on a quiet day in the Cardinals dugout before a game. "It was my rookie year, but that's kind of what I'm known for. I don't know if that moment can ever be topped, honestly."

That quiet day in the dugout, 11 years later after the curveball, Waino said friends still text him if MLB Network airs the Beltran at-bat. "I get way more nervous now, watching it back," he said. "I do always wonder what my career would've been like if I give up a double there or gave up a home run. It's not on just me. It's probably on Tony, who sends me back to the minors or trades me or whatever. Maybe things would've worked out the same way, but that started my career off in such a positive way."

Indeed, shortly after the '06 World Series ended, Wainwright went to dinner at Bandana's Bar-B-Q in St. Louis, and everyone gave him a standing ovation. During the next season, his actual categorical rookie season, he won 14 games and he just took off from there. And at the peak of brilliance and dominance in 2013, Wainwright's success helped a teammate get to the World Series for the first time. That teammate was Carlos Beltran.

But back in 2006, Beltran wasn't just a rival; he was an enemy. It wasn't personal, per se. It's just that he was Goddamn Babe Ruth every October he faced St. Louis. As a member of the Houston Astros in the 2004 National League Championship Series, Beltran belted four homers against the Cards with a .563 on-base percentage (OBP). He switched oranges, and in this 2006 NLCS, which also reached seven games, the Mets' Beltran hit three homers with a .387 on-base percentage. (His OBP would've been .406 if he had reached base against Wainwright.) And the night before, Beltran scored a key run in Game 6.

This set the New York stage for a show so big—Game 7—that billionaire Donald Trump got a seat behind home plate. The Cardinals, of course, weren't even supposed to be there. Injury-plagued that season, St. Louis only won 83 games. The Cardinals had the 13th most wins in baseball. But in the moribund National League Central, 83 wins was all it took for the title. And, as the story goes in St. Louis, the team got healthy. Mike Piazza dropped the foul pop, Albert Pujols homered, Ronnie Belliard's defense earned a gameball, So Taguchi homered, Jeff Weaver and Jeff Suppan pitched superbly, and the Cards ended up in Game 7 with the pennant on the line on October 19, 2006. "I was out there for that whole show," Thompson said of his bullpen view. "Endy Chavez bringing one back [to rob a Scott Rolen home run] and the emotions that just flowed through that game! Getting to the World Series was absolutely awesome, right? Beating the Tigers—that was great, but that Mets series was it. The Mets series, to me, was the playoffs. Game 7, I was standing up, pressed against the glass there, and every once in a while, peeking through the gate at old Shea. But that was definitely the visual, looking through some chipped-up plexiglass."

In the top of the ninth inning with the game knotted 1–1, Thompson suddenly looked straight up. As Yadier Molina thwacked the pitch, Molina's head was down for an instant, so you couldn't see his face. But as his head lifted up and he followed through on his swing, he was already smiling. He knew it. And his two-run homer sailed into, yup, the Cardinals' bullpen.

"We got to get three outs and we're going to go to the World Series," La Russa said on a 2017 day as he readied to discuss the classic change-up story. "Wainwright is our rookie closer, Izzy [Jason Isringhausen] is hurt, first two guys get on base. Dave Duncan makes a trip to the mound. That's an important detail. They pinch hit [Cliff] Floyd, strikes him out. [Jose] Reyes comes up, line drive to center field. Now we've got two outs. Paul LoDuca fouls off, fouls off. [Wainwright] walks him. Up comes Beltran. So I said to Dunc, 'You got to make the trip.'

"'Can't.'

"'Oh, shit.'

"And Dunc, he's the coolest dude in the room. He says, 'Don't worry, look.' Yadier goes to the mound. We always thought of Beltran: if you can get a sink down, that's good. But up and over the plate, he kills it. So Yadier says, 'Let's go to the sink.' As he's going back, he's thinking Wainwright has kind of a runner, more than a sink. He's got the bases loaded, you don't want to fall behind, and he's going to maybe elevate that ball. So he gets behind the plate, goes down in his crouch...Wainwright's in his stretch. I'm surprised he didn't balk. So I go to Dunc, 'What's he doing?'

"'Tony, relax.'

"Yadier called the first pitch change-up, a balloon, right there. And Beltran watches it go by. [La Russa's eyes get big as he imitates Beltran's.] And Dunc has taught that you can't throw a change-up on the first pitch because you're not changing anything up. But Yadi, man, he doesn't want to go curveball or sinker, so he goes change-up. Then Wainwright throws a curveball. Beltran fouls it off. It's 0–2 and one of the greatest hitters in postseason history.

"Curveball. Boom! That is Yadier Molina."

And that's Adam Wainwright, king of the hill.

6

BOB GIBSON

Pétrus, a grand vineyard in Bordeaux, France, is so sophisticated, so rarefied that I don't think they'd care for the likes of me even mentioning it. Jean-François Moueix oversees the estate once described by *Town&Country* as "a 28-acre blanket of mythic blue clay," which helps create a Merlot that is, "among oenophiles, Hermès in liquid form." The measured critic of *The New York Times*, Frank J. Prial, who has tasted absolutely everything, called it "nonpareil."

Tim McCarver's girlfriend works in wine, and her boss is the brother of Jean-François Moueix. McCarver pulled some strings, and on a November day in 2016, he and Bob Gibson were in Bordeaux to enjoy a private presentation at Château Pétrus. "It was," McCarver recalled, "graceful."

Moments after, they were greeted by a French winemaker. Sure enough, tucked in the back of his pants was a foreign object: a St. Louis Cardinals hat. The Frenchman pulled it out and asked Gibson to sign it. Gibson did...and then pointed to McCarver. "He played, too!" Gibson exclaimed.

"We laughed," McCarver said. "I was kind of like his valet in that scenario."

Gibson is an octogenarian now. It's been more than half a century since his '64 Cards won it all...and then won it all again three years later. And so I just love the imagery of Gibson and McCarver strolling around France, pitcher and catcher, forever together. "It was the most fun I've ever had on a trip," Gibson told me. "Usually, when I go on a trip, it's for working purposes. This was one of the few times

Nine-time All-Star Bob Gibson was known for his intensity on the mound.

I went on a vacation, drank a lot of wine, had a lot of good food. And I would have to say it was the trip of my life. I don't think I've had anything that I've enjoyed that much."

As a Cardinals pitcher, he was nonpareil. Gibson leads the franchise in pitching everything. How amazing was his Cardinals career? His Cy Young and no-hitter are just footnotes. His "1.12" is our town's "56." He was larger than life as a pitcher, and now his legend makes him, impossibly, even larger than that. "I remember the very first time I ran into him," said Art Holliday, a St. Louis TV journalist who grew up idolizing No. 45. "It was the '80s, and he was walking toward me in the press box. And I'm like, you know: here comes Zeus, down from Mount Olympus."

And he was my dad's guy, my dad's favorite player. Few things connect parents to their children like baseball, and few things connect a parent to their own childhood like their Favorite Player Growing Up. (Yes, it's capitalized.) So, talking to your child about your childhood hero is this beautiful thing, a verbal heirloom, a time-warping experience that takes you to the sunny sidewalk by your childhood neighborhood in front of Protzel's Delicatessen on a summer day.

And so it was literally standing in that spot a half-century later that my dad and I talked about Bob. "I don't remember every play of everything from growing up. I just kind of remember the whole picture," said my dad, Jere Hochman, who graduated from St. Louis' Clayton High School in 1970. "And what was so unique about him was whenever you'd see him pitch just the intensity and the determination—besides the fact that he struck out everybody. And then the unique moments, like when he drove in the only run in the game with a home run and would win the game 1–0. Or he'd field the bunt to the opposite side from the way he came off the mound, and it was like—*how* in the world did he do that? And that was pre-instant replay, too. So you'd either read about it or hear about it. That's what I remember: the aura of who he was. That was a unique time. I think of John Glenn. Anybody says 'three orbits,' you think of John Glenn. And we had heroes back then. They were just people you couldn't get enough of what was going on with them. And that's kind of who Bob Gibson was."

I also like the Pétrus story because it makes me happy to know that Gibson was happy. He deserves to be happy—as happy as he made Cardinals fans. He's a complicated guy. He played in an era of racism and tension and came off as aloof and even angry at times. Over the years you'd hear stories about how he wasn't always pleasant in public. So it was just nice to hear that Gibson was finding some happiness. The "trip of my life," he called it.

Another 1960s teenager adored Gibson. "Very vividly, I remember all of it," said Joe Maddon of Hazelton, Pennsylvania, who managed the Cubs to the 2016 World Series title. "There was '64 and then three more wins in the '67 series, including a home run in Boston, in the crease over the 379 sign. I can see the games mentally right now. I loved his delivery, I loved the energy in his delivery, I loved the way he'd fall off to the first-base side, I loved his intimidation. I always used to tell people that my favorite player was Gibson because of the way he competed. It was very obvious—even to me as a teenager. Fifth grade was Sister Agatha, sixth grade was Sister Theresa, and they used to roll the TVs in, you know, the big black-and-white ones, to watch the World Series. And you wouldn't have to sneak the transistor radio cord up your sleeve."

My dad actually did that once in class. He'd sometimes go to the games, too, taking the Redbird Express, a bus that would pick you up at Stix Baer & Fuller department store. To this day, Dad carries a Gibson baseball card in his wallet. He's done so since I was in school, and, as I write this, I'm 37. And when he got to meet Gibson, at a 2015 book signing, he showed it to him. "I was back to being a kid. I didn't know what to say," said my dad, laughing at himself. "I couldn't tell you today what I said. I just remember it was really cool to meet him and shake his hand and show him the card." My sister took a photo of the interaction. Gibson had a genuine smile on his face.

My first meeting with Gibson didn't go as smoothly. He's never been a fan of the media, these intrusive question-askers. At an event in front of a group of people, I stopped him as he walked by: "Bob, I just wanted to introduce myself. I'm Benjamin Hochman, the new sports columnist for the *St. Louis Post-Dispatch*!"

And Gibson said: "I don't care!"

It was perfectly imperfect, an awesome awkward feeling. I got Gibson'd by Bob Gibson because in a way it would've been all wrong if he'd instead said, "Benjamin, it's a pleasure. How's your day going?"

Being a badass is the perfect compliment for him and was the perfect complement to his skills. He even threw inside to (or at) former teammates. He once was hit by a ball that fractured his leg... and he still finished the inning. He seethed at Cardinals who tried to talk to him while he pitched—even poor McCarver. He wasn't anti-establishment or too verbally political. But the pitcher was a pioneer because of his captivating mix of aptitude and attitude, as much of weapons as his fastball and slider. "It's just all nostalgic, being a kid, growing up, and having those kind of cool heroes," said my reminiscing dad. "And the '60s were a time when people were breaking into a whole new arena. You've got the astronauts, you've got The Beatles, you've got a couple of ballplayers that were so much better, different, just more mesmerizing than everybody else in whatever their area was. It was a time to have something to look up to like that—and that was pretty cool."

7

THE FACES OF BUSCH STADIUM

His name tag said Marion. Or Marlon. I think it was Marion. And he would strut around Busch Stadium in the 1990s and bellow: "Anybody wanna sodee...and a *free straw*?" Marion (aka Maybe Marlon But Probably Marion) was a stadium staple, and his playful sales pitch was part of the soundtrack to my summers, everybody's summers. Decades later, whenever I've tweeted about Marion and sodees while trying to locate the old vendor, a deluge of tweets flood my timeline with stories of similar mirth. What a fun, silly memory it all was. "I remember the voice and hearing, 'Anybody wanna sodeee...and a free straw' under the radio booth," said Joe Buck, who worked with his dad at KMOX before graduating to national broadcasts. "And I remember the 'Buschy Wuschy Beer Man.' Better than 'Free Straw.' But, yeah, of course I remember those guys. They're a big part of my childhood."

You go to Busch Stadium to enjoy the pitchers and batters and fielders, but what complements the experience are the regular faces and voices, constants that you associate with happy pockets of time. They're people you never see anywhere else, as if they exist only to provide the backdrop to your ballpark experience. It's all the vendors, ushers, PA announcers, zany fans, and that Team Fredbird girl you totally know just made eye contact with you.

John Ulett is your narrator. Since 1983, "the U-Man" has been the public address announcer at Busch. It's his voice that starts each game day with: "Welcome to baseball heaven!" And he's the voice with the recognizable cadence:

"Now batting…[position, name]" In that same cadence, I even had the U-Man record the introductions of my wedding party—"Now introducing best man, Geoff Gloecker!"—and this was played loudly and proudly the day I hit my only home run ever.

Outside the stadium, on the same corner a block away, is "Snake the Scalper," who's been there for decades. "Got any extra tickets?" he'd say under his breath. Snake's more legitimate competition, so to speak? "Back in the day, before every game, my dad always—always— took me to the ticket window to say hi to Mary Tapella," said Tom Ackerman, sports director for KMOX Radio. "She's still alive today, about 94. When my dad was a kid, she knew him, just one of those familiar faces. She worked at the ballpark for 60 years. She's seen me grow up, and now I'm part of the team's radio broadcast. She lives right over here at St. Agnes retirement center."

There's another saint named Agnes. Aggie Ceriotti has worked for the Cards for more 30 years. She even has her own lobby. For real. The door for the stadium's VIP entrance says "Aggie's Lobby." And she's at the front desk, holding court, sharing stories about her grandkids to famous visitors. "Also at the stadium, you see the *same* ushers," Ackerman said. "They become like family to you. I love the fact that I can walk into Busch Stadium, and you feel right at home. And that's the thing the Cardinals do really well: they create great first-time experiences. They never take for granted it could be someone's first time. They've made kids, like us, fans by making us feel welcome."

At Busch Stadium there's honor in being on the ground crew. You work unhealthy hours, sometimes in triple-digit heat. But think about the fulfillment the average person gets after mowing his or her front lawn. Well, these folks prepare the city's lawn. And from the stands, we spot them, walking and chalking the baselines, evening the infield dirt—punctiliously and proudly.

Tim Forneris made $40 a game back in 1998. The groundskeeper was stationed behind the left-field fence on September 8, when a ball slipped through the small area above the wall but under the advertisements. It was No. 62. "Mr. McGwire, I think I have something that belongs to you," Forneris, 22 at the time, told Mark McGwire. It was a gesture they talk about to this day in St. Louis. The kid could've sold the ball for life-changing money but instead gave it to Big Mac.

In 2017 Forneris was a city prosecutor, though that job didn't stop him from continuing to work on the ground crew. That year, it was Forneris who encouraged the second most famous groundskeeper moment in Cardinals history. During the dog days of August, it involved a cat. Lucas Hackmann was a 20-year-old groundskeeper, a college kid working a pretty cool summer job. "So me and Tim Forneris, ironically, were at the steps, and the crowd goes wild," Hackman recalled. "I look out and go, 'Oh there's a cat, how cute.' And then I realized: no one's going out there to get it. I guess it's kind of our job, maybe the ushers, it's kind of in between. I looked at Tim and I can lose my rake real quick, so I said—'Tim, should I go get it?' And he said, 'Yeah.' So I get to the top step and I realized how popular this cat is getting. I looked back again and realized when I run out there it's going to be kind of a big deal. So I looked at him, 'Are you *sure* you want me to go out there?' He said, 'Yup, go get it.'"

He got it out in left field, as Yadier Molina waited in the batter's box, and the crowd cheered. And as Hackmann scurried off the field, the cat bit him. Like four times. In front of everyone. "The first one was easily the worst," Hackmann said. "He went into my finger pretty bad."

On the very next pitch in the game, Molina hit a go-ahead grand slam in the sixth inning. With that lead the Cards went on to win 8–5. The cat became Rally Cat. They sold T-shirts.

After the daring cat rescue, "My dad came up and took me to the hospital for shots," Hackmann said. "All the nurses all knew what happened. They were taking pictures with me."

Doggie, as well, had been a fixture at Cards games. J.J. "Doggie" Lynch began working for the club in 1926, the year the Cards won their first World Series. He first worked as an usher at Sportsman's Park but famously became the clubhouse guard all the way though the 1988 season. He passed away in February of '89. "Ask any player who played in the late '60s, '70s, '80s," Joe Buck said. "He was just this gruff, big guy with hanging, open eyes. His big moment was when they would have a team meeting, and he got to close the clubhouse and he'd go, 'MEETING! MEETING!' Walking around, 'MEETING!' If anybody walked up: 'MEETING! Can't go in.' He was like this bulldog literally in front of the clubhouse, and Doggie was his name."

Down the hall from the clubhouse is the Marty Hendin First Pitch Room, where hundreds of Wainwright wannabes prepare for their big moment each season. And in that hallway, Hendin's Trinket City is encased in glass. For decades, he was the club's vice president of communications, a forward-thinking Busch fixture who helped grow the popularity of Fredbird, the ultimate stadium staple. And he collected (read: hoarded) trinkets, thousands of obscure and fun Cardinals bobbleheads and pins and promotions. Many of them are on display there, along with photos of Hendin and visiting celebrities from Miss America to Mr. T. When Hendin died in 2008, the *St. Louis Post-Dispatch* headline read: "Cards lose a champion of the fans."

All these years later, I wanted a sodee and a free straw. I tried to locate Marion. The Cards even helped, but it was tricky because he stopped working as a vendor decades prior. After asking around the office, one Cards employee forwarded me this message: "[Busch Stadium worker] Debra Williams remembers him. He was picked up with a limousine at work and never returned."

What happened, I like to believe, is when the Cards switched to selling plastic-bottled sodas at games, Marion's straw shtick became obsolete. So he rode off in style.

RED
SCHOENDIENST

Three aren't many left who knew Red when he was red. Wally Moon is 87. He won the National League Rookie of the Year with the Cardinals in 1954. Of his redheaded teammate, Moon gushed over the phone: "Probably the smoothest hands I've ever seen in baseball, a natural second baseman, a little unusual, but he could pick that ball. He did a lot of backhand picks that you don't see in today's market, but he was just fluid."

Red Schoendienst could pick that ball. It seems like we've seen every play ever made by Ozzie Smith, the greatest shortstop to ever wear the birds on the bat. But with the team's greatest second baseman, we can only see what Moon describes for us. Sure, there are some grainy black-and-white highlights featuring the blatant sound of wood thwacking, which was created in a recording studio to simulate the sound of bat on ball. Still, it's hard to fully understand—and appreciate—just how smoothly Red played the game. "His play was beautiful to watch," Moon said.

In 1923 Red was born on 2/2 and now he still wears that red No. 2—94 years later.

Red's revered. The oldest living Cardinals World Series winner, who was 23 on the 1946 squad that won it all, is a rock star when he makes appearances at Busch Stadium.

And the coolest image of spring training is Schoendienst. I remember my first spring training as a columnist for the *St. Louis Post-Dispatch*. It was 2016, and there was 93-year-old Schoendienst, standing on the field in his immaculate uniform. If you stood behind him, it looked like the iconic 1984 *Sports Illustrated* cover photo of Yogi Berra in his full New York Yankees uniform, with his back to the camera, looking out onto the spring training green. The headline cleverly said of the rehired Yankees manager: "YOGI'S BACK!" And here was Red in his full Cardinals uniform, with his back to the camera, looking out onto the spring training green. Red's hat was, of course, red, though his old red hair color had faded into the new millennium. SCHOENDIENST screamed across his shoulder blades. His red spring training uniform tucked into his gray baseball pants. Red belt. Red shoes. And, perfectly, the old tall baseball socks up his legs with horizontal red and navy stripes circling his calves.

He shared his initial experience from 1943. "This was in my first full year in professional ball," Schoendienst said. "Sunday morning to Rochester, I traveled there all night. I went to the clubhouse, knocked on the door, and the trainer comes. He says, 'Yeah, can I help you?' And I said, 'Yeah, I'm supposed to report as a player for you.' He says, 'All right, good.' I walked in and I could hear [manager] Pepper Martin say to the trainer: 'I've got enough bat boys, I don't need him!' I was pretty frail, I weighed about 160 pounds."

Sure enough, Schoendienst hit .337 that season for the minor league club managed by Martin, the Cardinals great who was nicknamed "the Wild Horse of the Osage." Schoendienst served in the Army during much of the '44 season and then got the call-up to the Cards in '45. They didn't have the Rookie of the Year award at that time. Otherwise Red might've won it after leading the league in stolen bases with 26.

He made the All-Star team the next season and from 1946–55 he missed only one All-Star Game. A local hero, he became a national sensation in 1950. That season featured the first network-televised All-Star Game. The thing went 14 innings. Schoendienst won it with a home run. "From the first time I met Red to really talk to him, when the Cardinals took a barnstorming trip by railroad from St. Petersburg, Florida, immediately after World War II, I knew he had to be Huck Finn," wrote Bob Broeg, the Hall of Fame St. Louis sportswriter of the Hall of Fame St. Louis second baseman. "Heck, he even looked the way I knew Huck had to look. He was tall, loosey-goosey, freckled, and carrot-topped, and had a deep, Ferdy Froghammer voice, if you knew the caricature used in the movies then. Red didn't say much then because he was a bit shy, a bit uncertain because back in southern Illinois he'd played hooky, too, often whenever the catfish were biting on the Kaskaskia River. Or as a hunter, he'd sit with a stoicism for the thrill of blasting a mallard or a meaty Canada honker on a blustery day. And he knew more about the billiard angles of the township pool hall than he did any geometric figure this side of a pirouette at second base. Schoendienst was a beautiful athlete, playing so capably with his brothers and other kids in Germantown that they finally made him turn around and bat lefthanded to give the other fellas an even break."

His Cardinals origin story is famous in St. Louis. Two kids from Germantown, Missouri, about 50 miles from the Cardinals' ballpark, hitchhiked into town. They'd seen an ad in the newspaper for a tryout. And they were allowed to stay to watch that day's Cardinals game. Soon, the Cardinals made the drive to Germantown, a scout came to Red's home, and they worked out a deal. That was in '42. By '45 he was on the major league team.

It was a different world back then. It makes you wonder what other stars dotted the sandlots of the Midwest, boys who never got the opportunity to try out or get discovered. But it all worked out for the Huck Finn of Germantown, who ended up in Cooperstown. Schoendienst finished his major league career with 2,449 hits. He batted .289. And while defensive metrics back then were basically just errors and fielding percentage, he did have a .9934 fielding percentage in 1956, a single-season league record for second basemen that stood until 1986, when Ryne Sandberg broke it.

He later became part of the 1957 Milwaukee Braves, one of the great teams lost to history. They're often forgotten because the Braves are no longer in Milwaukee, and the Brewers have their own history there, and, frankly, folks just associate 1950s baseball with the New York teams of the Yankees, Dodgers, and Giants. But Schoendienst hit .310 for the 1957 Braves, who won the pennant behind the likes of Warren Spahn (21–11, 2.69 ERA), Eddie Matthews (.540 slugging percentage), and Hank Aaron (.600 slugging percentage). Milwaukee won it all, defeating the Yankees in the World Series.

Like Yogi Berra, Red once graced the cover of *Sports Illustrated* as well. The June 6, 1960, cover is pretty cool—a close-up of a hatless, smiling Schoendienst with the sun hitting the part of his hair just so. The headline read: "RETURN OF THE REDHEAD." Schoendienst missed the majority of the 1959 season, suffering from tuberculosis.

He indeed returned, hitting .257. But at 37, his playing career was fading.

Red became a coach and manager and made more history. From 1965 to 1976, he was the St. Louis skipper. So, yup, he's a World Series-winning manager. El Birdos, of course, won it all in '67. "The thing that I liked about Red most is he knew we can play, so he didn't try to over-manager us," Bob Gibson said. "And when there were times to do some things, he was smart enough to do it."

9

WILLIE McGEE

Willie McGee was 40. It was his final year in the big leagues, and he was playing hurt with an ankle injury that was unforgiving. During one at-bat at Busch Stadium, he hit a simple grounder and trudged toward first. But the infielder bobbled the ball. Since McGee, uncharacteristically, wasn't running with 100 percent intensity, the fielder recovered and had enough time to throw him out. David Howard, McGee's teammate on the 1999 Cardinals, was in the training room when Willie came in after the play. "He was very emotional," Howard recalled. "He felt so bad, thinking that's what the fans were going to remember of him. And I said, 'Willie, are you friggin' kidding me? Nobody will say anything. That's the one time I've ever seen you do that.' And it wasn't even awful. It was just that his ankle was hurt."

That was true Willie. Cemented as a St. Louis legend, he still worried that one play in his 18th big league season would be held against him. "He cared," Howard said. "Willie McGee was one of the best teammates I've ever had. He was a professional."

Cardinals center fielder Willie Dean McGee was, and is, beloved—perhaps disproportionately, considering he's not in Cooperstown and had only four All-Star seasons. "A few years ago, when they did the Willie McGee jersey giveaway, I was living in Denver and couldn't go to the game," said *Sports Illustrated* writer Joan Niesen, a St. Louis native. "But the minute the game was over, I bought one off eBay, mind you, knowing full well that this jersey would come down to my knees and I would never be able to wear it in public without looking like an idiot. But I have worn it in public. I wore it to a Cardinals-Cubs game last year at Wrigley knotted up, over leggings, still looked like a moron. I would tell that story to some people who weren't Cardinals fans, and they'd say, 'Wait, who's Willie McGee?' It wasn't like I bought an Ozzie Smith jersey, and everyone would be like, 'Oh yeah.' Whereas any Cardinal fan would've said, 'Did you pay like $400 for that? Because I would've!'"

At Cardinals games today, No. 51 jerseys are spotted as often as No. 4 or No. 1. To me, McGee is adored because he's one of the few players who transcended generations of fans. He was a vital part of winning teams from two different eras. That starts with the 1980s. As a rookie in 1982, he finished third in the Rookie of the Year voting and won the World Series. In 1985 he won the MVP. And the pennant. In 1987 he was an All-Star again. And they won the pennant again.

And even when the Cardinals traded him during a down year—on August 29, 1990, to the Oakland A's—McGee still had enough at-bats to qualify for the National League batting title, which he won.

But then the Cards *reacquired* McGee in 1996, the resuscitating season for the franchise (new owner, new manager, and redesigned grassy Busch Stadium). "I'm really glad they were able to get him back," Ozzie Smith said recently, "because this is the place he belongs."

That year, the Cards won the division for the first time since...1987. And McGee, age 37 in 1996, played an important role. It wasn't like he was this sweet, old guy they trotted out for a swan song. McGee was a key cog. He had 309 at-bats that year and hit .307. So because of his second campaign in St. Louis, this meant for a fan such as Niesen, who was born in 1987, that McGee was part of her memories, too. Yet for her parents, McGee defined the era of winning before their daughter was even born.

And the guy was just so damn likable. "The way he carried himself was the antithesis of a big money larger-than-life sports star," said Joe Buck, the FOX broadcaster, who has lived in St. Louis his whole life. "He just almost even walked kind of like he didn't want to overstep or he was shy. Such a humble person and yet was a fantastic switch-hitting center fielder and gave everything he had."

In the summer of 2017, he returned for the annual Cardinals Hall of Fame ceremony. Some joke that they created the Cardinals Hall of Fame just for Willie, a staple of St. Louis baseball who didn't have quite enough accolades to crack Cooperstown. And so, in addition to the Cards in Cooperstown, the Cardinals Hall of Fame has also inducted the likes of Tim McCarver, Mark McGwire, and McGee. At the '17 ceremony, each living Cardinals Hall of Famer was introduced individually on stage. When each Cardinals player walked out wearing his specially designed Brooks Brothers red jacket, he was greeted by thousands of frenzied fans at Ballpark Village. Yet, when Willie walked out, it was somehow even louder. But McGee stood humbly, almost seemingly like he was shrinking.

And later that day, there was a private setting in the dining room for media interviews. The 1985 National League MVP in his red jacket stood awkwardly in the back of the room, talking to the stadium chef in one of those big chef hats, avoiding the reporters and cameras.

"Obviously, we wouldn't be talking about him if he wasn't a great player, but I think St. Louis fans gravitate toward guys who are good guys," said longtime St. Louis sports broadcaster Art Holliday while sitting outside a coffee shop in St. Louis' Central West End. "Why do we revere Stan Musial? Obviously he's a Hall of Fame talent, but he was a Hall of Fame person. And so was Willie. He was just a really nice guy. The humility? That's different. And if he walked down this street right now, he'd get a standing ovation!"

From the gait of his run to the sway of his swing, everything Willie did was just a little different. Even the heave of the ball into the infield was distinctively his style. The swing, specifically, was something of lore. It was uncoachable. "Back leg bent, front leg straight," described Gar Ryness, the "Batting Stance Guy" who became an Internet sensation for replicating swings. "And he was bent over at the waist reminiscent of the last moment of exiting a diner booth before standing upright."

And Willie's swiping swing almost looked like he was holding a toothpick. Cards outfielder John Morris stole the show during a 1989 episode of *This Week In Baseball*. Wearing No. 51's full uniform, he did a McGee impression and gave a tutorial from the batter's box. "You got to look like you're in a lot of pain and having a miserable time out there and then make it look like your knees are killing you," Morris said. "And then lay out four line drives. That's Willie."

At the 30-year reunion for the 1987 team, Morris laughed at the batting-stance memory, sharing that: "Whitey Herzog was the one who egged me on about that because he knew that Willie and I were very good friends. And he knew that I had a way of making Willie laugh. I always tried to pick my spots in breaking it out—maybe if we had lost three of four, and guys were getting a little bit uptight, or if Willie was being too serious. What stood out about [the stance] was: it was so awkward, but it was so perfectly natural for him. It was Willie all the way. It was the pigeon-toed legs, it was the hands up and away from his body, it was him 'sitting on a toilet seat,' and then just generating this amazing bat speed, where it just seemed like a human being isn't supposed to do that, almost like where his wrists hurt, shaking his wrists. His hand-eye coordination was fabulous, off-the-charts fabulous. The fact that he was a switch-hitter, too?"

Fate is funny. If a few things had gone differently, the No. 51 retired by the New York Yankees might've been for McGee, not Bernie Williams. McGee was a first-round pick by the Yanks in '77, but on October 21, 1981, the minor leaguer was acquired by the Cardinals for Bob Sykes in a lopsided trade worthy of a trivia question. In '82 McGee began the season in the minors. "I had a manager in Triple A Louisville," McGee shared. "[He'd say,] 'You can't hit like that! You can't hit like that! You're chicken-winging it.' And I'm like, 'Oh. God. Here we go.' It's what I've done my whole life. Thank goodness, three days later, I was gone."

McGee was called up to St. Louis. Five months later came Game 3. "It was one of those games that kind of lives on in World Series history," teammate Tommy Herr said. "The quiet, unassuming rookie that no one really knows much about, and it was really his time to step onto the stage and become a nationally known player. And obviously later in his career he became an MVP and one of the most beloved Cardinals ever."

He hit two home runs. And he also robbed two home runs at the center-field wall. "That was kind of the opening act for Willie," Herr said.

The final act was 17 autumns later. It was actually on October 3, 1999, the Cardinals' last game of the century. It was the 19th birthday of Andrew Swinehart, who sure was born at the right time. He got Willie the first time as a larger-than-life childhood hero and then as a teenager got to appreciate the humanity and grace that made Willie great. A month or so into college, Swinehart returned home to

Fan favorite Willie McGee readies to bat during the start of his second stint with the Cardinals in 1996.

St. Louis. He went to the game with his childhood friends, Josh Smith and Dev Bala. "With it being my birthday, my mom gave me $40 to buy food and drinks," Swinehart recalled. "We bought three large pink lemonades and nachos with peppers. We were lucky enough to be treated to Willie's final game, and I got to share it with two of my best friends."

McGee grounded into a double play in his only at-bat that day. After the fifth inning, once all the Cards had jogged onto the field, manager Tony La Russa sent out a replacement for Willie. The great ballplayer had his moment. He jogged off with his head down before humbly hugging his teammates. He retired to the dugout—only to be called upon by the fans for a final curtain call. "Looking back, I realize it was the end of an era in more ways than one. You could say it marked the end of childhood," Bala said. "For the first time, we had all left the homes we grew up in and moved out into the world."

During one of his 2017 visits to Busch, McGee was asked to give a self-assessment of the fans' love. Visibly uncomfortable with the question, No. 51 finally said: "I don't dwell on stuff a whole lot. Every day I come around, I speak to everybody and try to be the best person I can be. I'm not perfect by any means, never have been. I don't think anybody is. But I've got to sleep at night, I've got to live with myself, and I'm conscious of who I'm around and what situation I'm in. One of the best things that happened to me when I retired was an umpire telling me, 'It was a pleasure.' That was like, 'Wow, okay.' That just closed the book."

After that final game, Howard asked McGee for a memento. "I said, 'You could give me a shoelace, I just want something!'" Howard recalled of that moment at their lockers. "And he gave me something that I cherish to this day. He took the uniform off his back and gave it to me. And you're thinking, *You've got the last* uniform *Willie McGee ever wore as a Cardinal.* I told him, 'No, no, no, no, you've got to give this to your kids or somebody.' And he said, 'No, I really enjoyed being your teammate.' It's in my house. My wife knows it's one of my favorite things that I have."

10

ALBERT PUJOLS

It was always the opposite-field ones that got me. Albert Pujols would just drill a baseball with such force or torque (or some science word) that it would catapult off the bat, seemingly as hard and fast over the right-field wall as a lefty could hit it. "He's certainly one of the best right-handed hitters of all time, one of the best hitters of all time," Adam Wainwright said, "also one of the most clutch hitters I've ever seen, probably the best hitter I've ever seen, actually."

His grandmother was named America Pujols. She had 11 children of her own but raised her grandson, too, in an impoverished section of the Dominican Republic. But in the 1990s, she immigrated to her namesake. In 1996, the year Tony La Russa became the manager of the Cardinals, 16-year-old Albert Pujols moved to America. First, fittingly, he came to New York City. Shortly after, he came to Independence, Missouri, the city near Kansas City that also gave us a president, Harry Truman.

He reunited with his grandmother, enrolled in school, and sought opportunities as a ballplayer. He went from an Independence high school to a Kansas City junior college to the 13th round in the draft to A ball to the cusp of the show in the spring of 2001. "I always remember that first spring training," said Deadspin founder Will Leitch, a die-hard Cardinals fan. "There was just this guy. There was some sort of Kansas City connection. And to think the rap on him was that he had been fat! That was actually one of the reasons he fell so far in the draft was they thought he was a little chubby, which is so funny to think that of Albert Pujols."

The first time I ever saw Pujols was at the Holiday Inn Executive Center in Columbia, Missouri, in January of 2001. He'd just finished a monster minor league season and he'd just turned 21 a week prior. I'd heard about him but didn't know much. It was an era before advance scouting sites, an era when word about a player didn't spread on

Twitter, but instead it was more like in a game of "telephone." It was just my second assignment ever for the newspaper in my college town. And in the article, "Cards caravan rolls into town," 20-year-old me wrote: "Right fielder J.D. Drew and pitcher Alan Benes were two of the marquee names in attendance. Other players included former pitcher Danny Cox, recently acquired reliever Steve Kline, and third-base prospect Albert Pujols. But Drew was clearly the fan favorite."

A few months later, my dad and I went to '01 spring training. I still have the program. On page 21 there are baseball-card shaped rectangles featuring the players, such as No. 77 Kevin Polcovich, No. 76 Luis Saturria, and No. 68 Albert Pujols. "We tested him so much at spring training once he started going well," La Russa recalled of the prodigious prospect. "Normally, a young player will expose where he's not ready. I would set up a lineup against a certain pitcher, and the coaches would say, 'You're trying to get him to go 0-for-4 so we can send him out.' During that process there was one really wonderful example to make the point. We shared the camp with Montreal, and they had this outstanding pitcher, Javier Vasquez. He was a veteran and had four or five ways to get you out. And I hit Albert fourth. I was thinking, *This guy's going to be a test for Albert*, making the ball do tricks. First time up, sure enough, fastball in, breaking ball away, and he strikes out. I'm thinking, *Yeah, maybe he's not quite ready.* Next time up? Fastball in, slider away, hits a line drive, one-hopper off the right-center field wall."

Opposite field. Pujols just has this tree-trunk base, so stupidly sturdy and strong, that he could drive a ball anywhere he seemingly pleased. "As the spring went on, it became obvious that he was so advanced," La Russa said.

Pujols made the club—La Russa said Albert would've been a Cardinal even if veteran Bobby Bonilla hadn't been injured—and Albert got a hit in his first game. And in his fourth game on April 6, 2001, Albert went 3-for-5 with his first double and first homer. "And then," La Russa said, "it was non-stop greatness for 11 years."

To me, here is the most astute way to capture his Cardinals career: Pujols played 11 seasons for St. Louis and in all but one he finished in the top five of the MVP voting. Yes, Barry Lamar Bonds marred some history by sometimes besting Pujols for the actual hardware (Pujols won three MVPs), but still every season except one—a decade of seasons—Pujols was a top five player in the whole league. And then in the seventh year, he finished ninth in the MVP voting.

Think about that. For most players one ninth-place finish in the MVP voting would be a defining career accomplishment. And in Albert's seventh year (2007) he hit 32 homers with 103 RBIs. He batted .327 with a .429 on-base percentage. That, ladies and gentlemen, was the worst of Albert Pujols in St. Louis. "Best I've ever seen," said St. Louis native Joe Buck, the longtime FOX broadcaster. "Best I've ever covered."

He hit a ball so hard that it broke a light bulb in the upper deck BIG MAC LAND sign at Busch. He hit three homers in a World Series game. He hit a homer against Brad Lidge that hasn't come down yet. And when he hit his 400th homer at age 30, Pujols was the third youngest player do ever do so (following Alex Rodriguez and Ken Griffey Jr.). That particular home run ball was "obliterated," as described by MLB.com writer Matthew Leach.

It went to the opposite field.

All along Pujols wore No. 5. (He dumped that No. 68 when he got the call to the show.) I find it symmetrically aesthetic that nestled neatly behind the iconic Man at No. 6 for the St. Louis Cardinals, Yadier Molina wore No. 4 and Pujols No. 5.

And today, No. 5 is an Anaheim Angel or whatever they call that team. It looks weird. It's him, but it's not him. Same stance, same glance, but upon Pujols what was once a lather of virility is now a froth of vulnerability. Yes, he occasionally uncoils that great swing, unleashing baseballs into the night—but not as often as he used to back when a Pujols homer was essentially anticipated. They all count the same, but they don't feel the same.

And maybe that's why there wasn't as much mystique surrounding Pujols' pursuit toward the 600-homer milestone. It happened during his 2017 season, in which his on-base percentage looked like a batting average, and his slugging percentage looked like an on-base percentage.

But with his career already Hall of Fame worthy, the Angel Albert trudged along to reach milestones that'll end up on his plaque. On June 3, 2017, two fellows named Ben Lively and Brad Goldberg made their big league debuts, the latter the 19,000th man to ever play in the majors. That very same day, Pujols became just the eighth player to *ever* hit a 600th home run in a career. Think about it. Only eight of 19,000 have done it.

But still, some St. Louisans remain miffed. How could he leave baseball heaven just to make more money after the 2011 season? "That's why my message has been—whenever I come back to town— that I've implored our fans to remember the 11 years and not have any negativity about the circumstances," La Russa said. "It wasn't smart for the Cardinals to make that kind of commitment and it wasn't smart for him not to go there. What he gave us should be forever honored and enjoyed."

11

1982 WORLD SERIES —CELEBRATION

The mayor hereby declared that if the Cardinals won the World Series, the bars could stay open all damn night. "Well," Ken Oberkfell said with a great guffaw, "that's the only incentive we needed!"

The starting third baseman for the 1982 Cards, Oberkfell still lived in Maryville, Illinois, his hometown that actually wasn't even classified as a town. And in the village, they drank Busch at The Village Inn. "I told everybody I was going to be there," Oberkfell said, "but a lot of people was like, 'He ain't going to show up!' So, when our game was over, after we did our celebration at the ballpark, I went back to Maryville, and the bar was open. [I] walked in, and people were like 'Wow!' They thought he's going to be over in St. Louis partying, but I came back and partied in Maryville. All my friends were there and my dad, too."

His father worked on the railroad for 42 years. His son had just won Game 7 of the World Series while playing for the family's favorite team just 17 miles down the road and over the river. It was completely surreal.

The 1982 Cardinals were dream-makers, creating a new generation of St. Louis history. See, the Cards hadn't been to the postseason since 1968, so even seventh graders in '82, such as Joe Buck, had never seen the playoffs in their lifetimes. "I was there with the Ken Reitzes of the world and Mike Tyson and Mike Ramsey and those guys," said Joe, the son of the Cards broadcaster Jack Buck, while seemingly sifting through his mental Rolodex of mustached 1970s infielders. "I was going down there with my dad every night, so I was lucky that I got to attend all those games, but the games weren't very fun to watch. I went from playing stickball in the inside part of the stadium down by the locker rooms with Jon Simmons and different players' kids to wanting to actually watch because they were good!"

They made a record about the '82 team, and it featured Jack Buck and Mike Shannon calls and such. The album cover was about as cool as it gets. I've got it framed. It's a tight shot of the players mobbing one another, but it's all bench players in red jackets except for the backs of side-by-side players in white jerseys: McGEE 51 and O. SMITH 1. And above the photo in red script similar to the "Cardinals" on the front of the jerseys, it read: "Celebration."

I was two years old in '82, so I have no memories of it happening, but in the coming years, my parents would play the record for me as I went to bed. My favorite lullaby was "Brummer's stealing home!"

So, Robert Bell was cool. His godfather was Thelonious Monk. Robert Bell was also Kool—that was his nickname. And Kool and his brother got together a gang of friends and made a bunch of hit songs: "Jungle Boogie," "Get Down On It," "Ladies' Night." But the best song by Kool & the Gang was "Celebration," which opened with four simple drum taps (tap, tap, tap-tap) followed by a funky guitar sound...and then an explosion of the most disco-y, R&B-y, awesome-y song ever (yah-hoo!) "Ceeeel-a-brate good times, come on! (Let's celebrate!)"

The song became a theme song for the '82 Cards and was played after wins. There were 46 of them at home that year—and exactly 46 on the road, too.

Now, the famous Ozzie Smith probably didn't even need SMITH on his jersey, but he had to wear the initialed O. SMITH because the Cards also had L. SMITH. Lonnie Smith had the most hits on the team (182), the most doubles on the team (35), and the most stolen bases (68). But the star and leader of the team was O. SMITH.

And the previous fall, during the 1981 World Series, Whitey Herzog made a deal to nab a wily minor leaguer named Willie. By the 1982 World Series, rookie Willie McGee was the Cardinals' starting center fielder. McGee was quiet, joining a Cards team laden with veterans. So Ozzie, already an All-Star and Gold Glove winner, would pick the kid up for work. "For Ozzie to do what he did," McGee shared, "it was just a blessing. [I] saved a lot of money [on gas]. But it was just special, getting a chance to ride with him to the park every day, learning the ropes. It sped up the learning curve for me. How many guys get to do that? You don't see that."

* * *

From the stadium's parking lot, you can see the Arch across the river. On a stunningly sunny summer day, Oberkfell sat on a bullpen bench at GCS Ballpark. He was 61, still coaching in 2017—and at the lowest of levels for the Gateway Grizzlies of the Frontier League, an independent professional league. "These kids," he said, "are hungry."

GCS Ballpark is in Sauget, Illinois, three miles from Busch Stadium. The World Series third baseman was home again. St. Louis, sure. But also Maryville, just up the way on I-55.

His dad passed away in '09. His mom is 85, living in a nursing home. "She's kind of slipping a little bit," Ken said, "but I know she's okay when I walk in, and she starts, 'Where you been?'"

Oberkfell hit .289 for the Cardinals in '82. Actually, from 1979 to 1983, his combined batting average was .296. And he could scoop. "We had great chemistry, we had the best infield in baseball, and we felt that way, too," Ken said. "We had good pitching and No. 42 closing. We had 67 home runs as a team. *As a team.* But we didn't beat ourselves. We were very fundamentally sound. It was hard to get the ball through our infield, and if they hit it in the air, our outfield was pretty fast, too."

And there was the bespectacled backstop, Darrell Ray Porter, a Missouri native. He was a fascinating man, a brilliant catcher who also battled drug addiction but was open about it, even writing a book. He became a born-again Christian but died at age 50 with cocaine in his system.

Porter's contributions to the 1980s Cardinals were that of lore. He worked magic with those pitchers and made magic in October. And in '82 he won the MVP awards for both the National League Championship Series and the World Series, à la another Cardinals Missouri native, David Freese. "I just remember watching Darrell Porter," said Mike Matheny, who became a Cardinals catcher himself and later the team's manager. "And that's when I was really trying to figure out if I could take this game to another level. I was watching the catchers more closely than I had done before. That was the position

I had really focused in on. I watched him more so than the team and was very, very impressed with how he went about it."

In the dugout during Game 7, Oberkfell recalled Joaquin Andujar was walking around, barking to his teammates: "You get me one run! One run and we're world champions!" Andujar threw forkballs to the opponents and then stuck a fork in them. He was a battler, a badass, and was cruising in Game 7 of the World Series against the Milwaukee Brewers. But so was their guy, Pete Vuckovich, the Cy Young winner. "Well, we got a run in the fourth," Oberkfell recalled. "So going into the top of the fifth, we throw the ball around. I took the ball. I said, 'There's your run, big boy! You wanted one, here's your run.' [I] threw him the ball. Ben Ogilvie hit the first pitch he saw out of the stadium and tied the game at 1–1. I walked up to Andujar and said, 'I think we need two.'"

The boys stayed loose, and by the ninth inning, St. Louis led 6–3. And No. 42 had the ball in his hand.

Bruce Sutter of Mount Joy, Pennsylvania, was a former Cy Young winner himself and a future Hall of Famer. He unleashed the final strike of the season—past Gorman Thomas' bat—into Porter's mitt. "Sutter from the belt, to the plate," Jack Buck announced that night, a quote forever audibly preserved on the "Celebration" record. "A swing and a miss, and that's a winner! That's a winner! A Worrrrrrld Series winner for the Cardinals! Porter throws his mask into the air, the players converge around the mound, the Cardinals have won the game 6–3!"

"Celebration" began playing, and a celebration began into the wee hours in Maryville. And 35 years later, Oberkfell was back in the village. "My wife passed away last September," he said quietly that summer day in 2017. "It was pretty bad. She had brain cancer. I basically retired to help take care of my wife. We were in Texas then, and I'd come back and forth here to see my mom. We decided if something happened to one of us, we would sell our house in Texas. And that's what I did. My step-kids are all grown, and I said, 'Well, you know what? My home is Maryville. Why not?' And so I moved back."

JACK BUCK

The kid's childhood had been narrated by Jack Buck, and here he was—Jack Buck—the voice of the Cardinals, the voice of the city, the voice talking *to him*. "I said, 'Mr. Buck, I'm Tom Ackerman, I just started here at KMOX, it's an honor. I've read your book—twice,'" recalled Ackerman of that 1997 day. "He reaches out his hand—a hand that's shook the hand of presidents and Hall of Famers— and he says, 'What kind of pizza do you like, kid?'

"'Pepperoni.'

"'I'll buy it if you go downstairs and get it.'

"So I brought the pizza up, and we started sharing a pizza and talking. I'm 22. He left the room, and I called my mom.

"'How's it going?'

"'It's incredible—I'm eating pizza with Jack Buck! Oh, he's coming back, I've got to go!'"

The kid became the boss. Ackerman is the sports director for KMOX, the Cards' flagship radio station. It's a dream job for a city of Tom Ackermans, each raised by Jack Buck.

As for the kid literally raised by Jack Buck? "He could talk to anyone," Joe Buck said. "He could plop down Vladimir Putin and he'd have a great interview with Vladimir Putin or he could do the same thing with [Cardinals pitching coach] Dave Duncan and he'd have a great interview with Dave Duncan. He liked people. He liked the human condition. He liked to get to know somebody with a microphone in his hand or without. It was really me eavesdropping on how he was 24/7 with people that he didn't know or wanted to get to know."

Jack Buck began broadcasting Cardinals games in 1954 and for decades—generations, really—he eloquently and passionately brought Cardinals baseball into homes and cars and even to beaches and prison cells. "KMOX is the soundtrack of summer," Ackerman said of the famed 50,000 watt station. "The strong signal is one part of it.

Growing up, I was proud of it, proud to be in a different city and could always hear my city on the radio. There was something cool about that. And we all know that for a while the Cardinals were the only team west of the Mississippi, and KMOX was blasting that signal to the south and to the west. It's part of the reason why they built such a large fanbase. And also the teams were good, and the personalities on the air were good. When I think of KMOX, it really was the voices that you heard. It's enhanced the lore, made it into a special place. It has brand name power like Cardinals or Budweiser. One time I was doing a postgame show, and on my call screener, it said 'John in Mexico,' so I said, 'Let's go to John in Mexico, Missouri, you're on KMOX,' and he said, 'No actually, I'm in Mexico—the country.'"

KMOX isn't a station; it's an institution. Even its commercials are famous. I don't know my wife's cell phone number, but I know that 314-645-2000 is Frederic Roofing—because for a hole in your roof or a whole new roof, call Frederic Roofing.

On a summer Sunday in St. Louis, Ackerman and I set up shop at Sportsman's Park, the bar and grill in Ladue, Missouri, known for its burger with the luscious pub cheddar atop. The dimly lit place is basically a Cardinals museum decorated with framed lore, and half of the back wall is a mural of photos just of Jack Buck. There is Jack behind the mic, with his wife, with his family. He was the voice of the community but genuinely felt that he was part of it, too. He was enshrined in Cooperstown and the orator of memorable sayings like "Go crazy, folks" and "I don't believe what I just saw," but in a way he was simply broadcasting for his fellow fellows who just wanted to experience the excitement. The voice of St. Louis was part of St. Louis. "Whether it was coming into this place and having a drink," Ackerman said, "or going to visit kids in the hospital or speaking to groups of people—because he felt like it was his duty to do it—his connection with the community made him larger than life. He was more than just a broadcaster. He was our ambassador."

He was a celebrity, really. In a baseball town, he was larger-than-life. So I've always wondered—why did Jack Buck care so much about the people? "I don't know. I think if he ever went to a therapist, which I'm sure he never did, they would probably focus on the time when he first came here and his relationship with Harry Caray," Joe Buck said of Caray, who also called the games in St. Louis in the 1950s and '60s. "Harry Caray was really hard on him, and I think he always went out of his way after that to make everybody feel welcome. So, he went up to players in the batting cage. He stuck his hand out and got to know who they were and where they were from. But why? Because I think he kind of made himself the de facto mayor or St. Louis or the de facto representative of the team because he was the guy that was there in the '50s, '60s, '70s. By the '80s it was kind of like 'Welcome to the group,' and they're just people. And I think they felt, I don't know, in some way honored that my dad bothered to get to know who they were. He just flung himself wide open, and there were very few really private moments with him."

At the 1987 reunion celebrating the team that won the pennant 20 years prior, the graying players gushed about Jack Buck, who in that '87 season was around the age they currently were. Tommy Herr said that Buck felt like "part of the team." Willie McGee said of Buck: "The best, man, the greatest. Not only the way he called the game, but what I liked about him was—he never made it personal or negative."

And Ozzie Smith's thoughts? "He was the fabric of the Cardinals," Smith said. "When I look back at it, Jack was always positive, no matter if we were playing good or bad, and that type of thing is always important. And we were able to go out there and do some magical things and give him something magical to talk about. Mr. Buck was Mr. Buck. One of the special things was when I was struggling a little bit. We'd be taking batting practice, and he'd walk by you. A lot of times he'd come by and say, 'Can I have two minutes?' But when things weren't going well, he'd just walk by you, wouldn't even really look at you and say: 'Keep your chin up.' And you know what? It's little things like that you remember from the great ones. They always knew what to say and they always said it at the right time."

Smith and Buck are forever connected, of course, because of that crazy homer. It was a beautiful sports marriage—St. Louis' version of Al Michaels and the miraculous 1980 U.S. hockey team or Russ Hodges and a pennant-winning Bobby Thomson.

Jack Buck was the voice of the Cardinals for several generations of fans. (USA TODAY Sports Images)

It was the playoffs. Dodgers at Cards, 1985 National League Championship Series, Game 5. Bottom of the ninth. The score and the series were 2–2. The Cards hadn't even mustered a hit—let alone a run—since the fifth inning. And in the bottom of the ninth, the wiry switch-hitting shortstop came to bat. Smith had logged 3,009 left-handed major league at-bats in the regular season and had never once hit a homer. "Smith corks one into right, down the line! It may go," Buck said. "Go crazy, folks, go crazy! It's a home run, and the Cardinals have won the game by the score of 3–2 on a home run by the Wizard! Go crazy!"

It's our town's call.

That day at Sportsman's Park, Ackerman did his best Buck, reciting the "Go crazy" line like so many St. Louisans do. Even at my wedding, the officiants were my sister, Emily, and brother-in-law, Mark. When the ceremony ended, my sister introduced the Hochmans to the guests and said: "Go crazy, folks!"

"Jack Buck had an incredible sense of timing," Ackerman said. "The great Hall of Famer Jon Miller described him as 'the John Wayne of broadcasting.' He could deliver a line. One of the great things about the 'Go crazy, folks' moment is his surprise at the home run, but also... he lets the crowd noise go for a minute. It's so awesome, and you hear the fireworks booming overhead. And he just sort of comes in and goes: 'Well...you can go to a lot of ballgames and never see one the likes of this one.'"

Toward the end, his health got bad. He suffered from Parkinson's disease. In May of 2001, the famous sportswriter Rick Reilly spent some time with Buck, who could still deliver a line, including:

- "I shook hands with Muhammad Ali recently," Buck told Reilly. "It took them 30 minutes to get us untangled."
- "I wish I'd get Alzheimer's. Then I could forget I've got all the other stuff."
- "I've given the Cardinals the best years of my life. Now I'm giving them the worst."

Of course, that wasn't true. Buck was always Buck. And four months later, in September of 2001, Buck read a poem to the Busch Stadium crowd, helping heal a post-9/11 community.

Jack Buck died nine months later. "He was a Depression-era guy that was a World War II vet and Purple Heart recipient," Joe said. "He died as an Army man. I swear I feel like the end of his life he was just obsessed with watching Army movies and Army on the History Channel and much more so than sports."

A few years earlier, Joe took his dad to see *Saving Private Ryan* at the West Olive movie theater in suburban St. Louis. "He said, 'The only time I cried was when the soldier and the priest pulled up the driveway to tell the mom that their boys were dead,'" Joe said. "The rest of it, he didn't like the loud conversation. He was like, 'When we were in the field of battle walking through the countryside of France, nobody was yelling at each other!' But yeah, he was much more obsessed with that than baseball, football. I mean, I guess when you get shot at, which you and I have never experienced, that has the ability to change you."

For Ackerman, directing the sports programming at KMOX means running the sports station of Jack Buck. There's honor to that because Jack Buck just cared so much. "One day I was sitting in there in the sports office by myself and I heard somebody open our sliding glass door," Ackerman recalled. "You could just tell who it was. It was 2 in the afternoon, just trying to finish up work. And he said, 'Hey kid, let's go to lunch.'

"'Yes, sir.'

"So we went downstairs to Max and Erma's, which was the restaurant right below on One Memorial Drive. We started talking. We both ordered chicken fingers. And about halfway through, he said, 'I heard your postgame show last night.' The night before Craig Paquette had a huge game. And he was filling in for J.D. Drew, who was hurt again. Drew's story was that he was always getting hurt. So I opened up the broadcast and said, 'What a night! J.D. Who?'

"He says, 'I heard your broadcast, I heard you say J.D. Who. If I were J.D. Drew's parents, I wouldn't like that very much, would you?'

"And I said, 'No, sir.'

"He said, 'You have a great sound, a classic type sound. But you've got to knock off trying to be cute and funny at the expense of somebody when you don't know what he's really going through.'

"I said, 'Yes, sir, I won't do that.'

"And I think about that all the time—that I would do it in a way that's fair. I had to pinch myself: here's this kid in his 20s, and he took the time to take me to lunch and explain to me how it should be. It showed me that he really did care. It was an amazing mentoring moment. And he did that for so many people."

13

1968

One day, in the fall of 1968, a white student bumped into a black student. Coffee splattered, and a fight erupted. The cafeteria manager at St. Louis' Normandy High tried to break up the fight. She was struck by a fist. Three days later, same cafeteria. A melee. Chairs were thrown, huge windows shattered, 140 students involved. During it all, "Someone jumped on my back," school security guard Elvis Braun told the *St. Louis Post-Dispatch*. "I got out of there as fast as I could and called police for assistance."

According to Braun, 100 of the students were white; 40 were black. "We were basically scared to death," said Mike Smith, a freshman at the time, in 2017. "We had just come to high school, and it was a huge high school, and within the first month, there was this, right there, in the middle of the day—whites squared off against blacks."

A school within a city, within a nation, all embroiled. The same September day, Lou Brock, the African American All-Star, tallied three hits for the Cardinals. He stole three bases, too. Teammate Curt Flood was hitting .300. St. Louis was in first place. And just 13 days later, the Cardinals would be in the World Series. "I got to say—despite these things going on, I do not remember ever hearing something like, 'There are too many of *them* on this team,'" Smith recalled. "It was all about the Cardinals winning."

It was a complicated and searing year. A war wouldn't end. Dinner tables divided. Police beat protesters at the Democratic National Convention. The music became angrier, heroes became complex. Hope was assassinated. "Racial strife," recalled Tim McCarver, the Cardinals catcher. "I remember Curt Flood saying, 'When you're driving now through certain areas, you ride low in your seat and high in your gear.' We had such an intelligent team, a team that went beyond just the game itself. From a social standpoint, guys were aware of everything that was happening. And we talked about it and were open about it. It made the team stronger, no question about it. Not only did we function well as a unit from an athletic standpoint, but we enjoyed each other…I do remember talking to Bob [Gibson] when Martin Luther King was killed. I told him, 'This isn't probably a good example, but I grew up with prejudice being Catholic in Tennessee.' And he said, 'Yeah, but you were white.'"

The best player on the best team in the league, Bob Gibson was having one of the best seasons baseball had ever seen. Velocity and ferocity. Asked if he felt pressure to match Don Drysdale's scoreless-inning streak, he told reporters in '68: "I face more pressure every day just being a Negro."

Five decades later the History Museum in St. Louis unveiled an exhibit. It was called: "#1 in Civil Rights: The African American Freedom Struggle in St. Louis." The exhibit was poignant, important. It captured the past: the 1819 demonstrations at the old downtown courthouse protesting Missouri's entrance into the union as a slave state; the 1917 massacre in East St. Louis, when white rioters burned more than 200 homes; the 1963 sit-in at Jefferson Bank, which wouldn't hire blacks, a sit-in that lasted seven months and led to the arrest of 500 people. And perhaps the most startling part of the exhibit was a simple black wall with white words. It was a quote attributed to a dairy owner, when asked to hire black delivery drivers: "I'll never hire Negroes as long as cows give white milk."

* * *

The 1968 Cardinals gave hope in nine-inning doses. They just won and won, and Gibson's ERA was in the 1s. Same with his opponents' batting average (.184 on the year).

Between June 2 to July 30—basically two months of starts—Gibson allowed two earned runs. Not two earned runs per start, which would have been astounding in itself. Two earned runs total.

"And I was into it like few of my classmates were into it," said Mike Smith, the Normandy student who in 2000 became the Cardinals' official scorer at Busch Stadium. "My dad had sports awareness. He studied it, read everything he could, so I did that, too."

Gibson wasn't just an intense pitcher. He was *the* intense pitcher, the standard. He started 34 games in '68. He finished 28 and was lifted for a pinch hitter in the other six, "which means he was never removed from the mound all season," Steve Rushin wrote in *Sports Illustrated*. "Just as well: given Gibson's menacing personality, a manager would have had to wear oven mitts to remove him."

His final start of the regular season was a shutout. Eleven strikeouts, not one walk. The outing put Gibson over 300 innings for the season, which means not only did he finish 1968 with a 1.12 ERA, but it also was the lowest ERA *ever* by a pitcher with more than 300 innings pitched. We sometimes find ourselves placing mental asterisks on statistical accomplishments—like a guy will have an amazing batting average, but it didn't top Ted Williams or Ty Cobb or one of those halcyon stars from a completely different era of baseball. But in 1968, Gibson's 300-plus inning season, not only was Gibson's ERA lower than any Cy Young winner, but it also was lower than Cy Young himself. And Walter Johnson. And Christy Mathewson. Gibson pitched their "amount" of innings and he pitched better than all of them.

The next season Major League Baseball lowered the pitching mounds. They changed the dimensions of the sport because Gibson was in another dimension. "I fell in love with the game in 1968 because when I was six years old at Our Lady The Pillar, my dad took me out of school and drove me to Game 1 of the World Series," said St. Louisan Frank Cusumano, who became a longtime sports anchor for the popular Channel 5 evening news. "I got to see Bob Gibson strike out 17 people, including Willie Horton on a slider to end it. And at that moment, I knew that this is what I was going to do for a living. So Gibby was my first baseball hero."

* * *

Detroit simmered.

Willie Horton was from there. And after one Tigers game the year before, he actually drove over to try to quell the racial protests, still wearing his uniform. But soon, the race riots of '67 enraged Detroit, engulfed Detroit, inflamed Detroit. They sent in the National Guard. Reporter William Serrin was entrenched with them and in the 2002 documentary, *A City On Fire*, he recalled what one guardsman told him: "Serrin, do you know how to deal with [n-words]? Machine guns and tanks."

When the riots ended, 43 people had died. More than 7,000 arrests were made, and 2,500 stores were looted. The following year, 1968, Detroit smoldered. But unlike a season prior, when Tigers fans avoided the downtown stadium, they came in droves in '68, escaping into baseball bliss—yet just blocks from where tanks had roamed. The Tigers were good in '67, but otherworldly in '68. They had the All-Star Horton, an African American hero in his community, and Denny McLain, who, preposterously, won 31 games. "It was like, 'Don't throw that brick, the Tigers are on,'" activist Gene Cunningham said in *A City On Fire*.

In Game 1 Gibson indeed set a World Series single-game record with his 17 strikeouts. But the 1968 series journeyed all the way to a Game 7. Mike Smith was in class at Normandy High that day. It was just three weeks after his classmates violently attacked each other. One teacher had the game on a television. The next class, the teacher played it on the radio. That's how Smith experienced the ensuing play.

Two on. Game was scoreless in the seventh. Gibson pitched to Jim Northrup, who whacked a ball into center. Flood, one of the greatest fielders of his generation, misjudged the ball, took a misstep, and just missed it. Both runners scored. Detroit would win the game 4–1 and the World Series in seven games. "I am not exaggerating," Mike Smith said in 2017. "It'll be 50 years next year, and I'm not over it. It seems like there's something immature about that, that I should've gotten over it by now. I'm 63 years old. I can't be the only person in this town who's still upset about that, can't be. It's worse than the Don Denkinger call [in 1985]. The Cardinals beat the Tigers in 2006, but that didn't take care of the wound from '68. I don't know what to say."

* * *

Walking through the Civil Rights exhibit at St. Louis' History Museum in 2017, I wondered if 50 years later they'd make a new exhibit. It would also be poignant, important. It would capture St. Louis in the

2010s. The police shooting of Michael Brown. Ferguson. The police shooting of Anthony Lamar Smith. The protests of the fall of 2017.

While I learned that day about history, history was being made in real time. Dozens of protesters were being arrested, some violently, at the Galleria, the mall I'd go to as a kid. There had been protests across St. Louis all week, following the acquittal of the cop who shot Anthony Lamar Smith. And during them, cops violently arrested *hundreds* of protestors, even a *Post-Dispatch* reporter with visible credentials, forcefully throwing him to the ground, spraying pepper spray in his face.

Since 1968 so much has changed. Since 1968, so much hasn't changed.

In recent years, athletes became activists, even kneeling during the national anthem, to bring attention to their causes and injustice. But then I think of the late 1960s—Horton in his Tigers uniform amid the Detroit protestors. Or Gibson's real and raw comment, baseball's best player saying: "I face more pressure every day just being a Negro." And, most famously, the halting image of the '68 Olympians, John Carlos and Tommie Smith, on the medal stand. As the national anthem began, the two African American men punched the sky, holding their gloved fists high and their heads low.

Sports have an eerie power. They can be a magical escape; they can magnify issues you can't escape. They can bring a city together; they can break a boy's heart. They can do all of the above. "The day that Flood broke in on that ball that Northrup hit," Mike Smith said, "I'm not over that one. I tell Detroit fans that to this day—'I'm not over '68.'"

14

TONY LA RUSSA

Mark McGwire was driving across the Bay Bridge when his car phone rang. It was 1997, back when they were still called car phones, and on the line was Walt Jocketty. McGwire knew Jocketty from the exec's Oakland A's days, and Jocketty was now the general manager of the St. Louis Cardinals. It was July of that season, the last season on McGwire's contract. He had 34 home runs but for naught—for the A's were in malaise, yet again. The Cards wanted that bat, but McGwire had the contractual right to veto any trade. "Walt kept talking," McGwire recalled. "'You don't understand, Mark, your *second dad* wants you to come play for him.'"

Tony La Russa. The great manager. Don Tony. It was an offer he couldn't refuse. "I sat there and said, 'Hey Walt, if I go there, I'm going to be a rental. I'm going to play the season out and then I'll go to free agency,'" McGwire recalled. "He said, 'That's okay. Your dad will take care of everything.'"

La Russa's wooing of McGwire to St. Louis shows so much about the manager. His power, his influence, the respect players had for him, his voracious hunger to win. Of course, they didn't win at first with McGwire. They missed the postseason in the famous home run years. But in 2000 many forget that Mac slashed .305/.483/.746 in 89 games. He also hit 32 homers, and La Russa's Cards won the division and the National League Division Series, too.

That began a 12-year run in which the Cardinals went to the postseason eight times. In six of those eight, they won at least one playoff round. In three of those six, they went to the World Series. La Russa won it all, of course, in 2006. And in the last game he ever managed—Game 7 of the 2011 World Series—he won it all again. "To be able to play for a guy like that—and then to be able to throw the last out in his final game?" Jason Motte said. "That's pretty cool. Every time I get to see him, I always give him a hug. And he says, 'You're like the son I never had!' And I say, 'You say that to everybody!' Playing for him, I went from someone who was a rookie and really young and not really understanding as much about the game. He had gameplans. He knew match-ups. It may not always be what someone else had in mind, but he had his gameplan and stuck with it. And the guy was a Hall of Famer, so he obviously knew what he was doing. It was an honor and a privilege to be able to play for a guy like that."

He was born in October and he was born for October. He became a legend behind those transition lenses. Even in a city with a famed five-star restaurant called Tony's, "Tony" in St. Louis means La Russa. He was the mastermind manager. His televised postgame press conferences even became part of the culture. "My favorite thing about La Russa as a manager was he took Cardinal losses as badly as I did," said author Will Leitch, a Cardinals die-hard. "And I love that. You just knew, even when he'd do things I didn't like, he was just so miserable because of Cardinals losses, and that's what the losses do to me! So I totally understand that."

Dave Duncan was La Russa's consigliere, the wise pitching coach. "When you look at my record, he is directly responsible for *hundreds* of wins," La Russa said. "We signed as rookies out of high school with the Kansas City A's, one year apart. I signed in '62, Dave in '63. We played together several years in the minors, roomed together several times. Dave always had a presence, very competitive, tough, smart. When we were all 18, he was 28. And he played 10 years as a legitimate major league catcher, and I spent 10 years as a legitimate minor leaguer."

Ballplayers, for however cocky they are when they're actually in their playing days, are often brilliantly self-deprecating afterward. La Russa, for instance, did get 176 at-bats in the bigs, 176 more than the majority of the human population, though he did maddeningly finish with a career average of .199, a tick under the infamous Mendoza Line. But he clearly understood the game, respected the game, and, as the story goes, retired as a player in '77 and became a minor league manager in '78 (while picking up a law degree on the side). He was promoted to the White Sox's Triple A dugout in '79. And on August 2, 1979, La Russa became manager of the actual White Sox. He was 35. It started his legendary managerial career and also led to a fun little

Tony La Russa celebrates after winning Game 7 of the 2011 World Series, which represented the second time he guided the Cardinals to a World Series championship.

trivia question: how many decades did La Russa manage in the big leagues? (Since he retired in 2011, the answer is five.)

His old buddy Duncan came back in his life for the '83 season. And this historic sports coaching union—in the same ilk of Bobby Cox and Leo Mazzone, Dean Smith and Bill Guthridge, Mike Ditka and Buddy Ryan—happened because of a poor (and cheap) decision by the Seattle Mariners. The White Sox had eight games late in '82 with the Mariners, and Seattle's skipper was Rene Lachemann, who La Russa knew from the old A's minor league days. Lach's pitching coach was David Edwin Duncan. "Lach told me, 'Dave wants a $5,000 raise, and the owner is not going to give it to him.' And Dave said he wasn't coming back because Dave's a very principled guy," La Russa said. "So Lach said, 'If Dave's going to go, I'd rather him go with you than go with somebody else.' And we had watched Dave grow, so he came with us for the '83 season. We had 99 wins and the Cy Young winner, LaMarr Hoyt. And Richard Dotson won 22 games when he was 24. One of the things that always pissed me off was when they would say, 'Dave doesn't work well with young pitchers. He always wants veterans.' And that's so much bullshit because he worked with whoever you brought him...as I came to find out. We were together from '83 to 2011. He was the complete pitching coach. Sometimes a guy might be strong in some areas but not others."

With the Cardinals, these two developed a litany of pitchers, squeezing the best out of guys (Kent Bottenfield comes to mind) or propelling a great pitcher to the next level (Chris Carpenter comes to mind). And of course, La Russa was an innovator—developing bullpen roles that never existed or sometimes batting the pitcher eighth—all while balancing intuition and integers. "Kind of like a mad scientist," said Motte, the rookie hurler whom La Russa named closer for October of 2011, similar to October of 2006, when La Russa named the rookie Adam Wainwright closer. "I feel like the more I get away from playing for him, the more I kind of see some of the other things he was doing that—not that I ever thought didn't make sense—but stuff that's like, *Wow, Tony was out there playing a chess match.* He was playing this chess match with people, and sometimes they were aware of it, and sometimes they weren't. I remember early on in my career, going to play the Cubs and watching him and Dusty Baker almost mean-mugging each other from one dugout to another. And it was just this big chess match between the two of them. Dusty would bring this guy in, and Tony would bring this guy in. From a baseball standpoint, Tony has done some amazing stuff."

That includes going to three World Series with the American League A's, winning it in 1989, and going three more times with St. Louis of the National League. He also won the fourth most games (522) in White Sox history, the second most in A's history (798 wins, second to Connie Mack's eleventy billion), and *most* (1,408) in Cardinals history.

And while he lets his guard down when it comes to his love of animals or talking about his all-time favorite players, such as Yadi and Carp and Big Mac, La Russa was a fierce, piercing leader of the Cardinals. "I'm still scared of Tony!" Brad Thompson exclaimed to me seven years after the pitcher had retired. "I'm still scared he's going to pull me out of a game. I never wanted to let Tony down. Tony to me, I knew how bad he wanted it and I wanted it even more because of that. He hated to lose. He hated to lose much more than he liked to win. There is no way around that. You've got to respect that, man. It sounds like it could be a grind through a whole season to have a manager like that. But when you have a manager like that, you tend to win more. You're not going to want to live through a week of Tony being pissed off...Going in, there's just the reverence around Tony. He's done special things. But when you're around it every day, you see the conviction that he manages with, the care he brings."

LOUUUUUUUUUU
BROCK

His first name had more U's than a college conference, and the U's caused even the baddest men in town to make kissy faces, cooing the "U" sound after yet another stolen base. Born in 1939 Louuuuuuuuuuis Clark Brock had a name destined for Cardinals glory. Louis became a Saint in St. Louis, playing at a ballpark on a street called Clark.

But first he was a Chicago Cub. But even before that, he was a student trying so hard to impress a college coach that he passed out from exhaustion. The famous tidbit about Brock, one of the greatest professional athletes of his generation or any generation, was that Brock went to college on a work-study academic scholarship. But when he lost that scholarship at Southern University, he decided to walk-on the baseball team in an effort to get an athletic scholarship instead. As the story goes, Brock volunteered to retrieve batted balls at practice. Hustling all over the place, he ended up passing out in the Baton Rouge, Louisiana, heat. Once he came to, the coaches allowed him to take five swings at batting practice. Brock mustered enough energy to hit one out of the park. He made the team and became Lou Brock.

Now, the casual baseball fan associates Brock with base burglary, and that's fair, but he could hit, too. Sure, he didn't walk much, but he could hit. In fact, Brock finished his career with a .293 average. And he did that in 19 total seasons. He eclipsed the 3,000-hit mark with 3,023. From 1965 to 1971, he averaged 33.7 doubles per season. And consider some of his finest seasons—in 1967 he hit .299 with 32 doubles and 21 homers and stole 52 bases, most in the league. In 1968 Brock led the league in both doubles (46) and triples (14), but he also found enough open bases to steal 62, a league-best, too.

But, yeah, what separated Brock from other talented hitters was his game-changing, season-altering speed. "Lou was just a genuine person off the field," teammate Al Hrabosky said of the Hall of Famer.

"And on the field, just a fierce competitor that had the ability to needle and get under the skin of catchers. He just had that arrogance that you would never associate with him off the field. On the field he would tell [New York Mets catcher] Jerry Grote, 'I'm going to get four off you today.' And the Texan would get so mad and everything, and Lou would get on base and start stealing and say, 'I got three more!'"

The 1964 Cards management wanted more speed. On June 15, 1964, St. Louis acquired Brock, Paul Toth, and Jack Spring from the Cubs for Ernie Broglio, Doug Clemens, and Bobby Shantz. But basically, it was Brock for Broglio. Brock then, famously, ignited the '64 Cards. In 103 games he stole 33 bases, hitting .348. They won it all. So he was a Cardinals legend before his first Cardinals spring training. Of course, he won another ring in 1967. He hit .414 in the World Series and he stole seven bases in the seven series games. And from 1966 to 1974, Brock led the league in stolen bases in every season but one. (The exception and trivia answer is Bobby Tolan in 1970.) "To do that over the course of the years?" Hrabosky asked aloud. "And back then, you didn't slide headfirst because an infielder would hurt you. He'd drop a knee on you. And Lou would slide so aggressively. I can't tell you how many times I thought, *Oh, that one broke his leg.* And middle infielders didn't want to hang in there because they knew he was coming in hot. At times, he'd even kick the ball out of their gloves. It was just so much fun to play with him. And then to see him as such a calm gentleman off the field, it was such a contrast."

Seventy-four. That's the most bases he'd ever stolen, entering '74. But some National League officials approached Brock about chasing the all-time single-season record of 104. Brock was 35 years old. But they told him about the rejuvenation of baseball in our nation—Hank Aaron breaking Babe Ruth's home run record, teammate Bob Gibson striking out his 3,000th batter. They wanted a season-long quest to captivate the fans. He said he'd give it a shot. And he was caught stealing 13 times in his first 25 attempts.

But then Brock called Maury Wills, the owner of the record. The Los Angeles Dodgers great told Brock that he was running in fear. That insulted Brock, but Wills meant that Brock was only searching for the perfect jump. Why not turn the tables on the battery and make the catcher make the perfect throw? Wills gave Brock some will, and by September, well, the old vet had stolen his 105th base. Brock finished the '74 season with 118 stolen bases, a National League record that still stands today. Brock kept on running through the rest of the decade while smacking hits and mentoring with grace. "Lou gave me my first pair of shoes actually," said infielder Ken Oberkfell, who was a rookie in 1977. "I think I actually still got them. Yup, when I first got to the big leagues, I had shoes, but he gave me a pair of shoes and I'm like, 'Lou Brock, I can't wear these shoes.'"

Brock retired at the end of the 1979 season, a fitting bookend to a decade he dominated. Louis Clark Brock finished with 938 stolen bases, the most ever by a National League player to this day. St. Louisans, even those who never saw him play, revere Lou. (They even reluctantly wore his "Brockabrella," the umbrella hat Brock invented and sold for years.) People have "I saw Lou Brock" stories like the "I saw Stan Musial" or "I saw Chuck Berry" stories shared by the wide-eyed.

And he would make public appearances—none more astounding than at Opening Day in 2016 after part of one of his legs had to be amputated in 2015. "I'd call him one of the toughest people I've ever met," said Tom Ackerman, sports director for KMOX Radio in St. Louis. "He and I have worked on some charity events together. I've seen him pull off some amazing things. At his golf tournament one year, it was just really hot. Some people had encouraged him to stay inside. He said, 'No, I want to be there.' And he's on the 10th tee box, visiting each group. And a couple years ago, I emceed a private nighttime event at Grant's Farm, and it was me, Whitey Herzog, and Lou. When Lou showed up, he had just had some dental surgery, a significant surgery. You could tell he was worn out. I thought to myself, *I'm going to keep an eye on him, and if there are any signs of difficulty, I'll wing it on stage.* Well, I introduce them, the lights come on the stage, and Lou is instantly engaged! His wit was just on, telling jokes, telling great stories, and I'm looking at him and thinking, *I can't believe this is the same guy I saw 10 minutes ago.* But that's who he was, tough. He puts on the show for the fans, just like he did as a player."

18

MIGUEL MEJIA CHANNELS ENOS SLAUGHTER

He may very well be the worst Cardinals player ever. One of his official positions wasn't even a position. On baseball-reference.com Miguel Mejia is officially listed as follows:

Height: 6'1"
Weight: 155 pounds
Bats: Right
Throws: Right
Positions: Outfielder and Pinch-Runner

Mejia was a 21-year-old wedged onto the roster of the 1996 division-winning Cards. This happened because Mejia was a Rule 5 pick, and the rule was those players had to be on the major league roster the entire year, or they'd be susceptible to being plucked by another franchise. Sometimes this works out. On the 2016 Cardinals, Rule 5 reliever Matt Bowman pitched well enough to become a go-to reliever the following season.

Other times, it works out like Miguel Mejia.

In his lone season, he actually finished with a negative WAR (wins above replacement). The whole point of WAR is to show how much better a player is than a marginal "replacement" player. Somehow, Mejia was even worse than one of those.

But on one mystical night in Los Angeles, he just didn't stop running. And it was reminiscent of a play made 50 falls before by one of the best Cardinals ever.

* * *

The 1946 World Series. Game 7. Bottom of the eighth. Tie game. The great Enos "Country" Slaughter was on first base with two outs when the Cards' Harry Walker smacked a Boston Red Sox pitch to left-center field. Slaughter had been running, so he rounded second, rounded third. He just kept running. They call it "The Mad Dash." It's some special stuff. It gets capital letters. Slaughter scored from first on the hit. (He, for all intents and purposes, scored on a single, but when the throw went home, Walker scooted to second, so the official scorer gave him a double.)

The Cards won the World Series, and the sliding Slaughter became an iconic image, one eternally bronzed as a statue in front of Busch Stadium. "Hard-nosed, hustling performer...Daring baserunner," it says on another eternally bronzed commemoration, which is Slaughter's Hall of Fame plaque in Cooperstown.

In May of 1996, manager Tony La Russa was asked about Mejia. Did he remind the skipper of someone from the past? "Possibly Paul Blair," La Russa mused of the old Baltimore Orioles player. "Mejia has as good a throwing arm as anyone in the league, has way above-average legs...If he hits .250, he can be a contributor in the big leagues. But we're shooting for better than that."

Well, Mejia hit .087.

But he was on the club all season, occasionally pinch-running, often pitch-watching. He was a cool story, though. The oldest of 11 kids, Mejia himself was married with a kid, and here he was in the majors, sipping 162 cups of coffee. "I guarantee you he's a serious player," La Russa had said.

As sports moments go, this has all the makings of an old fable, in which the details deteriorate, and the story plumps into the improbable. But it truly happened on September 13, 1996, and in the thick of a playoff race. And you have to remember, St. Louis hadn't been to the playoffs since 1987, going on nearly a dang decade. And while the Cards clung to a division lead, they had scored just four total runs in the previous 35 innings.

Scoreless game. Top of the ninth. Gary Gaetti, one of the best mistake hitters of his era, singled. La Russa called upon his pinch-runner. After another hit, Mejia went to second.

And so, trying to manufacture a run—and avoid a double play with the slow-running Danny Sheaffer—La Russa called for Sheaffer to attempt a no-out bunt.

Here's how the *St. Louis Post-Dispatch*'s Rick Hummel captured what happened next:

"Mejia from second base was running with the pitch on a sign he said he had from La Russa...But, like Enos Slaughter in the 1946 World Series, Mejia didn't stop at third. He roared past coach Tommie Reynolds and slid into catcher Mike Piazza...'My [jaw] sank to my stomach,' Tommie Reynolds said in the aftermath. 'I said—Holy cow, there's no way he can score on that.'...But umpire Gary Darling said Mejia bounced off Piazza's shin guard with no tag being made. When Mejia finally touched the plate with his hand, he was called safe, and the Dodgers went ballistic, losing manager Bill Russell and two players, who were ejected in the debate...'He didn't touch me,' Mejia said. 'Never.'"

As such, after Mejia's dash, the *Post-Dispatch* headline stated: "CARDS HEAR THE CALL, WIN 2–0 —'COUNTRY' MEJIA SCORES IN 9TH."

"Slaughter's play was not a surprise," 1996 team instructor Red Schoendienst, a player on the '46 team, told the newspaper. "There's no words for [Mejia's]."

The 1996 Cards, sure enough, made the playoffs.

Now, Enos "Country" Slaughter was famous—and to some, infamous—for his hard-nosed and hard-headed approach to playing baseball. Historians have written much about Slaughter's controversial infield run-in with Jackie Robinson.

In 1946 Slaughter returned after three seasons in the service. It really is remarkable to play the what-if game with stars of the 1940s like Slaughter and Ted Williams. Consider that Slaughter himself finished second in the 1942 MVP voting. He returned in 1946 and finished third.

Earlier in 1946 Enos beat out a throw to first, and Chicago Cubs general manager Jim Gallagher groused to the writer Bob Broeg: "That big-rumped baboon goes into service for three years, drinks beer, and comes out running faster than ever."

Slaughter slaughtered pitches. He finished 1946 with 130 RBIs and walked 69 times compared to just 41 strikeouts.

And the 1946 Cards were the first team to ever win a playoff series before the World Series. Since the Brooklyn Dodgers finished with the same record, they played St. Louis in a best-of-three. Slaughter had two hits in the opener against Ralph Branca, who surely thought after losing the game that nothing could ever get worse for him on a diamond. And in the second game, Slaughter tripled home Stan Musial and Whitey Kurowski, turning a fifth-inning nailbiter into a 4–1 cruise. Soon after, Slaughter scored on a hit by Erv "Four Sack" Dusak. St. Louis was headed to the World Series. And it was a dandy, going seven games and all.

After a previous disagreement about the decisions of Mike Gonzalez, St. Louis' third-base coach, Slaughter worked out a deal with the team's manager: if Slaughter felt it, he would run through a Gonzalez stop sign. And on his Mad Dash, Slaughter did just that.

There are often Boston excuses made about The Mad Dash. One is that crackerjack outfielder Dom DiMaggio had pulled his hamstring, so it was backup Leon Culberson who fielded the hit. Perhaps Dom would've been positioned differently. Perhaps Dom with a stronger arm could've thrown Slaughter out at third.

The second excuse, of course, is about Johnny Pesky, the infielder who hesitated upon cutting off Culberson's throw. Reports say that crowd noise kept Pesky from hearing teammates. So Pesky held the ball an extra tick or two before desperately throwing home as Slaughter slid.

Twenty-five years later, St. Louis hosted a reunion of both teams from that World Series. The players, including Pesky, played a couple exhibition innings that day in 1971. Sure enough, Slaughter hurried home. "They crossed us up," Slaughter told the *Post-Dispatch*. "They were supposed to get me out this time so that Johnny Pesky finally could be cleared."

"Country" retired to the country. He lived on a farm in his home state of North Carolina and died at 86. Longtime Cardinals beat writer Derrick Goold reported that Slaughter, who famously cried when the Cards traded him at an older age, was buried in a Cardinals jersey.

As for Miguel Mejia, he never made the majors again after 1996. In that '96 season, he had 23 at-bats and two hits. He stole six bases and was caught stealing three times. He played in the minors until 1999, becoming a what-if himself. But in Cardinals lore, he'll always be Miguel "Country" Mejia.

17

WHITEY

The only "perfect game" Art Holliday ever saw was a 9–5 Cards win against the Houston Astros. It was 1983. The Cards were defending world champs. "And Whitey Herzog was God in St. Louis," said Holliday, the longtime sportscaster for Channel 5. "I went to my news managers and said, 'Why don't I do an in-depth profile on Whitey?' And my idea was to put a wireless microphone on him during a game. Well, easier said than done. But [we] worked Whitey, worked him, worked him, and finally Whitey consented. I was kind of shocked, to be honest with you. So we're in the Cardinals clubhouse, wiring him up, and Whitey said, 'Aw, I don't know why you'd want to do this, I never say anything during the game.' And I'm getting paranoid. *What if he doesn't say anything?* But it was the perfect game."

Joaquin Andujar was pitching for the Cards that day. He was one tough Dominican. That's literally what Andujar called himself to the press. But Andujar was erratic against the Astros. So Herzog strolled to the pitcher's mound and, as Holliday described it, "just *lights* into him! 'You can't pitch as good as you did in the World Series and then all of a sudden get to be this horseshit, right? Take the fucking ball and throw the fucking ball the way you can throw it!' We had bleep half of it out, but it was gold."

Herzog's parents couldn't pick one name to give him, so they gave him three: Dorrel Norman Elvert Herzog. Whitey became Whitey in the minors. Born in New Athens, Illinois, a tiny town 40 miles from St. Louis, the blond bounced around in the bigs, beginning in 1956. After peeking at his stats, I was surprised to find he had a better career than I first thought. The great manager was wont to say: "Baseball has been good to me since I quit trying to play it," but he did stick for eight seasons. His two best came with the Baltimore Orioles in 1961 and 1962, when he combined for 586 at-bats, hitting .280 with a .379 on-base percentage.

When he took over as the Cardinals' general manager and manager in 1980, Herzog revamped and rejuvenated a franchise that had gone 0-for-the-1970s in regards to making the postseason. He traded big names, small names, seemingly any name any team would take. He made eight transactions from December of 1980 through December of 1981.

And he ended up with a title team.

Herzog and the Cards won it all in 1982. They lost the World Series in 1985 and 1987, and, though many make excuses about Don Denkinger ('85) and key injuries ('87), you can't tell the full story of those two World Series without bringing those up.

Whitey would finish 822–728 in his 11-year career in town. He filled his tenure with panache and personality and he won a bunch of ballgames with strategy and style and by bringing the most Herzog he could out of his hitters. See, Whitey walked a lot as a player, and only one National League team had more walks than the 1982 Cards, who also led the league in on-base percentage (.334) and stolen bases (200).

Sure enough, his '85 and '87 teams led the league in OBP and stolen bases, too. With the vast Astroturf as his personal playground, Herzog fielded a speedy, slap-hitting team that was always on the move. "I think of Willie going first to third, Ozzie with the flips, Vince Coleman stealing bases," said longtime St. Louis sportscaster Frank Cusumano. "And I think of Whitey in that powder blue, hideous Cardinal uniform, orchestrating it all."

The press loved him. "He would say, 'A fan's got a right to read the paper and find out what happened,'" pitcher Joe Magrane shared, "so he let the writers inside and didn't pull any punches and oftentimes got messages to us by what he would say."

The fans loved him. "It was like, 'Wait a minute, this is different. I can't get enough of these guys,'" said Joe Buck, Jack's son. "Whitey brought it back from the dead."

The players loved him. "One word that comes to mind is freedom," former Cardinals player Andy Van Slyke said. "He never stymied anybody's ability."

What fascinates me about Whitey is how he was a maestro. He orchestrated that mellifluous offense, sure. But he controlled every little facet, getting the right amount out of each option. He groomed his bench. He'd play cards with the Cards' 25th man just to make him feel comfortable. He'd tell John Morris: "Johnny, you do more with one at-bat than you do with four," which came off as an insult until Morris realized Whitey coveted Morris' keen focus when it mattered most. And thus Morris delivered when it mattered most. (According to baseball-reference.com, Morris hit significantly better in categorically high-leverage situations than any other situation.)

Herzog reduced pressure on his stars and starters. At times when Willie McGee was leading off, Whitey told him not to take extra pitches. A prototypical leadoff hitter would want to take extra pitches, but that's not what made McGee special. Willie was forever thankful.

And he strategized about future games during current games. "He has a photographic mind," said Magrane, who started Game 7 of the 1987 World Series. "Nobody else in baseball did this, but the day before we were going to start, pitchers would sit right behind home plate with a notebook of the baseball field and we'd draw dotted lines where the batted balls went. Whitey would process that information, and it affected how he positioned everyone on the field. This was before the over-shifting and everything that's done by a computer model now. He was such an incredible evaluator of talent. You would see players who played for us and then went to other teams, and the manager didn't know how to get the best out of them. I just felt that every time we played it was like we had a 10th man on the field because I've seen him so many times out-manage the other manager."

Over the years, the manager job in baseball has morphed. Today it's part psychologist, part sergeant, part innovator, part tone-creator. Forever enshrined in Cooperstown, Herzog was all of those things for the Cardinals. And sometimes the strategy wasn't sophisticated; it was just about feel. "Whitey had a way of relaxing players," said Rex Hudler, the scrappy Cards player whom Herzog acquired in one of his final moves with the club. "I would be a little uptight. I was trying to make some money, make a name, and he could tell. He'd say, 'Hey, kid, come here! Did I ever tell you about the time me and Red [Schoendienst] went fishing? Red! Red, get over here! We're in a boat, Red stands up, and the whole boat flips over!' And I'm getting wrapped up in his story, and about that time, he goes, 'It's time to play, kid. Get out there.' He knew how to take that pressure off. This was 10 minutes before the game. I'd have my game face on, and he relaxed me and he made me feel special, like I was somebody. I love the White Rat."

18

MARK McGWIRE

Her first crush wasn't a person but a personification. She was 10, ponytailed, and in love with baseball, the embodiment of childhood bliss. "I don't remember ever not being a Cardinals fan," Joan Niesen said.

Sometimes, her babysitter would take her to ballgames. Afterward, they'd wait to wave to the Cardinals, and by the players' parking lot, there was Mark McGwire whirring by. "It was the coolest thing ever," said Niesen, a St. Louis native, who became an acclaimed *Sports Illustrated* writer. "I was just so in awe of the Cardinals. They were like gods."

September 8, 1998. "[I] still remember the date. The night he hit 62," Niesen said. "I was at Jenny Albus' house, in her basement, playing. The game was on the radio. I was in fifth grade. She had this kids' rocking horse in her basement, and it had a pole like it would've attached to a carousel. It was the pole you held on to as you rocked. It was pastel colors, very girly. And I was just playing on it, and he hit the home run, and as it sounded like it was going to be the home run, I jumped up off the rocking horse, which caused the horse to tilt backward—if it was a real horse, it would've picked up its front legs in the air—and the pole whammed me in the mouth! And it chipped my right front tooth, the inner corner. I'm missing the inner corner. It's tiny, but you can feel it on the edge. There's a tiny triangle gone. But I didn't say anything to anybody that night. I was just so excited. So, I had the same dentist all my life in St. Louis and I'd told him at the time it was no big deal, and that was that. But after college in Dallas, I went to a dentist there, and they said, 'We can do a filling on that tooth to get that chip perfected,' and I was like, 'No! I would never want to fill that chip in!' And he looked at me like I was crazy. And I was like, 'That's Mark McGwire! I like that part of my tooth.' It just reminds me of that night, baseball. That was the season that made me. I read the *Post-Dispatch* every morning, and there was that box in the upper right-hand corner of the sports page that had Sosa, Griffey, and McGwire. I would look at the box. I'd memorize stats. It just reminds me of being that age and being just so excited and happy about something, so why would I want to change that?"

McGwire was the perfect thing to happen at the perfect time in the perfect place. You know the story: strike in 1994, game loses support. Then in '98 along come McGwire and Sosa, and the nation is captivated, captured, enraptured. A home run race to the home run record. Now this was bliss.

Baseball's home run is the most fascinating phenomenon in all of sports because it defies the constructs of the game. Here's what I mean. We play our games within parameters. There is, simply, a playing surface with denoted boundaries. Within those limits is where the sport happens. But if a baseball player proves strong enough, he can occasionally hit the ball so well, so far, that it breaks through the boundary, departing the confines. The baseball soars out of the controlled environment, into the world, perhaps smacking a seat, a step, or somebody or something unprepared for this flying projectile.

The home run is a spectacle to begin with. Yet when Mark David McGwire hit homers, his dwarfed the spectacle of the standard home run. This must've been what it was like to watch Babe Ruth. Or Roy Hobbs.

Of course, McGwire was juiced as hell.

In sports few players get better as they get older. And here was a guy in his 12th season somehow getting better *and* bigger. And in 2010 McGwire admitted his use of performance-enhancing drugs to Bob Costas.

From then on, we grappled. What do we make of Mark? He broke the unbreakable record of 61 homers, hitting 70 in 1998. (Shoot, he did it again in '99, hitting 65.) But how much of that was because of the PEDs?

We yearn for the larger-than-life. We're the humans on the outside, looking upon the confines of sports, desiring the superhumans to hit the ball out of the dimensions. But then we're pretty judgmental about how the sausage arms are made.

In St. Louis the debate intensified around McGwire's induction into the team's Hall of Fame in 2017. For a *Post-Dispatch* column, I sat with McGwire and pointed out that some fans felt he shouldn't be in the team's Hall of Fame because of PEDs. If he had the chance, what would he say to them? "If you go back in the game of baseball, there were no rules and regulations at the time," he said from the dugout that day. "Unfortunately, I did what I did. I've owned up to it. I'm truly sorry. If there were rules and regulations, I would've never touched it—even gotten close to it. That's the bottom line. Unfortunately, I did, I've owned up to it. Me knowing what I know and what I did in that box with the mental [side], the power of the mind, the preparation in the game, for that [PED] stuff to have any bearing on what I did? I don't agree."

Could he have hit 70 without them? "There's no question," McGwire said. "No question."

That's debatable.

When he first admitted steroid use, he said it was to heal from injuries faster, to stay on the field more. So if he hadn't used the PEDs, wouldn't he have been out with injuries more often? Would he have even had the necessary at-bats to total 70 home runs?

And then, of course, there's the aspect that PEDs make you really, really strong. McGwire was a strong slugger before he began using PEDs. But he wasn't the exact same player after using them. He was enhanced.

Okay, okay, okay.

As we sift through it all, maybe this is the best way of handling the conflicting emotions—putting everything out there, warts and all, talking about it, getting stuff off our chests. He cheated. He cheated you and me. But the experiences still happened. Seventy balls went over walls. That tingling feeling of wonderment? You felt it. That can't be erased. So we just encompass it all. "There is that little—ugh, it's too bad it's not perfect," Joan Niesen said. "But it's not like Mark McGwire was some nobody who couldn't do anything, took steroids, and then did what he did. I do appreciate what he was as a baseball player. In the end sports are a game, and cheating is despicable.

But it is just a game, and does it really matter? Am I going to curse Mark McGwire for it? No, it's a game. And I really do think they saved baseball in a lot of ways. Was it right that they were taking steroids? Absolutely not. But at the same time, before that baseball was an old man's sport. It was hard to get people who were younger in other cities into it, especially in cities where NFL is king. It was really important to get a generation of fans on board. I do think it's not a perfect story because of that. But at the same time, baseball needed that."

19

VINCE COLEMAN VS. THE TARP

A t Cardinals' Fantasy Camp, you're a Cardinals player without talent. You live the life of a major leaguer. You get a full Cards uniform, your last name on the back, the famed birds on the bat on the front. You play in actual games at the actual stadium, batting from the Busch batter's box. You even get to pick your own walk-up song. And during the day, you just hang around Busch Stadium with pretend Cardinals and the real Cardinals, the retired players who return to make your baseball dreams come true.

And so in the summer of 2016, I was sitting in the clubhouse, talking base-stealing with some retired Cardinals, when Vince Coleman walked by. One of the guys in the conversation was Tyler Greene, who swiped 11 bases for the 2011 World Series champs. Not once that season was Greene thrown out stealing. He meticulously explained the math of the base swipe, utilizing the pitcher's release time clocked by the first-base coach. If a guy took 1.3 seconds or more to deliver a pitch, Greene would consider stealing. But if it was 1.2 seconds or faster, no way. "What is all this?" Coleman chirped.

Greene fumbled through a quicker version of what he'd explained and was interrupted again by Coleman: "Nah, come on, man, you just go when you feel you can go."

This juxtaposition of generations showed the changes to the game from the 1980s to the 2010s. And it also summed up the panache that was "Vincent Van Go." The point of getting on first base is to steal second.

In 1985 Coleman, then a rookie outfielder, stole 110

bases. He was also thrown out 25 times—they had 1.2 second pitchers back then, too—but that's shooed aside when it comes to what's inside his shoes, the mystique of these fleet feet in cleats.

Fittingly for the St. Louis area code, the '85 Cardinals stole 314 bases. That was the most in the National League. Since 1920. "I don't think there's been a player like Vince Coleman since Vince Coleman," said St. Louis native Jason Sklar, who was 13 in 1985 and is now part of a popular L.A. comedy duo with his twin brother, Randy. "I can't imagine how intimidating that was for a pitcher. You think about that impact. Right now, my son is in a seven-to-eight-year-old league, and for some reason, they allow stealing in this league. It's the weirdest thing in the world. So basically any time anyone gets on first base, in two pitches they're on third. And that's how I felt about Vince Coleman that year...It was a magical time."

In the '85 National League Championship Series, the Cards were down 0–2 to the Los Angeles Dodgers. But back at Busch, Vince was Vince. In Game 3 he tallied two hits, stole a base, and scored two runs.

The Birds headed into Game 4 on October 13, 1985, a day that'll live in the infirmary.

"I'm thinking, *Here's the fastest guy on the field, and I've never seen a tarp roll faster than my garage door*," Jason Sklar said. "How the hell is Vince Coleman getting caught by a tarp? None of this makes sense."

There was a chance of rain. So the Busch Stadium automatic tarpaulin rose from the Busch Astroturf and then began to roll, trapping the left leg of the oblivious Coleman. In the coming nights, Ozzie Smith made St. Louis go crazy, Jack Clark made Pedro Guerrero throw his glove to the ground, and Don Denkinger made even nuns curse. But the Cards lost the 1985 World Series to Kansas City. Would St. Louis have won it all if Vince never hurt his foot in the tarp? "I would like to think so," Coleman said.

I first met Vincent Maurice Coleman in 2015, a year prior to the aforementioned Fantasy Camp. We sat for an inning in a private box at Busch, talking tarps. He then began to tell the story, which is still crazy after all these years. I first asked how many times he was interviewed and *not* asked about the tarp. Coleman laughed and said: "Never.

If I had a quarter for every time that question has been asked, I'd probably be a millionaire."

Before Game 4 of the '85 NLCS, the Cards were on the field. Coleman and Terry Pendleton were coming toward the dugout to get bats for batting practice. It began to drizzle. "And [coach] Hal Lanier said, 'I'll get your bats. You guys stay right here.'" Coleman recalled. "We were positioned between the foul line and the pitcher's mound. Now the tarp is right where the first-base box is. There's a guy down midway in right field, and you have to hook it up to a truck and drive it out. He started doing that, we're not paying attention—just like you and I talking. It would've either gotten me or it would've got Terry because you can't hear it.

"Next thing I know, it was tugging on my leg. It knocked me down. And you know how they say, 'When you're in fear of your life, you

Vince Coleman writhes in agony after the tarp machine inexplicably injures his leg prior to Game 4 of the 1985 National League Championship Series.

don't feel a thing?' This thing weighed a ton, and I didn't feel anything because I'm thinking it's going to crush me."

It was 1,200 pounds spread over 180 feet. And the massive tarp did what seemingly no catcher could do—keep Coleman from stealing bases. "I'd seen a lot of things take athletes out of commission," Mitch Albom, the author of *Tuesdays with Morrie* who also covered the 1985 playoffs, shared with me. "Injuries, freak accidents, a guy putting his hand through his headlights, cutting off a finger with a steak knife, shooting himself in the leg—literally—but, honestly, that was the first time I'd seen a piece of equipment try to eat a player alive. There was nothing to do but shrug and say, 'When you think you've seen it all...'"

At first, Vince's injury was ruled a contusion. He missed that night's game, and the media had some fun while writing from their TRS-80 Model 100 portable computers. Kevin Horrigan of the *St. Louis Post-Dispatch* wrote: "He'd seen the Killer Tarp in action before. Like a Zombie it rises from its grave, a three-foot-wide, 180-foot-long section of the stadium floor that comes up, unrolling a motorized aluminum tube on which the rubberized canvas infield tarp is stored. One night, the Killer Tarp got stuck halfway across the field, forcing postponement of a game. But usually the Killer Tarp is kindly. Not Sunday afternoon."

And Albom, then writing for the *Detroit Free Press*, described the fictitious arrest of the tarp for "attempted man-smother." The tarp finally broke down to the media, admitting: "This ain't an easy life, you know. How would you feel if every time you came out, people booed?"

But an MRI soon revealed that Coleman's left tibia was cracked. His season was over.

The Cardinals not only won Game 4 in St. Louis, but also Game 5, thanks to Ozzie's walk-off homer.

Deprived of a chance to be Mr. October, Coleman spent a day off in Los Angeles looking for Miss October. "I was a guest at the Playboy Mansion. I go over to Hugh Hefner's house," Coleman said. "Hefner knew exactly who I was. And he said, 'You're the guy that the female tarp was looking for!'"

At this point, all they could do was laugh. After all, Coleman had suffered perhaps the most inexplicable injury in baseball history.

St. Louis won the National League pennant. And then, seemingly everyone—whether they call it Missour-ee or Missouri-uh—in Missouri knows what happened next. The Kansas City Royals won Game 6 after Denkinger blew a ninth-inning call at first. And Kansas City won Game 7 after the Cardinals unraveled under pressure. "We could've won it in six games if we get the call," St. Louis manager Whitey Herzog said during a visit to Busch in 2015. "But we got shut out again in the seventh. That's the worst night I ever spent in baseball."

St. Louisans forever ask "what if" in regards to Coleman in 1985. Herzog did show some levity when asked about it. "I don't know," the skipper said, "he wasn't what you'd call Babe Ruth."

Coleman finished his career with 752 stolen bases. During six seasons with St. Louis, his stolen base totals were 110, 107, 109, 81, 65, and 77. Coleman played for five other teams, but asked if he'll forever consider himself a Cardinal, he said: "Oh, of course. This is where everything started for me. It's a special privilege to play for the Cardinals. There's nothing better. I'm honored and proud and can easily say I was part of one of the best baseball teams that have ever been assembled, being on the '85 team. It was probably the fastest team ever assembled."

20

THE 1964 WORLD SERIES

For 50 cents, the blind man let you park on his lawn. You'd honk two times to let him know you'd arrived, and he'd wave his arm like a third-base coach. So on gamedays, Ed Smith's Rambler rambled down Page Boulevard to Grand Avenue, though sometimes he'd detour to Natural Bridge Road because he wanted to show his son the ballfields of his youth. They ultimately were headed to the ballfield of Ed's son's youth.

They'd park off Grand before going to the park on Grand. The blind man lived on Sullivan Street, and as Ed Smith paid him, the next thing you knew, they were in some drawn-out, heated discussion about some Cardinals lineup move. And antsy Mike Smith, 10 in '64, just wanted to get in the danged ballpark because "the whole thing was built around for me anticipation of going to see Ken Boyer."

In 2017 Mike Smith turned 64 in October, fittingly since he was gushing about October of '64. The 2017 season represented his 17th season as the official scorer at St. Louis Cardinals games. His office was Busch Stadium, but on this day, his mind was back at Sportsman's Park, where Ken Boyer roamed, where the Cardinals somehow won the pennant, and where the Cardinals won the World Series. "We'd sit third-base side, upper deck," Mike Smith recalled. "Dad was on an upper-deck budget. He was a civil engineer. And the upper-deck seats were reserved to a point, and then there was a railing there. It was like a line of demarcation and then general admission seats, and they would cost a buck. I remember the outrage when they raised the tickets to $2. So he would make sure that we got there in time, so we'd be right by the railing, so I would be closest to Ken Boyer, so I could get a good look at Ken Boyer because I wouldn't shut up about Ken Boyer."

Kenton Lloyd Boyer, of Alba, Missouri, drove in 119 runs during that crazy season of '64. He won the MVP and was the captain and catalyst of an offense that did the impossible. The Cards were so far back that summer that they made a seemingly desperate deal, trading a starting pitcher with a 3.50 ERA who also had ERAs of 3.00 and 2.99 in the previous seasons. Newly traded to the Chicago Cubs, Ernie Broglio told reporters, "I'm glad to join a winning team."

Then the guy who made that trade was fired. It was August 16th. The Cards were nine-and-a-half games out of first place, and general manager Bing Devine was out. By the 23rd of August, they were 11 back of the first-place Philadelphia Phillies. But on the next night, Bob Gibson started for the Cards.

He went all nine, allowing a lone run, striking out a dozen. Ken Boyer thwacked a solo shot. And Lou Brock, the kid nabbed in the Cubs trade, tallied two hits and two runs. He stole a bag, too. The Cards beat the Pittsburgh Pirates, while the Phillies lost to the Milwaukee Braves.

It had begun.

* * *

The boys were born into the Dust Bowl. Edward Collins Smith was named after the great ballplayer Eddie Collins. He had an older brother, Tyrus Raymond Smith, who was named after Tyrus Raymond Cobb.

It was the Depression. Their family went from West Texas in the 1930s to Arkansas to Missouri. This new town of theirs, St. Louis, had two teams for which the Smith kids could root. Ty took the Browns. Ed ended up with the Cardinals. Those were his guys.

As a ballplayer himself, Ed had some high school highlights over at Fairgrounds Park. Into his adult years, he'd play and play well in a fast-pitch softball league. "I felt like Boyer was a taller model of my dad," Mike Smith said. "My dad had Popeye forearms. And he saw my interest, so the first glove he bought me was a Ken Boyer six-fingered model...There was just something about Boyer...He would launch balls into the left-field seats. He would make the stunning plays at third. He had a great throwing arm, and the whole thing looked so effortless. I was trying to play when I was little and I wasn't very good, and then there was this guy, and it was all effortless, just, like, born to play."

One of the first memories Ed shared with Mike was a Boyer grand slam back in 1956. At that point it had been a long decade since Ed's team had won a pennant, let alone a World Series. And by 1964, still nothing. Year after year after year.

But something started to stir. After Gibson's win against the Pirates, the Cards were 10 games back. The very next night, in the bottom of the 13th inning, Brock hit a walk-off homer. And then they completed the sweep of Pittsburgh. Boyer knocked in two; Brock homered again.

Louis Clark Brock. Man, he changed the game. He energized the Cardinals, a forerunner to the four runners: Lonnie Smith, Ozzie Smith, Willie McGee, and, of course, Vince Coleman. They played for the Runnin' Redbirds. Brock *was* the runnin' Redbird and he spearheaded the inexplicable '64 run. From that Pittsburgh series until the end of the '64 season—a 39-game stretch—Brock hit .360 with a .400 on-base percentage. He hit eight round-trippers, stole nine bases, and the Cardinals went 28–11. The Phillies fell apart, fell in the standings, and fell on their faces. It was historically tragic. "It was inconceivable that the Cards would catch up in the race," Mike Smith said.

But on the very last day of the season, they did. The Cardinals won their last game and won the pennant. And Ken Boyer, of course, had the biggest hit of the game—a double that drove in one, tying the game at 3–3. Their opponent in their first World Series since 1946? The New York Yankees, who also had a third baseman named Boyer.

* * *

Down in the mapdot town of Alba, Missouri, Vern Boyer grew ballplayers. He had seven boys, and all of them went on to play professional baseball of some kind. Three—Cloyd, Kenton, and Cletis—made the majors. The Boyers of Jasper County were the first family of third base. Ken won five Gold Gloves; Cletis, who went by Clete, was one of the more underrated fielders of all time. And the 1964 World Series was their family reunion. "When they asked my mother who she was rooting for in the series, she told the media: 'The fellow on third base,'" Clete Boyer told the *Tulsa World*.

It was, of course, Ken's first World Series as a player. Clete had been in the previous four. The New York Yankees were a machine. And '64 was Mickey Mantle's last great season: 35 homers and 111 RBIs to go along with his .303 average, his league best .423 on-base percentage, and a second best .591 slugging percentage.

The New York–St. Louis series was tangled in storylines. The famed National League franchise against the hallmark of the American League; the fifth time the two faced each other in the World Series, and that series was tied 2–2; the Boyer brothers; the Yankees catcher, Elston Howard, was from St. Louis; the old Yankees catcher, St. Louis native Yogi Berra, was now the Yankees manager; and after the series ended, more fascinating facets, notably Roger Maris later joining the Cards...and Cards manager Johnny Keane replacing Berra in New York.

The Cards snatched Game 1. New York won the next two and led 3–0 in Game 4, as the Smiths got home from church. It was Sunday, October 11, 1964. Top of the sixth inning. "My dad would always sit there, arms folded, a real student of the game," Mike Smith said. "They load the bases, and Boyer comes up. Al Downing throws that pitch, and Boyer launches the ball, and there weren't like 27 camera angles back then, and there wasn't even the angle from center field looking in. It was just the view from above and behind home plate, so you couldn't tell how launched it was. But you saw him follow through with the swing and you saw the ball take off on a high trajectory. And my dad—not demonstrative ever, even about sports—leaped out of his chair!...So, finally the camera catches up to the ball going over the left-field wall, and the next shot is down at home plate. One run, two runs, three runs, here comes Boyer. And then off to the dugout he goes. I'm like, *This is unbelievable. Boyer saved the World Series!* And it was my first World Series. And my dad had been waiting 18 years for another one."

Ken Boyer, who grew up in a family of talented third basemen, led the Cardinals to the 1964 World Series title.

After the Ken Boyer grand slam in Game 4, the Cards won the contest 4–3. And, of course, they won the World Series 4–3, too. In that Game 7, Gibson pitched a complete game. Lou Brock homered. So did Ken Boyer.

* * *

Each January, as the temperatures resemble Cardinals retired numbers, thousands of St. Louisans unite to talk some baseball. The Baseball Writers Dinner in St. Louis is a time-honored event, an annual gathering of the great Cardinals of this year and yesteryear. It's a big deal. In the old days, the local chapter of baseball writers in every city would host these grand dinners. Now, they only have them in a few true baseball towns.

At the dinner in January of 1982, Gibson and Ken Boyer were honored with the distinguished Dr. Robert F. Hyland award for meritorious service to sports. Six months later Boyer died at age 51 from lung cancer.

In the coming years, Mike Smith sometimes attended the big dinner. Although he proudly proclaimed he worked unbiasedly as an MLB official scorer—serving at the pleasure of the commissioner— around his family and friends, he cared for his Cards. So for Christmas gifts in 1992, Smith bought his dad and mom tickets to the big dinner. How cool was this? Ed Smith was going to see and meet the Cardinals. That night, at the 35th annual dinner, Stan Musial was there. Ozzie Smith, Joe Torre, and so many others were, too.

There were 2,000 fans there that night, but the Smiths were at a table front and center. The dais of stars looked down upon them. The dinner portion of the evening had begun when "there was something wrong," Mike Smith said of his dad. "And he rolled over onto me. I had to lay him down on the floor. Somebody on the stage saw what was happening, ran up to the microphone, and said, 'We need a doctor!' A couple of doctors came running, some nurses, too. It happened front and center in front of everybody. I remember putting him down on the floor. Everybody's rushing up. They're ripping his shirt open, giving him CPR. It took a long time for the emergency people to get there. I remember, all of a sudden, the noise subsided for me, and Todd

Worrell got up and said, 'We need to pray for the gentleman,' and the room got silent. And we started praying for him. I looked over at my mom, and she was just watching Todd Worrell because she didn't want to look down. He was gone when we put him down on the floor.

Of all the things…he could've had a heart attack anywhere."

The obituary in the *St. Louis Post-Dispatch* began: "Edward C. Smith, a lifelong baseball Cardinals fan, died Tuesday night, surrounded by the players he had always admired." He was 64. All those years later, in 2017, Mike Smith said of his dad's passing, "Time heals the wound, but below the scar, the wound is still there. You're over it, but you're not really over it."

21

EL BIRDOS
OF 1967

In the spring of 1966, the moribund North Siders were in talks to acquire the San Francisco Giants' Orlando Cepeda. The former All-Star was beleaguered by knee pain, leaving his future in question. The "Baby Bull" had just 34 at-bats in 1965, so the Chicago Cubs offered to trade Dick Ellsworth, an average starting pitcher. Conflicting reports were published that April of '66. One said the Cubs got greedy and wanted an additional player with Cepeda. A different report said earlier newspaper leaks of the trade talks infuriated the Giants' general manager, who thus called the whole thing off. Either way, the Cubs kept Ellsworth, who went 8–22 and was gone the next season. And a couple weeks later, the Giants indeed traded Cepeda... to the Cardinals.

In that '66 season, Cepeda was the Comeback Player of the Year. And in '67? Cepeda was the Most Valuable Player in the National League. "*Cepeda*," Tim McCarver gushed. "Talk about a feel for the game. We had two additions that were extraordinary in the scope of what was given up. Charley Smith for Roger Maris and Ray Sadecki for Orlando Cepeda."

Sure, Sadecki had a couple good years for the Giants, but the MVP, Cepeda, was key to the Cards winning the World Series. "To his everlasting credit, Mike Shannon moved to third base," McCarver said. "If he doesn't do that, it doesn't work because we had to make room for Roger Maris in right."

Coach Joe Schultz taught Shannon the new position. And Shannon held his own while also driving in 77 runs that year, not bad in a pitchers' era. Shannon's

77 were the second most RBIs on the team, trailing only the "Baby Bull," who led the whole damn league with 111.

El Birdos. The 1967 Cardinals got their nickname from Schultz, who smashed together two languages to create the famous moniker. Indeed, the Cards had a strong Latin influence, notably Cepeda from Puerto Rico and Julian Javier, the sturdy second baseman, from the Dominican Republic.

Cepeda hit .325 with 25 homers, winning the MVP award unanimously. "And he was an underrated fielder at first base," McCarver said. "An underrated base runner. And probably the best example of having Lou Brock rub off on someone the right way, he made Cepeda a better base runner. Orlando had bad feet, bad ankles, and bad knees—not really good things to be a good base runner, but he would kind of limp off the bag at first and then *boom!*

"It was a smart team. We learned a lot from Lou about how to run the bases. We weren't as fast as Lou, but he taught us how to be daring on the bases and we didn't make mistakes. We didn't beat ourselves."

The 1967 Cardinals led the league with 102 stolen bases...while hitting into a league-low 105 double-plays. Surprisingly, one of the Cards who stole the least was actually a tremendous defensive outfielder. Curt Flood had just two stolen bases in '67, but think of all the base hits he stole. He won one of his seven Gold Gloves that season. Oh, and he hit a career-high .335. Of course, Flood's impact on baseball history transcends a couple championships. He famously and controversially challenged the reserve clause. He helped ultimately change the game. Flood should be remembered and revered for doing so, but he was also one heck of a Birdo.

And while Bob Gibson is remembered for his World Series that season, not everyone remembers he missed a bunch of games that same season. Roberto Clemente thwacked a liner that broke Gibby's leg. "Everybody was worried about [Gibson's injury]," Cepeda said on a recent visit to St. Louis, "but Dick Hughes was amazing. Nelson Briles. You can't think about the past. You've got to take care of business. And we did it."

ST. LOUIS CARDINALS

St. Louis' original Nellie, Briles won nine straight starts after the All-Star break while filling in for No. 45. And Hughes, a 29-year-old rookie from Louisiana, started 27 games for the Cards, leading the whole league with his 0.954 walks-and-hits-per-innings-pitched (WHIP). Looking back at the stats, he lost the Rookie of the Year, perhaps unfairly...to Tom Seaver.

Another kid hurler for El Birdos was Seaver's Cooperstown contemporary, Steve Carlton. In his first full season in the bigs, "Lefty" went 14–9 with a 2.98 ERA. Controversially traded to the Philadelphia Phillies after the '71 season for Rick Wise, Carlton won the 1972 Cy Young and became an icon. Gibson was still an ace in '72, which prompted this comment from Gibby in 2017: "If that pitching staff had stayed together, there's no telling how many series or playoffs we could've won. I think we could've probably done at least three more."

But at least they won one. During that storied October of '67, they faced the Boston Red Sox, these adorable dreamchasers from Fenway who snatched the pennant in the season's final days. They had Yaz. And Tony Conigliaro—until the infamous beanball ended his season in August. And Reggie Smith, who later became a venerable slugger for the Cards in the mid-1970s. And Jim Lonborg. The towering righty later became teammates with "Lefty" on some quality 1970s Phillies teams, along with a veteran catcher, McCarver. But in 1967 Lonborg was Boston's ace and he held the season in his pitching hand.

Kind of lost in history is Lonborg's Game 2 start. (He didn't start Game 1 because they needed him to win the last regular-season game). Down 1–0 in the series, Lonborg had a no-hitter into the eighth inning. With two outs, too! And then Javier doubled. And so Lonborg finished with a one-hit shutout to even the World Series. He was their Gibson for a year.

Back at Fenway for Game 6, the Red Sox saved their season, setting up another Cardinals-Red Sox Game 7. The previous Game 7 between the teams featured Enos Slaughter's famed "Mad Dash" in 1946. This one featured Gibson-Lonborg, a matchup that defined this era of great pitchers. McCarver, Gibson's dear friend, had been one of the leaders of the team that season. In fact, the MVP runner-up was featured on a September cover of *Sports Illustrated* with the headline:

"THAT ST. LOUIS SPIRIT." It wouldn't be the most famous headline of the season.

"I remember 'Lonborg and Champagne.' That upset us," McCarver said 50 years later with genuine competitiveness in his voice. On the day of Game 7, a Boston tabloid featured that headline in red... along with a cartoon of a choking bird. "That's all we needed," McCarver said. "With Gibson going and white shirts and the crowd in center field, there was no batter's eye. And it was tough from a catching standpoint to even see the ball. Before Game 7 'Lonborg and Champagne,' that headline upset us, and we didn't need any impetus on that team."

And with Lonborg pitching on two days' rest, the Cards hit him hard. Javier walloped a three-run homer. Gibson himself smacked a solo shot. And Gibby, of course, threw the final pitch of the season, a swinging strike. *Viva!* El Birdos were world champions. "We were confident and a very close-knit group," McCarver said, "perhaps the most viciously competitive individuals of any team that I was ever a part of, a ruthless competitive team."

As for the 1967 Cubs, Ellsworth and the boys finished in third place.

22

DIZZY
DEAN

He was a yokel-like version of Yogi. His country-fried mantras, malapropisms, and mangling of the language made Dizzy Dean a forebear to Berra. In fact, while Jay Hanna Dean pitched from atop the St. Louis hill, young Lawrence Peter Berra listened from The Hill, the time-honored Italian neighborhood in St. Louis. Yogi Berra was in elementary school during Dean's days with the Cardinals. But perhaps the best way to capture Dizzy Dean is to start at his last start. And that occurred, if you can believe it, all the way into Berra's rookie season.

It was 1947, and Dizzy Dean was the broadcaster for the St. Louis Browns of the American League. The Browns were bad at playing baseball. All summer Dean denigrated the pitchers in his Arkansas twang. He'd pronounce that at 37, and six years retired, he could pitch better than some of the Browns.

So, on the last day of the season, they had him pitch for the Browns. It was unprecedented, preposterous, and delicious.

Actually, it was Browns executive Bill DeWitt Sr. who made it happen. His son, of course, would become owner of that other St. Louis team in 1996. DeWitt Sr. figured it would be good publicity for his club, which drew dozens, not thousands. Sure enough, nearly 16,000 folks showed up on September 28, 1947, to watch the team's broadcaster pitch in an actual major league game.

And Dizzy dizzied. He pitched four innings, and all were scoreless. And at bat he even thwacked a single. It had been six years, and he just hopped into a big league ballgame and pitched his butt off. It was the stuff of lore. After his fourth inning, a hamstring pull forced him to call it a day. Still, his final start encompassed all that was Dizzy Dean—pristine pitching, bratty bragging, and a ballgame that seemed more like an old folktale. "Talking's my game now," Dizzy Dean said. "And I'm just glad that muscle I pulled wasn't in my throat."

When it all began, the Hall of Famer was first scouted on a sandlot because of course he was. Soon after, Dizzy Dean showed up to a tryout camp in Shawnee, Oklahoma. It was there in 1930 that one of baseball's most bizarre relationships—the sophisticated, bespectacled Branch Rickey and the sophomoric spectacle Dizzy Dean—commenced. "I completed college in three years," the team executive Rickey wrote in *Branch Rickey's Little Blue Book: Wit and Strategy from Baseball's Last Wise Man*. "I was in the top 10 percent of my class in law school. I'm a doctor of jurisprudence. I am an honorary doctor of law. Tell me why I spent four mortal hours today conversing with a person named Dizzy Dean?"

It was a relationship like the one sometimes seen in a comedy, where the sophisticate is caught in the orbit of the dope. Frasier Crane hung out with Norm and Cliff at Cheers. Or, perhaps, Sean Penn's iconic Jeff Spicoli, the high, high schooler in *Fast Times at Ridgemont High*, verbally sparring with the buttoned-up teacher, Mr. Hand.

Before he revolutionized baseball, Rickey revolutionized minor league baseball. With the Cardinals, Rickey created a farm system to develop young (and affordable) talent. It changed the game and produced some of the Cardinals stars of the 1930s, and there wasn't a bigger star than Jay Hanna Dean. Or was it Jerome Herman Dean? The former is what it says on his Cooperstown plaque; the latter is what it said on the 1935 cover of *Time* magazine, featuring his famous face.

This was the allure of Dizzy Dean, who was tough to pin down. (Was he born in 1910 or 1911? In Arkansas or Oklahoma? Or maybe Mississippi?) He was the son of a cotton picker and had two brothers, one you've heard of. That was Paul Dean of "Me an' Paul," Dizzy's Cardinals teammate, and a fine hurler in his own right. Little known is Elmer Dean, the Cooper Manning of the clan. But it was Dizzy and Paul who pitched for the great Gashouse Gang, the ragtag ragamuffins who won it all in 1934. "The dumber a pitcher is, the better," Dizzy Dean said. "When he gets smart and tries to experiment with a lot of different pitches, he's in trouble. All I ever had was a fastball, a curve, and a change-up and I did pretty good."

He did pretty well indeed. From 1932 to 1937, Dizzy Dean dominated the National League, winning the MVP once and finishing second in the voting twice. He led the league in strikeouts in four consecutive seasons. He continually and publicly demanded more money from Rickey. And he pitched with panache, famously asking batters which pitch they would like to miss.

Hall of Fame sportswriter Bob Broeg told the story of a particular game against the New York Giants. With two outs in the ninth inning, Dizzy Dean purposely walked a batter so he could face Bill Terry. This seemed, for all intents and purposes, dumb. Terry would be inducted into the Hall of Fame the year after Dizzy Dean. But earlier that day, Dizzy Dean promised some sick children in a hospital that he would strike Terry out. "I hate to do this, Bill," Dizzy said, "but I promised the kids I'd strike you out." And he did.

When you think of the old days of baseball, you often think of purity, love of the game, a fun bunch of teammates all playing together for the same goals. Maybe it was the way movies depicted baseball. Or the fact that the modern game got so greedy and cocky that in comparison surely the older days were, if you will, sweeter. But they weren't. Guys were assholes. Teammates weren't always best buddies. Which brings us to the story of Dizzy and Ducky. "There was no one like Dizzy Dean," Gashouse Gang pitcher Jim Mooney told writer Bob Hood. "One time Diz goofed off in Pittsburgh, and Joe 'Ducky' Medwick got mad at him, went after him with a bat. Oh listen, Diz was all the time getting in fights after ballgames if he'd lose one. He'd come in that clubhouse. We'd be taking a shower, and he'd be griping about someone not getting a base hit at the right time, something like that, and Rip Collins and Pepper Martin would jump all over him. I saw them beat him up, never hurt him, but you know, they didn't like him blaming the other players."

In the 1934 World Series against the Detroit Tigers, the Dean brothers were suddenly the center of the sports universe—quite a ways from an Arkansas cotton field. In *Baseball*, Ken Burns' epic documentary series, I love a particular scene from the field before the first World Series game. A lot of the old-timey baseball footage doesn't include audio, but there were Dizzy and Paul in black-and-white. Someone surely had "drug"— to use a Dizzy Dean word—the two of them over to the camera and then made them say certain lines. "This is my brother, Jerome, better known as Dizzy," Paul Dean said to the camera in a syrupy Southern accent. "This is my brother, Paul

Dean, better known as Daffy," Dizzy said, not once looking toward the camera.

And then, the two said simultaneously: "We're both full of ambition against those Tigers." However, Dizzy Dean stopped talking about halfway through. His face conveyed: "What is this crap?"

Or maybe he just forgot his line.

In that '34 Fall Classic, Dizzy Dean forever left his mark on baseball, like a tobacco stain on a Gashouse Gang jersey. He won Games 1 and 7. And Paul, a pretty sturdy second fiddle, was the winning pitcher in the Cards' other two victories in Games 3 and 6. A photo from the series showed Dizzy Dean in the Gashouse Gang's clubhouse, wearing a white safari helmet, playfully chewing on a toy Tiger. "As a ballplayer Dean was a natural phenomenon, like the Grand Canyon, or the Great Barrier Reef," the legendary Red Smith wrote about Dizzy in *The New York Times*. "Nobody ever taught him baseball, and he never had to learn. He was just doing what came naturally."

Of all places it could have happened, Dizzy Dean's All-Star career changed forever—and for the worse—in the All-Star Game. It was 1937, and the great right-hander's pitch was promptly smacked back at him, striking his toe. As the old story goes, someone informed Dizzy Dean that his injured toe was indeed fractured. "Fractured?" Dean cried. "Hell, the damn thing's broken!"

He changed his pitching mechanics to avoid pain in his foot but ended up disassembling his great motion. The next year, he was traded to the Chicago Cubs of all teams. In 13 games he was Dizzy Dean once again. He finished 7–1 with a 1.81 ERA. His walks-and-hits-per-innings-pitched (WHIP) was a microscopic 0.95.

And in a what-might-have-been, the legendary Cardinal almost changed Cubs history.

Chicago had won the pennant but lost Game 1 of the 1938 World Series to the New York Yankees. Dizzy Dean started Game 2 and he allowed only two runs in the first seven innings. His Cubs led 3–2 heading into the eighth inning. Dizzy Dean was going to even the series up, as the Cubs tried to win their first World Series since all the way back in 1908.

But Dizzy Dean, pitching at home, allowed two runs in the top of the eighth inning. And in the top of the ninth, he allowed a two-run homer to Joe DiMaggio. The Yankees won Game 2, the next two games, and the World Series.

Ol' Diz pitched sparingly the next few seasons for Chicago, and according to Robert Gregory's book, *Diz,* Dizzy Dean resorted to throwing "floaters" and "sidearm twisters" that couldn't "break the crust of a custard pie."

So, he broke into broadcasting where he became beloved for being blunt. And you never knew what new word he'd modulate. "Slud" became his most-famous one, as in "Phil Rizzuto slud into third." Dizzy Dean declared that a "slud" meant sliding but with great effort. Local English teachers were reportedly aghast at Dean's mutilation of language.

Sure enough, Ol' Diz slud into a new gig—a broadcaster for nationally televised games. He was forever folksy. Sometimes, he'd start singing "Wabash Cannonball" on air and he ended up making a record of the old song. He made an appearance on *Hee Haw*. Thriving because his voice wasn't all uppity and refined, he was a voice of the common man.

He died in 1974 in Reno, Nevada. A few decades later, the Hall of Famer was inducted into another Hall of Fame. It was the St. Louis Sports Hall of Fame, and at the banquet, Paul's son spoke on behalf of the Dean family. (Dizzy did not have any children.) In a bolo tie, Sandy Dean shared some old stories that night, ending his speech with a favorite from Dizzy Dean's broadcasting days. During one game the TV camera occasionally caught a couple kissing in the stands. The other broadcaster wondered aloud if they were newlyweds. The camera kept going back to the couple, and the unaware couple just kept on smooching. Finally, Dizzy said, "I think I've got it figured out. He's kissing her on the strikes, and she's kissing him on the balls."

It's a perfect Dizzy Dean quote. Fun and folksy. Was Dizzy Dean aware that he accidentally made a pun and sexual innuendo? We'll never know, but that's the fun of it all. We don't necessarily know what was going on in Dizzy Dean's noggin, but the stuff he'd say was often fun and dizzying.

23

THE 1987 SEASON

ack from commercial an ABC camera zoomed in on a fan—
my dad. "Well, the 1964 Cardinals! A well-worn button," Al
Michaels said, as the camera showed a nostalgic button on my
dad's red sweater and then zoomed out to show my dad next to his
brother. "Tim McCarver would know all about that."

It was 1987. Game 3 of the World Series. As McCarver, the other
broadcaster, began talking about the '64 team, the phone rang in my
home. On the phone my dad's dad spoke to my mom. "Just saw your
husband on TV!" Grandpa gushed. "How neat! So who was he with?"

This was my first season as a fan. I turned seven on May 5th of that
year—the Cards lost 10–6 to the San Francisco Giants at Busch that
day—and my first baseball memories involve Topps cards with "wood"
frames, Jack Buck's omnipresent voice, and of course that autumn
night at our home on Watkins Drive when we watched the playoffs in
the den and saw Dad (and my apparently unrecognizable uncle) on
national TV. The '87 Cardinals will forever hold a special place in my
heart—albeit broken that October before being mended by memories
over time.

It was such a fun season, man. Ozzie on the cover of *Sports
Illustrated*, Buck getting inducted into Cooperstown, Tommy Herr's
walk-off grand slam on Seat Cushion Night, Tom Lawless' bat flip in
the World Series, Vince Coleman's drunk celebration on Channel 5, the
chameleon Jose Oquendo nicknamed "the Secret Weapon" playing
seemingly every position (and, except for catcher that year, he did).
And this club was so good. Besieged by injuries the Cards still won 95
games, even though no pitcher won more than 11.

The Runnin' Redbirds led the league in on-base percentage, stolen
bases, and high-fives. "I remember in camp just seeing how great
the team was," pitcher Joe Magrane said during a quiet moment at
the 30-year reunion. "Normally in spring training, you've got guys
playing themselves into shape, but we were kicking everybody's ass

in spring training, too. The thing that was so amazing to observe on a daily basis was how much pressure we put on the opposition by how we ran the bases. It's a thing that's extinct now. You just had such an appreciation for how it affected how everyone in the lineup was pitched to. As one of the only rookies on the team, it felt like it was almost suspended, pinch-myself animation, just boat-racing all the way into the postseason, and me just wondering—*Where the hell did I come from?*"

And there was Jack Clark, who should've won the 1987 National League MVP. He certainly looked the part. Strapping, dark hair, this look of intensity—he probably would seem serious even eating Froot Loops. He was the slugger in every baseball movie ever made. From his knees to his waist, those trunks weren't made out of regular leg stuff. They appeared bionic or Bunyan-ic. And this guy wasn't a hitter; he was a slugger.

In my childhood mind, Clark got singles accidentally. He was up there to homer, and every motion in his swing was based on the notion of hitting the crap out of the ball. He had incredibly high walk rates, and while maybe it was because he had this keen eye for the strike zone, I like to think that he just wasn't going to swing at anything that possibly couldn't be homered—as if he'd rather walk than slap an opposite-field double. Jack would thwack. He'd cock back and use his forearms and bionic thighs and step into one. He batted right-handed, and upon contact his left knee would bend into a right angle, "while squishing a bug with right cleat in back," said Gar Ryness, the famous batting stance imitator nicknamed "Batting Stance Guy."

Clark would trot around the bases with his head down, as if to imply: "What is this shit? I thought the point of homering was so that you don't have to run?" "Jack Clark, to me, was like a big brother," said John Morris, an outfielder on the '87 team. "Probably the most important day of the season was the day I came back from my father's funeral. It was in late September. After being off for a week, Whitey inserted me into the lineup on my first day back. And it was the only game of my major league career that I had four RBIs. Shawon Dunston could've caught three balls if they were just three feet to the right or the left. It was a magical day. After the game I was overwhelmed by the attention I was getting around my locker, and Jack Clark was right next to me and he just stepped inside, made sure that I was okay, got me a beer, sat with me, and said, 'Just do this [interview] once, do it right, you'll never have to do it again.' Those are the things you don't forget. It's very emotional."

As Morris told the story, 30 years later, his eyes watered.

Clark's 1987 season is underappreciated in history. Folks only seem to talk about MVP Andre Dawson, who hit 49 homers for the Chicago Cubs, while in St. Louis, the talk is often about Smith, who hit .300 for the first and only time—and came in second in the MVP voting. "That was one of my goals coming into the big leagues in 1978: to win myself a Silver Slugger and, hopefully, win a Gold Glove," Smith said. "The latter part I was able to do a few times."

I chuckled when he said it. Yeah, Ozzie, you did win a Gold Glove a few times—*13 times in a row!* Along with 43 base steals and his countless stealing of hits, he was extremely valuable, but Clark's season should have made him the MVP not only of the Cards, but also the league. Jack The Ripper played in only 131 games and yet he crushed 35 homers with 106 RBIs, while hitting .286. He walked 136 times, most in the NL. He led the league in on-base percentage (.459) and slugging percentage (.597), thus leading the league (obviously) in on-base-plus-slugging percentage (a 1.055 OPS, quite better than Dawson's .896). Heck, in Mike Trout's historic first five seasons, Trout never had an OPS of 1.0 or higher.

But Clark finished third in the MVP voting. Now, as you grow up, baseball gets Santa Claus'd. Or demystified. We find out truths. Some ballplayers, for instance, were liars, cheaters, or just assholes. Or you read about collusion in baseball in the mid-1980s, in which owners' actions fought free agency, affecting roster balance. I was always wide-eyed about the 1987 season, this fantastical show of power in my first foray into baseball. But as I got older, I occasionally wondered about the numbers. Dawson hit 49 homers? So did rookie Mark McGwire? Yet into the late '80s and early '90s, players weren't doing that—not until the steroid boom of the mid-1990s.

So what was it about this one year of 1987? In Denver, where I was a columnist for *The Denver Post*, I got to know pitcher Mark Knudson. He firmly believes that baseballs were juiced in the 1987 season in the minors and majors. Others around the game have the same inclination. SB Nation writer Larry Granillo, for instance, astutely pointed out that 28 major league players hit 30 or more homers in 1987. Yet in 1988? Only five did. Also, in 1986 there had never been more homers hit in the majors, yet the following season in '87, that record number was up 20 percent. Wade Boggs, for instance, who never before or after hit more than 11 homers, hit 24 in '87. In the minors Denver Zephyrs slugger Joey Meyer hit a homer into the night (and into the altitude) that went a reported *600 feet*.

Which leads us to my guy, Clark. In 1987 he hit 35 homers—in just 419 at-bats. Never before or again did he eclipse 30 in a season. But

Ozzie Smith performs one of his trademark flips prior to Game 1 of the 1987 National League Championship Series.

you know what? He was still our guy and to be fair he still hit 20 to 28 homers an astounding 10 other times in his career. And you know what? In the end, juiced ball or not, it didn't matter. The Cards didn't even have Clark anyways. A lone strikeout in the National League Championship Series notwithstanding, an ankle injury prevented him from playing in the postseason.

* * *

Whitey Herzog had a penchant for preparing his bench for a pinch. This helped save the season because everyone got hurt in '87. I think even organist Ernie Hays pulled a finger muscle. *St. Louis Post-Dispatch* writer Bob Broeg wrote that with all the injuries you would've thought St. Louis would've finished seventh in the six-team division. Instead, they were in first place most of the season.

But in the playoffs the Cards were without Clark. And they had Terry Pendleton for only seven World Series at-bats. And while the injuries allowed two reserves to have classic moments—homers by Oquendo and Lawless—it caught up to the Cards in the end. "If Jack and Terry stay healthy," Smith said, "I think we had enough to beat the Twins."

But they did first beat the Giants, who were managed by the weathered Roger Craig. When told he used to pitch for the Cardinals, I figured they meant for the Gashouse Gang. But Craig, who was "only" 57 in 1987, pitched for the famed 1964 club, logging a 3.25 ERA in 166 innings. Craig's Giants were tough. They'd been in beanball battles and brawls with the Cardinals before. Chili Davis called St. Louis a "cow town," while slugger Jeffrey Leonard trotted around the bases with "one flap down." Upon hitting a homer, he'd leave his left arm all the way down during his trot. After three homers—and interrupting a Magrane wind-up with his curtain call—Leonard was finally beaned by Bob Forsch in Game 3. They still talk about it in St. Louis.

Leonard, who had four homers, a .417 batting average, and a .917 slugging percentage in the series, would actually win the National League Championship Series MVP. As of 2017 he was the last player on a losing team to win the award. The Cards took the series to Game 7, winning at home. Coleman, infamously injured by the tarp in the 1985 playoffs, caught the final out, promptly holding the ball into the air. He was finally headed to the World Series. And in St. Louis, they sang along to that cheesy song. I still sing it. I think it's awesome.

> "We're shooting for the top, we're never gonna stop, it's St. Lou-is—got to be St. Lou-is! Tell everyone you know, everywhere you go, I'm sold on St. Louis, I'm sold!"

In the mid-1980s, there was a promotional slogan in town—"The state of St. Louis," but it confused more people than it inspired, so they changed it in 1987 to "Sold on St. Louis." They made shirts. There were banners on street lights. And Ralph Butler, a St. Louis staple for decades as he sang Motown and standards and pop songs around town (and probably at your cousin's wedding), performed the song. The music video was just perfect—Ralph rockin' the mic, Fredbird playing the sax, spliced-in shots of Herr homering, and Smith Ozzie-ing. The song and video were released in October right after defeating the Giants. It really was a cool time in town. An article in the *Post-Dispatch* said that at St. John's hospital, newborns got tiny T-shirts that said: "The Cardinals and My Mom: Both Delivered." At a pep rally, Butler performed the big song. Two years after St. Louis was snookered out of a World Series title, the Birds were back in '87.

They would play the Minnesota Twins, who played in a stadium seemingly out of *The Jetsons*. The Hubert H. Humphey Metrodome was modern but an oddity with those high walls and low ceiling and exceedingly loud crowd waving white "homer hankies." "Playing up there was very challenging for us. We had a couple misplays on fly balls," Smith said. "And we also had to deal with the blowers, which we felt were on at certain times. It was one of those kind of weird years. We probably should've won, but we didn't."

Thirty years later, Willie McGee complimented the "no flash" Twins on their grinding style of play. The center fielder also said that the Metrodome in October was "the scariest position I've been in as a baseball player. We all know that one game can make a difference, and the roof in the Metrodome was the color of an egg or something. So if a ball is hit up, you can't see it. So you couldn't take your eye off the ball and you're running, and the ball's in between you and another outfielder and with the noise level in that dome you couldn't hear anybody call the ball. It's just a train wreck waiting to happen. We're fortunate that we got through there without any complications."

After losing the first two games at the Metrodome, the Cards returned to St. Louis. They won Game 3—with dad and my uncle in the stands—and also won Games 4 and 5. They were a win away from winning the World Series—just like when the Cards went to Kansas City in '85 for Games 6 and 7. But it had the same outcome. "I went to Minneapolis for Game 6," said KMOX Radio's Tom Ackerman, who was a student at the time. "I was in the bathroom when Kent Hrbek hit the grand slam. You could feel it in the walls, the whole place, shaking."

And Game 7 was the culmination of a coronation. Pitcher Frank Viola won the game, won the World Series, and the World Series MVP. "They deserve it. They won. It's not their fault that we weren't at full throttle," McGee said. "And even if we were at full throttle, who knows if we even would've won. But you would've liked to see your team at full throttle in a series like that."

One season into this baseball thing, I was sold on St. Louis. But sadly the Cardinals wouldn't make it back to the playoffs until I was 16. Clark was gone that winter, signing with the New York Yankees. And just a few weeks into the '88 season, the Cards traded Herr—to the Twins. "It was a shock," said Herr, a staple of the three World Series teams in the 1980s. "I remember tears flowing as the plane was leaving the runway from St. Louis to Minnesota. It came as a big surprise to me. It took me a while. It took me a long while to get over just the emotional hump of that trade. And quite honestly, it shouldn't have taken me that long. I should've understood that this game is a business. But, you know, my heart was still with the Cardinals."

24

MIKE SHANNON

They've got plump shrimp and Krispy Kreme donuts in here. The KMOX booth isn't a booth. It's a spacious lounge that resembles one of the VIP suites here at Busch Stadium with a spread of fun and fancy foods, cold frosty drinks, and framed photos of Cardinals legends on the wall. The difference is most of the photos are of the same legend, Thomas Michael Shannon. "The way this is built, you can talk back here and can't be heard down there on the air," Mike Shannon explained to me an hour before a ballgame against the Chicago Cubs. "And everyone who enters, I make them sign the guest book. Last night we had two little girls in here. I made them sign the book. They said, 'Why?' And I said, 'Because you're going to be famous someday, and I'm going to sell the book!'"

And there was that laugh. Famous and folksy. Recognizable and relatable. It's the comfort food of guffaws. Mike Shannon. Born in 1939. The man is from St. Louis, became a World Series hero for St. Louis, and then became the voice of St. Louis. "It's more than a job and it took me a long time to realize this, but there's an unbelievable responsibility to the people who tune in to this game every night," said Shannon, who began broadcasting in 1972. "You have to fulfill that responsibility. And if you don't, you're letting down a lot of people. And I'm not talking about the players and coaches and manager. I'm talking about the fans. And there are people that set their day by Cardinal baseball."

For decades, he was paired with Jack Buck. They were different, but they shared a passion for the fans and for storytelling. Buck passed away in 2002. Shannon has remained in the booth, forever pleading homers to "Get up, baby, get up!" In fact, in 2017, a promotional giveaway one game was a Cardinals alarm clock. You could set it, and when it went off, it was Shannon's voice, telling you to get up, baby. "I'm fairly certain I've heard him say more words than any other person in my life, and that includes my wife," said author Will Leitch, who follows the Cardinals intently and intensely. "She's catching up, but only because Shannon doesn't travel as much anymore. My favorite Shannonism is still, 'He hails from the island of Puerto Rico. Puerto Rico is an island, isn't it? Well, just try swimming off of it, and I guess you'll find out.' That is oddly brilliant."

As a player, they called him "Moonman." Sure, he hit some "moon-shot" homers. But he was also, um, out there. It plays perfectly on air. He's a knowledgeable former ballplayer who can also be quick and quirky. And sometimes he'll say something that's just categorically goofy. Moonman's most-famous one, fittingly, involved the moon. As said from a New York broadcast booth, "I wish you folks back in St. Louis could see this moon!"

There are actually numerous blogs dedicated to Shannonisms. Some of Mike's best from behind the mic include:

- "It's raining like a Chinese fire drill!"
- "I just want to tell everyone 'Happy Easter and Happy Hanukkah.'"
- "Back in the day when I played, a pitcher had three pitches: a fastball, a curveball, a slider, a change-up, and a good sinker pitch."
- "The Yankees and Mets are playing tonight at Shea. After four innings, New York leads 3–2."
- "He tried to sneak that fastball by Rolen. That's like trying to sneak the sun past the rooster."
- "Would you believe Andujar Cedeno is not related to either Joaquin Andujar or Cesar Cedeno?"
- On Randall Simon: "Even if he didn't have a bat in his hands, he'd take a swing."
- Talking about a road game in Montreal: "This game is moving along pretty quick, it must have something to do with the exchange rate."
- "*Graaand Slaaaaam!* Nope, nope, nope, it's gonna be caught at the warning track."

And right before those 10-second station identification breaks, Shannon will always give a shout-out to a random town in the Midwest: "This one's for the folks in Suchandsuch, Arkansas!" It's a fun, simple thing, but it connects him to the everyman listening. And Shannon also gleefully speaks about the sponsors, notably *"Bud-why-zah!"* "I'm convinced that nobody has sold more Budweiser, more hotel rooms, more Cardinals tickets than Mike," said Tom Ackerman, sports director at KMOX. "You talk about a great St. Louis ambassador, grew up here, great athlete here, has a little bit of that St. Louis accent, loves St. Louis food, will rave about anything St. Louis any time, big personality. He became kind of like everyone's uncle, a family member you could always enjoy and laugh at. And you talk about a unique broadcast style. There's not a broadcaster like him. There's a great comfort level listening to Mike. His cadence, his little sayings, they make you feel warm—and back in St. Louis. The other thing is he's really taught all of us the intricacies of this game. I strongly feel this way. He's put in so many years in that organization. He should be in Cooperstown."

In the KMOX booth that day, as I eyed the donuts, Shannon shared a story. President George W. Bush visited for an inning. Shannon was going to interview the nation's First Fan on the air. "They always have their PR people," Shannon recalled, "and I said, 'Well the first thing I'm going to ask him is—and it was about whatever was going on in politics at the time. And they said, 'No! You can't ask him that!' I was just kidding, of course. We've had some fun. You've got to have fun. There's been I don't know how many tens of thousands of baseball games, and there's never been two the same. So we don't know what's going to happen!"

Shannon has been there, for instance, for both no-hitters by Bob Forsch, for when backup catcher Glenn Brummer stole home to win a key game in 1982, for when Mark McGwire hit No. 70, and for all the World Series moments of this century, including this one: "Swing and a long one into right. *Get up baby, get up! get up!* It's at the wall, it iiiiiiiis—off the wall! One run in! Here comes Berkman! Over to third goes Freese! We're tied 7–7! How abooooooooout that! Unbelievable!

Freese hit it off the right-field wall, and listen to this crowd. They have gone *bananas*!"

In a great baseball town, the broadcasters are as famous as the players. You grow up with them. You grow old with them. And Shannon, a regular fellow who was remarkably blessed, has been the narrator of memories for generations of St. Louisans, as well as all the folks in Suchandsuch, Arkansas, and all over Cardinals country and, really, depending on how clear the night is, the actual country. "Mike Shannon is on my short list of St. Louis celebrities to go have a beer with," said Brad Thompson, a pitcher on the 2006 World Series champion Cardinals. "He's just the perfect guy to chop it up with, and it doesn't have to be just about baseball. It could be about life. It could be him playing back in the day. He's a special individual. Listening to him on the radio, the sound is iconic. Hearing him call something that you're doing is pretty special, knowing how far back he goes here in St. Louis Cardinals history. I listen to a lot of baseball games driving to and from work and I hear a lot of different broadcasters, but you don't hear anything quite like that. And sometimes you might not know what happened in an inning, but you sure were entertained! He's just a fun guy to be around. He's old-school baseball, and I love every second of it."

25

VINCE COLEMAN'S LIVE CHANNEL 5 INTERVIEW

It's perhaps my favorite moment from my childhood, but I never even saw it live.

It was only decades later that I was introduced to "the Vince Coleman video," and I'll tell you: it was kind of like the time I first heard Pearl Jam's "Ten" or saw *Hamilton* on Broadway. I instantly knew this thing was iconic.

The date was October 1, 1987. With a victory the Cardinals would clinch the National League East, and sure enough, the mustached Danny Cox hurled a complete-game, 8–2 win against the Montreal Expos. And so Channel 5 went live to the winning clubhouse.

For generations in St. Louis, Channel 5, the NBC affiliate with the call letters KSDK, has been a prominent part of sports, the local NBC sports version of must-see TV. Personalities such as ESPN's Trey Wingo and NBA TV's Matt Winer did stints in St. Louis. Frank Cusumano, a hometown hoopster turned homegrown newshound, got his start on-air in 1993. He remains the venerable face of Channel 5 Sports. "I previously worked in Kentucky and Tennessee," Cusumano said. "I reported sports there. *I feel sports here.*"

Back in '93 Cusumano was first hired by Mike Bush. That was my guy growing up. Bush was confident and charming and spoke like he was just speaking to you. Bush was responsible for the strong stable of reporters over the years, notably Cusumano, Wingo, Winer, and another local fellow, Art Holliday. So, on that October night in 1987, Bush sat at the anchors' desk. Holliday was down at the stadium. "Well," Bush said into the camera, pausing for one of his signature lines. "You gotta love it! For the third time in six years, the St. Louis baseball Cardinals are the National League Eastern Division Champions!"

They showed some earlier footage of the players celebrating on the Astroturf and then again showed Bush, who was about to send it live to Busch. "And the celebrating continues!" said Bush while a screen appeared over his right shoulder.

And there was Holliday inside the Cardinals' clubhouse. His mic was off, but as Bush introduced him, you could see Holliday in his 1980s sweater, pressing the ear piece in his ear. And Coleman stood right next to him. It looked like the outfielder was screaming. Just what the hell was going on in there? "Going into it, you're just trying to get an interview—whoever," Holliday explained one morning in 2017, 30 years later. "Coleman comes over, Mike Bush tosses to me, and Vince starts yelling: *'we've got an All-Star at every position!'*"

Coleman was, Holliday recalled with a laugh, "drunk off his ass." Now, Ol' Vince had reason to celebrate. He was a key player on the division champs, finishing 1987 with an astonishing 109 stolen bases. As Holliday began to speak into the mic, Coleman stopped

FRANK CUSUMANO

He was known for his knowledge, a six-foot St. Louis sports encyclopedia. Frank Cusumano yearned to be the Channel 5 sports director, sort of a "pope job" in St. Louis. Since 1968 only three people held the position. But in 2003 when the job opened, Cusumano was passed over.

But he remained on-air for Channel 5 for—give or take a year—forever. Actually, he was there throughout the St. Louis Rams' entire tenure in town from 1995 to 2015. Finally—finally!—Cusumano got the sports director gig in 2016. The headline on the station's website featured an exclamation point: "Frank Cusumano lands his dream job!" And in a video on the site, Frank humbly spoke about his pride in becoming sports director, explaining: "I would give anything in the world to be able to tell my dad about this job. Who knows, maybe they get Channel 5 in heaven."

screaming, freezing his body while holding a champagne bottle in the air.

But halfway through Holliday's intro—"Well, the champagne and beer is flowing here in the Cardinals' locker room..."— Coleman suddenly stumbled. He caught himself, looked at Holliday, and hollered, "What else you wanna know?" He said this while the champagne bottle remained raised in his right hand.

Holliday tried to continue, but Vince, with his eyes popping wide, slurred into to the camera: *we've got the best team in the world!*"

So Holliday replied, "Best in the world, is that right?"

And a giddy Vince screamed into the camera like a used car dealer in a commercial, pointing each time he named the Cardinals' "All-Star at every position! Jack Clark! Tommy Herr! Ozzie Smith! Terry Pendleton! Willie McGeeeeee!"

As Vince started to say the name "Tony Pena," a teammate splashed Vince right in the face with a cup of champagne. Unfazed, Vince wiped off his face and loudly said to Holliday: "What else you wanna know?"

But before Holliday could even ask the next question, Pena himself jumped into the shot, fake tackling the inebriated outfielder while others fire-hosed champagne on not only Coleman, but also on Holliday. It was madness. "I've got this ear piece in my ear, and because of all the moisture, it's starting to short," Holliday recalled in 2017. "So I'm getting little jolts of electricity in my ear. But sometimes you got to play hurt."

Coleman then spotted one of the team's coaches, pointed, and screamed: "Everybody dressed at 6 o'clock!" He laughed uncontrollably.

It was chaos. Sweet, beautiful chaos. "I let him go because I'm thinking, *This is pretty good,*" a laughing Holliday said in 2017. "Don't get in the way because sometimes that's the smartest thing you can do. But at some point, I've got to ask him something, a serious question, and it's like somebody flipped the sober switch!"

After Vince burped twice, saying "excuse me" right into the camera, Holliday got a question in, asking him about the team's perseverance while overcoming so many injuries during the 1987 season. "We bounced back and played consistent baseball," Vince said, stoically, "and I think that's the most important word associated with the game right now. And when you have guys coming off the bench and being consistent every day; and consistency with the offense, pitching, relief pitching, and defense; and when you have those categories, it's what it's going to take to win a championship."

It was like the scene in *Old School* when Will Ferrell's character, Frank "the Tank," had to debate political expert James Carville. Inexplicably during the debate, Ferrell spoke eloquently about biotechnology and the government, to which Carville said, "I have no response. That was perfect." (And Ferrell turned and said, "What happened? I just blacked out.")

But just as Coleman finished his own eloquent answer, someone poured out yet another a cup of champagne, but this time it was right upon Holliday's head. It was incredible, and the newscaster tried to remain serious as foamy champagne spilled down his skull. They sprayed Coleman again, and shivering from the champagne's temperature, the outfielder shrieked: "Ohhhhhhhhhhhhhhhhhh! We're No. 1! We're No. 1!"

Drenched, smiling, and squinting, Holliday said to the camera: "While the Cardinals reload, we're going to pitch it back to the studio. I'll be back later on in sports, a little dryer. Reporting live from a very soggy locker room, Art Holliday, Channel 5, Eyewitness Sports!"

Back at the studio, Bush and anchors Dick Ford and Karen Foss tried to keep their composure, somehow processing the insanity they just witnessed on live television. "From the looks of tonight," Ford said to Bush, "tomorrow's game might be interesting."

Like myself, Cusumano didn't get to see it live. But over the years, the story of the insane Coleman video has been carried like a keepsake at Channel 5 and passed down like an heirloom. In the Channel 5 newsroom, Cusumano walks past a picture every day of Holliday interviewing the animated and inebriated Coleman, whose arms are in the air. "I think," Cusumano said, "it captures the essence of the man and the moment better than every interview I've ever seen."

Wait, which man? "Mainly Vince," a chuckling Cusumano said. "But Art, too."

I'd always been curious about something. So I asked Holliday—just how much did it cost to get that sweater dry-cleaned? "Oh," Art said, "it never recovered because they ran out of beer and champagne and started throwing fruit juice. So by the time I left the locker room, it was pink."

26

THE ORIGINAL BAT FLIP

Sometimes a thing will happen, and with our jaws dropped and our eyes popped, we'll start to calculate the odds to categorize the proper level of preposterousness. During the game you'll wonder: "Does such-and-such a better chance of happening than this?" Well, in this instance, the such-and-such was anything. *Anything* had a better chance of happening than this. One thousand, two hundred, and seventy-three days had passed since the dude hit a home run.

Back when he played for the Cincinnati Reds, the little infielder Tom Lawless hit a solo shot against the Atlanta Braves back in April of '84. Lawless went on to play for the Montreal Expos and the Cardinals. "Play" being a curious word, considering he seldom actually did. In 1987 Lawless had 25 at-bats for the Cardinals, but he was on the team the entire season, as if he had won a contest or something. "I was an extra infielder," he said, "and we had Ozzie Smith, Tommy Herr, and Terry Pendleton. You're probably not going to play very much. But my job was to be ready every day."

Jose Oquendo, who could play any position, was the Cards' secret weapon. Lawless, an infielder and third catcher, was essentially just a secret. "I'm still trying to find out who Tom Lawless is," Reggie Jackson, working the '87 World Series broadcast for ABC, told a *USA TODAY* writer.

Lawless was the only big leaguer ever out of Penn State Erie, the Behrend College of Pennsylvania State University. Suddenly thrust onto the biggest stage of his sport, Lawless was 30 years old.

The third baseman, Pendleton, was banged up, so against a lefty, the Cards wedged Lawless into the lineup for Game 4. He batted eighth that night in St. Louis, though I bet Whitey at least considered batting him ninth.

On a frigid night suited more for the then-St. Louis Cardinals of the NFL, the baseball Cards hosted Game 4 at Busch Stadium. The Minnesota Twins led the series 2–1. Bundled in their red turtlenecks under their home-white V-neck jerseys, Tony Pena stood on third, and Oquendo was on first. Bottom of the fourth. At the bat, with nary an out, was Tom Lawless.

Earlier in the dugout, injured slugger Jack Clark had whispered to Lawless to take a couple of pitches against Frank Viola, the Minnesota ace. Ball. Ball. Then, Viola fired a 2–0 fastball. "He just missed his location with it," Lawless said. "Viola was really good, really good. But I was just lucky enough to get the barrel on it. After that, it was 40 degrees outside, so it was—is the ball going to carry far enough? All those things go through your head, but if you play baseball long enough, when you hit baseballs and you really feel good, you know they're probably going to go pretty far. Or far enough."

And so, as the ball sailed toward the left-field fence, Lawless didn't run. He slowly stepped toward first base, his eyes on the ball the whole time. The 10th step coincided with the ball over the wall, and Lawless, holding the bat in his left hand, flipped it high into the October sky. "I have no idea why that happened," Lawless said. "No idea. It just happened. Just the moment."

"I assume," I said to Tom Lawless, "that wasn't your style."

"I had no style!" he exclaimed. "I hit three home runs my whole big league career, so you don't have no style."

The three-run homer was mustache-on-mustache crime. Lawless broke open Game 4, as the Cards scored six in the inning and won the game. And I don't think that bat has landed yet. "When he has that reaction after he hit it, you're watching it and thinking, *Oh my God, he hit it 550 feet*," recalled Will Leitch, die-hard Cardinals fan and founder of the website Deadspin. "It's an amazing bat flip for a guy who had, what, 25 at-bats that year? And then to realize that it just barely went over the wall? That's the best part about it!"

ST. LOUIS CARDINALS

The scenario, the celebration, everything, it was just ridiculous. Used to broadcasting sports miracles, Al Michaels said on ABC: "Did we really see that? He hit .080 in the regular season!" Busch burst. As Lawless crossed home, stadium organist Ernie Hays played "Here Comes The King." Many of the Cardinals came out of the dugout to congratulate Lawless, almost like a college team. "Barely hit the back of the wall, and he's bat flippin'?" Ozzie Smith said. "It was fun, and when you can get that type of production from your extras, that's very important."

Mr. October now knew who Tom Lawless was. Afterward, in the losing clubhouse, Minnesota's Don Baylor was asked about Lawless' flinging of the bat. "I never saw Reggie Jackson do anything like that," he said. "Or Hank Aaron, or Frank Robinson, or Harmon Killebrew. Tom Lawless? You've got to be kidding me."

It was his only hit of the World Series. He finished 1-for-10, and the Cards lost the series in seven. But in St. Louis the Lawless homer became part of lore, as kids in Fenton and Festus flung Wiffle Ball bats in backyards. "I wonder," Leitch said, "how differently I would've experienced that moment if he would've just done 'the Scott Rolen,' if he would've just hit it and put his head down and started running to first base. The fun of the moment is partly that it's such an unlikely character to do it, but the real thing that makes it transcendent is the bat flip. Of *all* people to do a bat flip? To me, that's always the joy of that moment."

And it was Lawless' lone moment. He'd only hit one more homer in his career. It was in 1988 off Tom Browning, who, perhaps so embarrassed by allowing a bomb to Lawless, had to make amends and 19 days later pitched a perfect game.

Lawless was also known as a prankster and an elite trash talker from the dugout. When he was manning third base, he once brought a cheeseburger out to the field. He carefully placed it upon third base, where umpire Eric Gregg, who was a larger gent, was positioned. "Yeah, that was me," Lawless said. "Back then, we had a lot of fun. The umpires, most of them, you could joke around with. The umpires were in on it, so it was just a fun thing. It's part of baseball. If you don't have fun and you're grinding too hard, nothing good is going to happen."

Lawless will occasionally get calls and texts from buddies who see the bat flip on TV or at the Birds game on the big screen. "Over the years, everybody's had a good time with it. It settled down for a while," he said. "And then Bautista decided to throw his bat, and it stirred it all back up again! So it's always fun to be in the conversation."

Indeed, in the decisive game of the 2015 American League Division Series, the Toronto Blue Jays-Texas Rangers game was 3–3 in the bottom of the seventh with two on, and "Joey Bats" was at bat. Jose Bautista had already delivered an extra-base hit in the game, which was mired with some controversy over calls. The Blue Jays' slugger drilled his second homer of the series, watched the thing soar, and aggressively threw his bat sideways. Twitter exploded.

All I could think of was Tom Lawless.

27

THE MAD HUNGARIAN

FACES TWO BATTERS AT THE SAME TIME

I leisurely sipped my Carrot Kale Dream smoothie when I encountered a mad man.

Unbeknownst to me, I'd parked a little over the line at Smoothie King. So as I sat in my driver's seat, sucking down the carrot kale goodness, a car tried to pull in next to me but couldn't fit. This fellow pulled back and tried again. And again. I did, admittedly, feel bad and I wanted to reposition my car, but if I pulled out, I would've hit his car. Also, the smoothie was really good. So I watched as the guy finally squeezed into in the spot on the third try. I presumed he might be mad. Sure enough, he literally was. Of all the humans in St. Louis, the guy was "the Mad Hungarian."

"Oh shit, it's Al Hrabosky!" I whispered to myself. Moreover, I actually sort of know him from my work as a columnist. So, as a 37-year-old man, I decided the best course of action was: to hide! I couldn't let Al Hrabosky know I was the buffoon who parked over the line. So I threw on sunglasses, kept my head down, and voraciously guzzled the smoothie as he squeezed sideways between our cars, huffing his way into Smoothie King.

Alan Thomas Hrabosky is as much a part of St. Louis culture as toasted ravioli. He pitched for the Cardinals from 1970 to 1977 and has been on game broadcasts since 1985, as St. Louisans have watched his famed Fu Manchu mustache go gray. I sat down with Al for this book a couple months after the "incident." He was very willing to help. I was very unwilling to admit I was the idiot at Smoothie King.

His best year for the Cards was in 1975. Hrabosky finished third in the Cy Young voting, tallying a league-best 22 saves with a 1.66 ERA. He pitched 97⅓ innings and tallied an eye-popping 13–3 record out of the pen. And he did it all by annoying the hell out of opposing batters with his "Mad Hungarian" antics.

It actually all started when they'd first made him the closer in '74, even though he couldn't close. At one point broadcaster Jack

Buck came up to Hrabosky and said, "Simmons saved you." Turns out the Cards were prepared to send him to the minors, but catcher Ted Simmons had faith in the hairy hurler. "I had a horrible first half, so that's what was the advent of 'the Mad Hungarian,'" Hrabosky said of this crazed persona, in which he'd step off the back of the mound and pump himself up. "It was realizing I had to do something to get my concentration and use it as a weapon to get hitters out. Before that, I was going through marital problems and stuff, my mind was wandering, and I'd be out saving the game and thinking of something else."

How did he come up with his concentration plan? "As silly as it might sound, I'd chipped a tooth," he said. "And I'm not the biggest fan of dentists. So I'm sitting in that chair and was just focusing on anything other than what was going on. I started concentrating and kind of came up with a routine where I was going to go behind the mound and really get into visualization and self-hypnosis or whatever it was. The other closers may have had more of a physical ability than I, so maybe they didn't have to do the mental stuff that I did. If I was on the road, I'd be greeted to a standing boo. And people would say, 'Don't let this donkey do that to you.' Well, that still puts pressure on the hitter. The odds are with me that I'm going to get him out, and he feels like he still has to do something special. If a guy stepped out, then okay, he's accepted a challenge. I really tried to make it a one-on-one challenge with every hitter."

Which leads us to his one-on-*two* challenge. There's a still shot of the moment, and it's one of the craziest images I've ever seen. It doesn't show Hrabosky, who'd just fired a fastball from the mound. Instead, in the picture there's Simmons crouched behind home—and the ump behind him. And in the right-handed batter's box are *two* Chicago Cubs. Each Cub has his bat cocked and ready to swing. And just outside the other batter's box is the Cubs manager screaming at the umpire.

How did this happen? Well, it was September 22, 1974. Bob Gibson actually started that day at Busch, and when Hrabosky took over for him in the eighth inning, it was a 5–5 game.

And it remained 5–5 entering the ninth, when tempestuous Bill Madlock came to bat. It was "Mad Dog" vs. "the Mad Hungarian."

Madlock was actually a rookie in '74. He'd finish third in the Rookie of the Year voting behind the Houston Astros' Greg Gross and the hardware winner, the Cardinals' own Bake McBride from Joplin, Missouri. Madlock would go on to win the batting title the next two seasons—and two more seasons down the line, making "Mad Dog" the only player with four batting titles *not* in Cooperstown. But his nickname wasn't just because his surname had the word "mad." Famous for numerous run-ins with umpires and other players, he was a fiery fellow.

So here he was, coming to bat in the ninth inning of a tie game, and part of his focus was about rattling "the Mad Hungarian." "In the eighth I threw three line drives," Hrabosky recalled. "It was a tie game, and I realized I might need a little extra help. So Madlock was the first hitter. I went behind the mound, got ready, came on the mound, and he stepped out. I'd been waitin' for somebody to do it. People were trying to figure out how to get one step ahead of me. I actually had hitters sometimes thinking through it all and I'd throw a pitch and they're not ready for it. Or, all they want to do is knock my head off, so they forget about situation hitting."

On this day, Madlock then stepped back in the batter's box and smiled because he thought Hrabosky was thrown off. So Hrabosky then stepped off the mound and did his mad routine again, and Madlock walked all the way back to the on-deck circle to apply some pine tar. "Shag Crawford, Jerry's dad, is the home-plate umpire," Hrabosky said. "He went to him and said to get back in the batter's box. Whatever Madlock said, he didn't like."

It was chaos. Three Cubs—Madlock, on-deck hitter Jose Cardenal, and manager Jim Marshall—were barking at Crawford. Fed up, Crawford stormed back behind the plate, set up behind Simmons, and pointed to the pitcher. "Shag told me to throw a pitch!" Hrabosky said. "Now, I'm not the smartest guy in the world, but if an umpire tells you to throw a pitch, I'm going to pitch. And if it's an automatic strike, I've got a pretty good chance there."

Without a batter in the box and both Cardenal and Marshall shouting from behind, Crawford called the strike. Still holding his bat, Cardenal lingered near the batter's box, so he began screaming for the cocky Madlock to return to the plate. Mad Manager Marshall moved a couple feet from the plate over in the left-handed batter's box. Suddenly, a scurrying Madlock came into the right-handed batter's box as Hrabosky delivered.

It was all happening so fast. Madlock pushed Cardenal with one arm as the pitch zoomed toward the plate, and, suddenly and instinctively, both ballplayers cocked back their bats. Each was ready to swing from the *same* batter's box. The ball whizzed by, Simmons caught it. Three seconds later, he shoved Madlock in the face, and a brawl erupted. Hrabosky sprinted in from the mound. Simmons got another swing on Madlock before an opponent from the dugout tackled Simmons, as if the Chicago Cub was a Bear. "I asked Teddy, 'What did he say to you?'" Hrabosky recalled. "And he said, 'I dunno, man, there were just too many bodies around me.' It was a good 20-minute brawl. When it was all said and done, I was pitching, Teddy was catching, Cardenal was on deck, Madlock was the batter. And Jim Marshall got thrown out for arguing."

Hrabosky struck out Madlock, Cardenal popped up, and Dave LaRoche struck out to end the inning. Sure enough, it was Simmons who won it for the Cards. With Lou Brock on second, Simmons singled to center, and Brock zoomed home for the winning run.

28

SCRAPPY CARDINALS

The Assistant U.S. Attorney explained in the federal courtroom that the defendant, who illegally accessed the private database of a rival executive, had done so with a password dedicated to an old ballplayer. The player was described as "scrawny," Michael Chu said to U.S. District Judge Lynn Hughes, saying it was a player "who would not have been thought of to succeed in the major leagues. But through effort and determination, he succeeded anyway. So this user of the password just liked that name, so he just kept on using that name over the years."

Later it was suggested in court that the password ended in "123." And so, it was discerned that the password Cardinals executive Chris Correa used to famously hack his former Cards co-worker, now with the Houston Astros, was: Eckstein123.

As if David Eckstein wasn't already part of Cardinals lore, the name of the scrappy 2006 World Series MVP was forever a part of a delicious 21st century crime and ensuing court case.

The shortstop is on the "Mount Rushmore" of scrappy Cardinals, though, perhaps it should be a scrap heap instead of a mountainous monument.

The 5'6", 19th-round pick first became a World Series hero with the Anaheim Angels. Eckstein then became an All-Star with St. Louis, swatting three doubles and eight overall hits in the 2006 World Series, earning a trophy to go along with his newest ring. "He didn't have the greatest arm, and everyone probably said he couldn't do this or couldn't do that," said Greg Garcia, the scrappy Cardinals infielder of the current era, "and he goes on to have a great major league career. So fans like that. The Cardinals like those kind of players because at the end of the day those are baseball players, and that's what we do here. And you look around this locker room. There are a lot of guys who maybe don't have the best tools, but they're baseball guys."

While the only Hamilton to ever play for the Cards was the 6'4" Mark, the Cards have had many players who were "young, scrappy, and hungry" just as the musical's "My Shot" melody indicated. What are the characteristics when compartmentalizing scrap? Does the player have to be under 6' tall? Does the player have to be fast? Can a pitcher be scrappy? Can there be a brawny, scrappy player, or is that an oxymoron?

I like how the fellows from the Cards blog, On The Outside Corner, put it. Defining a scrappy player is a lot like it was for Supreme Court Justice Potter Stewart back in 1964 when he helped define obscenity by saying: "I know it when I see it." For instance, Jose Oquendo was clearly scrappy; Jose DeLeon was not. Rex "Hurricane" Hudler? Yes. Mike "Spanky" LaValliere? No. And while Mark "Big Mac" McGwire (not scrappy) had an upper-deck landing spot called "Big Mac Land," 1999 teammate Joe "Little Mac" McEwing (scrappy) had a just-over-the-fence landing spot called "Little Mac Land."

The Cardinals fans, of course, have become known for their adulation of scrappy players—almost to the point where it's a little much. There's even a T-shirt for sale that looks like the script font that says "Cardinals" but instead says "Scrappy." In 2017 the human gusto Harrison Bader made his big league debut against the Colorado Rockies. In Bader's first at-bat, he grounded out but ran so hard he nearly beat out the throw. Fans gushed on social media, as if his first at-bat was a triple. And then in the bottom of the ninth, Bader tagged up from third on a fly, sliding home for the game-winning run and then leaping into the air with dirt-caked joy. "Bader looks like the next easily hate-able Cardinal," tweeted Denver-based sports journalist Will Petersen, "who their fanbase will just fall in love with."

Indeed the fanbase unabashedly hangs its red hat on the adoration for the adorable, the guys who are smallish, scurrying, gritty, and gutsy. "Being a Cardinal," Hudler said, taking a breath to gather his emotions. "Being a Cardinal—you were somebody. Even the 25th man, I'll never forget how the fans made me feel...I'd do it again for those people. I'd do it again...I loved leaving freckles out on the turf."

Adron Chambers, the wispy, 5'10" outfielder, is one of my favorites of the scrappy Cardinals. He only had eight at-bats in the 2011 season. But one of those was on September 20 in the seventh inning of a 7–6 game. At this point in that season, every game was a must-win game.

Bases loaded. Two outs. Two strikes. And Adron Freaking Chambers whisked a liner to right, far past the unsuspecting outfielder. All three runners scored. The third, Yadi Molina, touched home while grinning as wide as the plate itself. It was a triple for Chambers.

Others who made brief appearances include Stubby Clapp, whose name exudes scrap. The 5'8" infielder, who would do pregame backflips for the Memphis Redbirds, had five hits in 2001 for the St. Louis Cardinals. And there was Bo Hart with a scrappy name right out of a movie script. In June of 2003, the St. Louis second baseman tied a 102-year-old record with 28 hits in his first 15 games. And his .460 average after his first 10 games broke a record set by Kirby Puckett. "It's great when people come out of nowhere and they have success. It's absolutely a great story, no matter what the sport is," Hart told me by phone. "It could be a quarterback coming out of college, a late-round pick, and all of a sudden they're throwing touchdown passes and winning games. There are always feel-good stories because there are just so many players, and you always hear about the prospects and then? You have someone who gets an opportunity because of whatever circumstance, and they take advantage of it."

The entire Gashouse Gang itself epitomizes scrappy, especially Pepper Martin. "The Wild Horse of the Osage" was famously filmed making a headfirst slide right into the camera back in the 1930s. To him, dirt was a food group. In the field the 5'7" peppy Pepper would put his body in front of balls at third base and he'd gamble on the base path, too. But he's in the Cardinals Hall of Fame, which leads to the question: can someone be too good to also be scrappy? For example, Mike Trout and Bryce Harper throw their bodies all over the field, but since they're superstars, do they count? "People like scrappy players because they can relate to them more than a Mike Trout," Garcia said. "That guy is one of maybe three people in the whole world who can do what he does. People maybe relate to me more because they see *themselves* in me—the undersized guy, not the strongest or the fastest. And not to say these other guys don't work hard—because Trout works hard, these superstars work hard—but their abilities are higher than mine. So people relate more."

So, yes, a player can have scrappy abilities but be too good to be categorically scrappy. It also helps to play a scrappy position, namely second base like Garcia does. For the past 20 years, it's as if the Cards are continually heisting feistiness for their second-base position. They've had Delino DeShields, Tony Womack, Aaron Miles, Mark Grudzielanek, Skip Schumaker, Daniel Descalso, Kolten Wong, and Fernando Vina, who was hit by so many pitches (a league-high 28 in 2000) that the *St. Louis Post-Dispatch* newsroom used to chart where he was hit on the life-size Vina poster procured from a Cardinals game.

"Hurricane" Hudler played some second and also shortstop and even outfield for the Cards of the early 1990s. He was six feet of spitfire. He'd run through stop signs and run through walls. When he was traded to the Birds early in 1990, he flew out to Los Angeles, threw on his No. 10 jersey, and just hustled around the field during warm-ups. "I took all my ground balls. I'm out there at Dodger Stadium, I'm taking fly balls, I'm just running all over the place," said Hudler, the fast-talking Kansas City Royals broadcaster, on a visit back to St. Louis. "So I get in after batting practice, and there's a big, tall glass of milk at my locker. That means drink some milk to calm down. So then Tom Pagnozzi said, 'Hey, Hud, come here, I got to introduce you to somebody.' Joe Magrane was pitching that night. I had a little history with Joe Magrane. I hit some home runs off of him, and he had drilled me. I didn't like him. Now I'm on his team. So Pagnozzi brings me into the training room, and there's Joe Magrane. He looks at me, and I look at him. He said: 'Just because we're teammates doesn't mean we have to be friends.' The hair on the back of my neck stood up. I'm ready to throw down right there! And then I turned around, and there was the whole team. They had set that up. So I'm thinking, *This is going to be fun.* They knew I was a live wire, a wild man. I played aggressive, I played hard. And now I'm on their team. So I attacked. I played hard. I once dove into some gravel in San Diego."

Hudler's three seasons in St. Louis added up to about a season's worth of at-bats, 522 in total. He hit .253. But he was a human hurricane, Category 10. The fans loved it. He played the game the way they wish they could, with hardscrabble scrap.

First bottled in 1916, Vess Soda is a local treasure in St. Louis, and generations of St. Louisans have guzzled a Vess Orange Whistle. Well, Vess had a promotional deal with the Cardinals, and they approached Hudler about a life-size poster. "Usually, those things are reserved for Ozzie, Pendleton, McGee, Coleman," Hudler said. "They wanted to do it like a hurricane. 'We'll put some palm trees in the background, rip your uniform up a little bit.' They said they wanted to get me dirty, so they'd have some dirt in the studio. And I said, 'Nah, I'll make it real and original.' So I showed up here at the ballpark, an hour before the shoot that morning with my whole uniform on. The ground crew is sitting there, hanging out, drinking their coffee. I ask them to lift the tarp off and I go to third base. I act like I'm tagging up on a fly ball. I come home and I do a head-first slide into home. I pop up, and they're just watching, and I said, 'Hey, quit standing around, give me high-fives! Let's go! I'm not going to slide here and not get no love!' Then I said, 'Okay, one more, I gotta get my backside.' So I did a feet-first slide. Then I showed up at the photoshoot, and they go, 'Oh my gosh, that's perfect!'"

Hudler played the game like he was from a different era. While with the Cards, he bonded with Red Schoendienst, the old manager and coach who made Cooperstown as a gritty player. Back in World War II, the story goes, Schoendienst suffered an eye injury while shooting bazookas. The Cards in the early 1990s joked around the clubhouse that the red-headed Rex was Red's illegitimate son. "Trainer

Gene Gieselmann would kid: 'Where was your mom about this time and this time?'" Hudler said.

And Hudler can still feel the bruises on his shins courtesy of Schoendienst's grounders during practice. "He was sooooo strong," Rex said of Red.

Forever versatile, Hudler can do a variety of impressions. Spot-on. He encapsulated the gruff voice of an elder Schoendienst, sharing this anecdote: "He once said, 'Hey kiiiiid, you woulda been great in my day.' That's the greatest compliment anyone's ever given me in my entire career."

29

THE
GASHOUSE
GANG

This one time, Ducky met the Pope. It was on a USO Tour in 1944. The retired ballplayer Joe "Ducky" Medwick was given an audience with Pope Pius XII. And the old star from the Gashouse Gang told Pope Pius XII: "I was once a Cardinal myself, Your Holiness."

It seems too good of a story to have actually happened. But sure enough, there it is on page 35 in *Man of Peace: Pope Pius XII*, a book written by Sister Margherita Marchione. And there's no way Sister Margherita would've made something up about the Pope. (It reminds me of that day in the Denver Jewish Softball League, in which I played for my temple team and made, if I may, an Edmonds-inspired catch in center. But there was just one umpire, who was stationed behind the plate, and he said the ball had first hit the ground, to which I came running in and said: "I swear to God I caught it and I wouldn't lie. The shortstop's my rabbi!")

The Gashouse Gang. Ducky. Dizzy. Daffy. The Lip. The Fordham Flash. The Wild Horse of The Osage. That's an incredible nickname— even if I'm not really sure what the Osage is. Upon review, it appears that the Osage was a Native American tribe based in Oklahoma, the home state of John "Pepper" Martin, whose birth name is Johnny, not John, which means he was one of the rare men to be bestowed a nickname for a nickname for a nickname.

In 1934 the Cards won it all, and this team did so with carefree flair. They're remembered more for their persona than their accomplishments. Every year there's a champion, but very few champions transcend. The Gashouse Gang symbolized a style, accentuated an attitude. The fellows wore dirt-caked uniforms with tobacco stains, and the gang played the game with grit and grime. They said they'd beat you and then they'd go out and beat you. They were the forebearers to braggadocio. The 1986 New York Mets come to mind. And in our halcyon minds, the '34 Cards played the game like you'd want the game to be played—hard but happy. "They became an identity. They were kind of the anti-Yankees," St. Louis-based historian Ed Wheatley shared with me. "They were kind of the underdog, common guys. They weren't the aloof New Yorkers. And they were broadcast with such strong radio signals—they covered the South, they covered the Midwest, they actually would go to the West Coast. And people could relate to them and feel good. The Cardinals were there for people. Thirty-four, the Depression. What was there to look forward to? It's going to be a shit day tomorrow, too. But radio and newspapers brought the stories of this crazy team."

The best of them all was Dizzy Dean, and Dizzy Dean would've been the first to tell you that. The great gangly right-hander whirled and whirred pitches past batters, sometimes asking them prior to delivery what pitch "they'd like to miss." Dean was a bumpkin's bumpkin. He wasn't a thinking man, but he sure shared his thoughts. He would tell it like it is but probably do so with some grammatical errors. "Me an' Paul are gonna win 45 games," he proclaimed prior to the 1934 campaign. Paul Dean—called Daffy by some—was his little brother. They didn't win 45; they won 49. Dizzy finished 1934 with a 30–7 record, the most wins in the National League and the best winning percentage. Paul won 19, but his walks-and-hits-per-innings-pitched (WHIP) was 1.18, astoundingly close to Dizzy's 1.16.

Yet on August 9 of that year, the Cards were actually in third place, six games back. "What the Cardinals need," it said in the *St. Louis Post-Dispatch*, "is more Deans." But the Gashouse Gang made an enrapturing rush toward the pennant, grabbing it on the final day of the season. The Cards needed the Brooklyn Dodgers to beat the New York Giants, and sure enough, Brooklyn pulled it off in the 10th inning. At the Cardinals-Cincinnati Reds game in St. Louis, spectators suddenly heard factory whistles from afar. Folks were celebrating the news that the Dodgers victory meant the Cards clinched the pennant.

The factory whistles were a fitting tribute to the Gashouse Gang. "Gashouses" referred to the coal plants in towns that produced gas for electricity. They produced, as numerous writers eloquently alliterated over the years, "putrid plumes." And it was these plants that inspired the "Gashouse Gang" nickname for the local nine. Leo "The Lip"

LEAP YEAR BABY

Gashouse Gang member Pepper Martin was born in Oklahoma. "The Wild Horse of The Osage" had the distinction of being born on Leap Year Day in February 29, 1904. There have been more than 19,000 men to play in the major leagues; 14 were born on a Leap Year Day. A four-time All-Star, including in 1934, Martin was the best of them all.

So for fun, I decided to write about him on Leap Year Day of 2016, which was Martin's "28th" birthday. I was in Jupiter, Florida, at the time, covering Cardinals spring training. The 93-year-old Red Schoendienst was visiting camp, and Red had played for Pepper Martin when Martin managed in the minors. I asked Brian Bartow, the longtime Cardinals public relations director, if I could interview Red. Soon after, Bartow asked about the immediacy of my interview request. "Well, basically, if I don't get him today," I said, "the next time I could do this story would be in four years."

And so a few minutes later, I was summoned to Bartow's office. There was the great Hall of Famer, wearing his full Cardinals uniform even with his high red socks with horizontal stripes. He's a living legend. To paraphrase the writer Rick Bragg's famous line about Bear Bryant, Red was so beloved, they named a color after him. I asked him about Martin. "Balls didn't get by him at third base, he'd knock 'em down," said Red, who was an 11-year-old boy in nearby Illinois in 1934. "He was strong. His destination, when he walked on the field, was to win. After listening to the ballgames in the big leagues—no television in them days—when I first saw him on the field of play, he was just about finished. His better days were over, as far as playing. But he could run so fast, so quick. And he could stop on a dime. He wouldn't go more than two steps hardly when he was flying to first base when he hit a ground ball. I don't know how his legs could stand it. But I followed him back when he was with the Cardinals, 1934, when they were in that World Series. He'd get your attention. That's what he did in that World Series."

Indeed, Pepper Martin hit .355 that fall against the Detroit Tigers.

Durocher said of the stuffy American League, "They wouldn't even let us in that league over there. They think we're just a bunch of gashousers."

Durocher previously had a taste of that league over there. He'd actually been a New York Yankee. But in St. Louis he epitomized the Gashouse Gang, playing the game with a fury. As explained by the author Daniel Wyatt: "The pool-hustling Durocher was a fiery, all-ego, all-glove, no-hit shortstop, who left a trail of bad checks that he needed to finance his expensive tastes for food, drink, clothes, fast women, and slow horses."

Growing many of these ballplayers in his revolutionary farm system, Branch Rickey was the general manager. Of Durocher, the great Rickey said he had a special capacity for "making a bad situation worse."

In 1934 Rickey's strongest crop from the farm was James Anthony Collins, aptly referred to as Ripper. Collins is somewhat a forgotten Cardinal in lore. But in 1934 Ripper ripped 35 homers with a slash line of a .333 batting average, .393 on-base percentage, and a league-leading .615 slugging percentage. The St. Louis star was born, fittingly, in the year 1904, often considered the grandest year in city history because of the Olympics, World's Fair, and all those Judy Garlands singing on the trolleys.

Dizzy Dean, naturally, won Game 1 of the World Series against the Detroit Tigers. In Game 4, with the Cards up two games to one, Dizzy served as a pinch runner, but upon sliding into second to break up a double play, the throw hit him right in the head. He was sprawled on the field unconscious. Imagine the fans, listening to the account. *Was he dead?* And if he was alive, would he even be able to pitch again in the World Series? Fortunately, he was alive and taken to a local hospital, and the city and the nation awaited results of his tests. According to the great *Baseball Anecdotes* by Daniel Okrent and Steve Wulf, a headline the next day read: "X-RAY OF DEAN'S HEAD SHOWS NOTHING."

He actually pitched that very next day, but the Cards lost 3–1 and trailed in the series 3–2.

For a franchise that has had its share of thrilling Game 6s, this one deserves to be in the conversation. Paul Dean saved the season. He pitched a complete game and even drove in Durocher for the would-be winning run. And so the Cardinals were in Game 7 of the World Series. Only 11 times have they ever played in Game 7 of the World Series.

And Dizzy Dean pitched the game of his life. On the road, too. Complete game. Shutout. Six hits. No walks. The Cardinals won Game 7 of the 1934 World Series by the score of 11–0.

But the game will be forever remembered for the fruit delay. Medwick was on pace to set a record for hits in a World Series. In the sixth inning, with the Cardinals up 9–0, an unlucky Ducky got tangled up with the Tigers' third baseman. When Medwick trotted out to left field for the next inning, the fed-up faithful pelted him with fruit and other items from the stands. It was a debacle. The commissioner of baseball, Kenesaw Mountain Landis, actually removed Medwick from the game for the player's safety. It was an unprecedented decision by the commissioner.

Medwick, thus, never got a chance to break the hits record. But he won a World Series ring. Three years later he won the Triple Crown. As of 2017 he was still the last National League player to have done so. And thus, even at the Vatican, this old ballplayer was an esteemed Cardinal.

30

THE PLAYING OF "HERE COMES THE KING"

To incorporate two of my favorite tastes at the same time, I wanted to invent a burger that had ice cream sandwiches as the buns. This was culinary creativity, the brainchild of some Julia Child-like brain—or just a childlike brain. So I pulled some strings, took my idea to a local burger joint, and they actually prepared my ice cream sandwich burger. It tasted like shit.

But years later, with a renewed spirit for mixing favorites, I decided to combine one of my favorite thrills with presumably another: hearing "Here Comes The King," the famed organ song played at Busch Stadium...and getting married. I had always told my sister that the Busch Stadium organist would play my wedding. And so on July 1, 2017, I walked down the aisle to "Here Comes The King."

Ernie Hays played the soundtrack of my childhood. At Busch Stadium II, or "old Busch," you would walk into that gray and drab concrete concourse until you spotted the little opening for your certain section. When you walked through it and into the red sea of seats, it felt as if sunshine had been spilled upon your body. The ballpark. Synonymous for a synagogue. The sprawling green AstroTurf, the electronic scoreboard, the peculiarly blue-colored outfield walls. The waft of hot dogs—you even relish the relish. And the sound, percolating through the stadium, of the organ. It was something like a carnival—or a revival. When you're 10 in St. Louis, baseball feels as religious as religion. And on the scoreboard, the dotted yellow lights spelled these words:

FOR YOUR LISTENING PLEASURE
THE CARDINALS ARE PLEASED
TO PRESENT
ERNIE HAYS
ON THE YAMAHA ORGAN
PROVIDED BY LUDWIG-AEOLIAN
PIANO EXCHANGE

Hays was this mysterious figure to me as a boy. You never saw him. You just heard his music, this breathtaking whomping of organ keys. He was our Van Cliburn. (Admittedly, it's hard to come up with a go-to superstar pianist. Cliburn was the best I could do.)

In later years, I became acquainted with Hays a few different ways. First, I remember reading about how he would always tell these dirty jokes to people, which sort of demystified him to me. But later, I saw the YouTube video of him playing "Here Comes The King" at his home, wearing a shirt with the U.S. flag, and gleefully plucking at the keys. I've probably watched that YouTube more than any other video. Sometimes I'll listen on the treadmill to pump me up. And I definitely play it around the house on Opening Day.

And the third Hays connection came in 2009, when I got to interview him on the phone. I was writing for *The Denver Post* at the time, and St. Louis was hosting the All-Star Game later that summer. So I wrote a piece from a Cards game, capturing why my hometown was the best baseball town: "To my right, my sister sips a Bud Light, which always seems to taste better at the ballpark, like champagne at a New Year's party. Behind me, a young boy is seated between his father and grandfather, all three dressed in red, like there was even a choice. In front of me stand nine men, hailing from Pennsylvania to Puerto Rico, each man now one of us—Cardinals in Cardinal Country, saints in St. Louis."

Before I turned in the piece, I reached out to ol' Ernie. He was 74 at the time. Getting to speak with him was just, well, fun. "Baseball," Hays said, "is close to being a religion. People live, eat, and breathe baseball in St. Louis...These people were idols and my idols," he said of the Cardinals players of lore, "and to be able to have met them—and picked their brains—gives me goose bumps right now just thinking about it."

Hays died in 2012 in the autumn after the season.

Six years prior, Hays needed some new ivories. The Cardinals contacted a fellow named Dwayne Hilton, who worked in St. Louis for Lacefield Music. The Music Man sold the St. Louis Cards a Lowrey Inspire, a $70,000 state-of-the-art organ, though Hilton begrudgingly admitted that Lowrey is based in Chicago. Hilton impressed the Cards with his organ savvy. Soon, they asked him to occasionally fill in for

Hays. "As a little boy, my parents would bring me up here to watch Cardinal baseball, and, of course, I would hear Ernie Hays playing," Hilton told me at Lacefield Music. "And it's kind of funny, I remember as a kid thinking: *Man, wouldn't that be the coolest thing?*

"It was baptism by fire. They brought me up there the second or third day of the season. They said, 'Take notes, watch what he does.' The next day, 'Okay, you're in the hot seat, kid.' Truly it's a dream job. I'm getting paid to watch baseball, play 'Here Comes The King,' make people happy. What more could a person want?"

After Hays passed away, Hilton got the gig full time. And so, it's arguable that Hilton's hands are the 26th most important hands at Cardinals games. Yes, pop music is also played, but the Cardinals still understand that the organ connects with its fans, it connects fans to their pasts and their parents' pasts. And so, at the end of every seventh inning, Hilton plays the E-flat (but never flat) masterpiece, "Here Comes The King." Originally a beer jingle, the song was written by Steve Karmen, an ad man, in 1971. "It's more of a polka, like that German, beer-drinking, clap-along song," Hilton said.

Of course, we're all well aware of what we're doing: helping beer sales. The song has taken on a life of its own. While it's the sound of a stadium and a city—a song that links you to home—it's forever connected to Budweiser beer. What jingle has had more lasting power in advertising history? On a national scale, there's the "Buy the World a Coke" song. But from a regional scale, consider that in St. Louis *generations* of children have clapped and sung along to this song:

Here comes The King, here comes the big Number One!
Budweiser beer, The King is second to none.
Just say Budweiser, you've said it all.
Here comes The King Of Beers, so lift your glass, let's hear the
    call.
Budweiser beer's the one that's leading the rest,
And beechwood aging makes it beer at its best.
One taste'll tell you so loud and clear.
There's only one Budweiser beer, there's only one Budweiser
    beer!

ST. LOUIS CARDINALS

Okay, so kids sing about beer. But then again, St. Louis is a beer town. And St. Louis is unabashedly proud of St. Louis things. So even if we're aware that our song "Here Comes The King" promotes a beer company, at least it's our town's beer company. "It's always been a funny, chuckling, ironic thing for me," Cardinals president Bill DeWitt III told me for a *St. Louis Post-Dispatch* column. "We use it as a signal to the concessionaire workers and the portable workers that it's time to cut off beer sales. In the past there was never a way to tell the whole building it was time for the beer cut-off. But that song is at every game. So when they hear it at the end of seven, it's time to cut off the beer sales. And I always laugh at the irony of that—it's the quintessential 'go drink a Bud' song, but for our timing, it actually means 'no more beer.' But the song is big part of our gameday entertainment, always has been, and I think it always will be. Even though it's not the sole thing it used to be—now there are walk-up songs and all kinds of other multimedia intrusions into your senses— but it's still there. To me, it's that link, that link to the past. Even if it's somewhat diminished over the years, it's still there and it's still important. And for that reason, I love it. It does remind you of bygone days. Anything that links us to how things were 20, 40 years ago, I'm all for it."

And on Opening Day? Holy moly, what a show. Fans fueled by Busch at Busch eagerly anticipate the reins and not the rain; the only reigning, if you will, should be "The King." Before the first pitch, the team trots out the Budweiser Clydesdales and the complementing Budweiser wagon, featuring the Dalmatian and the gents taking the horse by the reins. And Hilton plays "Here Comes The King" for about 15 minutes, as the Clydesdales parade the exterior of the field, followed traditionally by the Cardinals themselves on stools in the beds of trucks.

The Clydesdales are St. Louisans, living in the stupendous stable at the Anheuser-Busch Brewery. For our engagement photos, my wife and I got the chance of a St. Louis lifetime—to be photographed with an actual Budweiser Clydesdale. Down at the stable, we were introduced to Chief, this majestic horse with the trademark white fluffy hoofs, which gracefully stride.

And like I'd told my sister, all those years ago, the Cardinals' organist would indeed play my wedding. Hilton was there on July 1, 2017, seated at the piano in the historic Central West End home where Angela and I were married. I'll never forget standing at the top of the stairs, waiting like a pitcher at the bullpen door. Hilton played sweet songs for the bridesmaids and groomsmen before me, and then, as I heard those time-honored first eight beats of "Here Comes The King," my goose-bumped body began to walk down the stairs and then down the aisle. Our smiling guests began clapping along. It was the coolest moment of my life—until about 10 seconds later.

31

THE RAJAH

He was an ass.

Perhaps Rogers Hornsby was just perpetually tormented by his quest for perfection. In a game in which failing seven out of 10 times gets you in the Hall of Fame, Hornsby failed just six out of 10 times in three seasons, but dang it if that still meant he was .600 away from his desired clip. Or perhaps he was just unwavering—forever in disbelief that others couldn't play at his level or live life with a similarly maniacal dedication to baseball.

Or perhaps he was just an ass, a miserable man who was great but grating. In *Sports Illustrated* the great wordsmith Ron Fimrite once wrote: "Ty Cobb was a bona fide monster whose racism and contempt for humankind were virulent. Hornsby was, by contrast, merely cold-blooded, pigheaded, humorless, and obsessive, a curmudgeon who regarded as utterly worthless anything that did not involve throwing, catching, or hitting a baseball."

The Rajah hit a career .358. The only player with a higher career average? Cobb. That's it. One guy. Hornsby was considered the greatest right-handed hitter in history.

But some modern fans simply associate him with his influence on a famous movie scene. "There's no crying in baseball!" Tom Hanks' Jimmy Dugan shouted in *A League of Their Own* to one of his players. "Rogers Hornsby was my manager and he called me a 'talking pile of pig shit.' And that was when my parents drove all the way down from Michigan to see me play the game. And did I cry? No! And do you know why?...Because there's no crying in baseball!"

Hornsby was born deep in the heart of Texas—well, an hour or so from it. His tiny hometown of Winters is 86 miles from Brady, the city geographically considered the center of the state. In 1915 Hornsby was making $90 a month for Denison in the Western Association, a league featuring teams from Muskogee, McAlester, and Paris. In an exhibition game, the Denison Railroaders had played the St. Louis Cardinals.

Impressed, the Birds plucked Hornsby at age 19. His first full season in the bigs was in 1916. The kid hit .313.

* * *

"Check this out," sports historian Ed Wheatley told me one day at Kaldi's Coffee in St. Louis. "You're gonna need white gloves for this puppy."

It was a St. Louis publication succinctly called *Baseball Magazine* and it was from early 1917. "This is a very, very, very rare publication," said Wheatley, who collects artifacts from baseball history. "This is stuff you can't find on the computers. Here's a picture of Hornsby, and the interview is from Miller Huggins."

Now this was cool. The legendary New York Yankees skipper first managed the Cardinals, and this magazine quoted Huggins about the young second baseman: "Hornsby was the big sensation of the club. He is one of those players the manager dreams of finding among his recruits but seldom does. He is still a young player, of course, and it is never safe to make predictions. But he looks to me like a real slugger, one who will improve rather than fall off in his work."

Huggins nailed it. In the 1917 season, Hornsby turned 21 and led the league in slugging percentage. And on-base-plus-slugging percentage. And triples. Hornsby was stupendous. And superstitious. Or just weird. He refused to read or go to the movies because he was afraid it would affect his vision for batting. He was engrossed with the sport of baseball, in the spirit of a Pete Rose in a later generation. And like Rose, Hornsby was a compulsive gambler. The ponies were his pleasure. At one point in Hornsby's career, his team's ownership hired a private detective to follow him, even setting up a wiretapping of Hornsby's conversations.

As a ballplayer, there are so many different ways to capture Hornsby's brilliance. Perhaps most efficiently: he's the only player ever to hit 40 homers and hit .400 in the same season. And two years after that, he hit .424 in 1924. No player has hit higher since.

And a particular six-season span pops off the page. baseball-reference.com bolds any player's stat that led the league in that category. From 1920 to 1925, it looks like someone typed his stats

Rogers Hornsby, a .358 career hitter, poses in 1926, the year he led the Cardinals to their first World Series title.

without realizing the bold function was on. In that six-season span, Hornsby hit .397. *Three-ninety-seven!* His on-base percentage was .467, while his slugging percentage was, perhaps appropriately for his personality, .666.

Wheatley, the historian, pontificated during that day with me at the coffee shop. "Planning for our meeting, I kept searching for one word to describe Hornsby," he said. "It would be—perfection. Rogers was almost perfection as a ballplayer. And they say he was the best double-play turner of his era. But as a hitter, there was nobody. There was a Hall of Fame pitcher, and he started screaming at the umpire because the umpire called it a ball. And the umpire said, 'Mr. Hornsby knows the strike zone. If he says it's a ball, it's a ball.' But that perfection? It was with everything. And that's where he fell apart. His teammates had to be as perfect as he was, and he could not deal with people inferior to his abilities."

And those people consisted of, well, all the people. The Cardinals won their first ever World Series the following season in 1926. Hornsby was the Cards' manager, too. It was a "down" year for The Rajah. He only hit .317. With 93 RBIs.

But even as a championship manager, in just his first full season as a player-manager, Hornsby managed to bungle managing. Fimrite wrote in his *SI* piece about a day when the Cardinals owner, Sam Breadon, was hanging around the team, and Hornsby kicked his boss out of the clubhouse. The owner never forgave the manager. After the Cardinals' first ever championship, Breadon traded Hornsby. Think about that. The best player on the best team, who is also the manager of the best team, was traded because he was such an asshole. And then Hornsby was traded again the next year. And again the next year, too. "Four teams, four years—at the peak of his Hall of Fame career!" Wheatley exclaimed. "He kept getting traded. They didn't want him on the team. He was kind of a cancer."

Decades later, Hornsby wrote a book. It was an unapologetic, nostalgic look at his career titled *My War With Baseball*. Chapter titles included: "Why I'm Ol' Hard-Boiled Hornsby," "The Game's Not The Same," and "The General Problem—General Managers." "I've never taken back anything I've ever said," Hornsby wrote, "and I've never failed to say exactly—and I mean, exactly—what I was thinking. To everybody—from the owner to the bat boy."

It was published in 1962, the season Hornsby took a new job as hitting coach for the new expansion team, the New York Mets. The '62 Mets were the worst team ever, recording 120 losses. The best right-handed hitter of all time was coaching the worst team of all time.

Hornsby retired as a player in 1937 and the next year took, reportedly, the only job he was offered. That was as a spring training hitting coach. The Double A Minneapolis Millers descended on Daytona Beach. The Rajah was 41. But he bonded with one particular player, a 19-year-old who seemed to care as much about hitting as he did. "Boy, I picked his brains for everything I could," Ted Williams wrote in his book, *My Turn at Bat*. "Something Rogers Hornsby had told me in Florida the year before was fast becoming a cardinal rule for me: get a good ball to hit…I've always felt Rogers Hornsby was the greatest hitter for average and power in the history of baseball."

* * *

Hornsby played for the Cardinals from 1915 to 1926 and he actually returned to St. Louis toward the end of his career. He played with the St. Louis Browns, the team he also managed for five years until the middle of 1937. They were not good.

That day at the coffee shop, Wheatley handed me a photo. I recognized the guy in the middle. It was the famed owner of the Browns, Bill Veeck Jr. Surrounding him in the photo were 10 Browns players in uniform. Everyone was smiling, and Veeck Jr. was holding a trophy. "The team was thanking him," Wheatley explained, "for firing Hornsby."

32

1940s

Stan Musial could see a pitch and make something out of nothing, and apparently the same was the case when he'd hear one. Before his harmonic harmonica days, the musical Musial would play the coat hangers. He'd listen to teammate Harry Walker play a slide whistle, and Stan The Man would clack those things in the Cards' clubhouse after a 1940s win. They also had a drum with a rope attached to it. And sometimes after turning on the phonograph, team trainer Doc Weaver would tap his scissors on the medicine bottles to a ditty such as "Pass the Biscuits, Mirandy." "That was our favorite song!" recalled Musial in *The St. Louis Cardinals—The Movie*, a VHS released in 1985. "I played the coat hangers, and it was fun. We'd carry on after every game! 'Pass the Biscuits, Mirandy.' What is Mirandy?"

Actually, Mirandy was a character in a song by Spike Jones & His City Slickers:

In the hills of Tennessee, sittin' 'neath a hickory tree,
There's an ornery rifle shootin' mountaineer.
He loves mountain feuds and he also loves good food.
And when he goes home to supper you will hear.
(chorus): Oh pass the biscuits, Mirandy,
I'm just as hungry as sin.
Oh, pass the gravy, Mirandy,
I need some stuff to sop 'em in!

The Cardinals loved that damn song so. It was a silly one. Mirandy's biscuits were so hard that the mountaineer started using them as bullets. And like "The Heat Is On" four decades later, "Pass the Biscuits, Mirandy" became the soundtrack of the pennant winners from St. Louis. From 1942 to 1946, the Cards played in four World Series, winning three. And Musial wasn't the only Cardinal thwacking the ball like it was a Mirandy biscuit.

The '42 Cards led the majors in doubles and triples, swooping around the bases so often that they earned the nickname "The Swifties." And because of different ages and wartime service, 1942 was the lone season in team history that regularly featured this iconic outfield: Musial, Terry Moore, and Enos Slaughter. Stan and Enos are in the Hall of Fame, while Moore—the Cards' captain and a brilliant fielder in center—is in the Cardinals Hall of Fame.

Now, as in the Cardinals' version of "Talkin' Baseball,"—as sung by Terry Cashman—"Mort pitchin', Walker catchin'—St. Louis was another Cooperstown."

The Coopers' hometown was actually Atherton, Missouri, but in the '40s, the All-Star brothers were St. Louis royalty. Burly and brawny and ballsy, Mort Cooper pitched with fire in 1942, one of the better seasons by any Cardinals hurler ever. Consider that as the league MVP, Mort had a 1.78 ERA...in 278⅔ innings pitched.

He'd never won more games than 13—his uniform number—and for a while in '42, it seemed like he wouldn't get past it again. As the story goes, Mort switched his jersey to No. 14 on August 14 in an effort to get his 14th win. He sure did. So each game up to win No. 20, he wore the number of the win he needed. And he eclipsed that mark, too, finishing 22–7. His brother was behind the plate for the whole run. Walker Cooper had his best season the next season, finishing second in the MVP voting. Alas, Musial prevented a consecutive trophy being sent home to Atherton.

Some say "The Swifties" were the best team St. Louis ever had. Thanks to a torrid final two months, they finished with 106 wins in the 154-game season. And they won the World Series, thanks in part to the Cards' George John "Whitey" Kurowski. Musial wasn't the only 1940s Cardinals player from Pennsylvania. Kurowski grew up in Reading, where at age seven he fell onto glass and infected a bone in his right arm. Even as an adult, he had a misshapen right arm, which was a few inches shorter than his left. But he persevered, and in September of '41, both Pennsylvania boys made the big club. The next year, they won it all.

How good was Musial? He had a .397 on-base percentage in '42. It was his *worst* on-base percentage until 1956. As for Kurowski, he had his biggest moment against one of the better pitchers he'd ever faced—future Hall of Famer Red Ruffing of the New York Yankees. Whitey came to bat in the top of the ninth of Game 5. The Cards led the '42 Series three games to one, but this game was tied at 2. With Walker Cooper on second, Kurowski read Ruffing's pitch perfectly and smacked a two-run homer. Johnny Beazley closed out the Yankees in the bottom of the inning, and when it was over, Kurowski led the Cardinals in a rendition of, yup, "Pass the Biscuits, Mirandy."

> Oh, pass the biscuits, Mirandy,
> I'm a-gonna load up my gun.
> I'll use your biscuits for bullets,
> I'll put them varmints on the run.

One October later, New York won the Yankees-Cards World Series. This time it was four games to one. During that '43 fall, there was a pall on the Cards because the Coopers' father died during the series.

The 1944 season was weird. Many stars were at war. In the American League, the Yankees had been in seven of the past eight World Series, but during this particular year, the best team was actually the St. Louis Browns, who captured their lone pennant (though they did so with a pennant-winning low .578 winning percentage). Dubbed "the Streetcar Series," the St. Louis vs. St. Louis World Series was played at the shared Sportsman's Park. The Fall Classic featured fascinating facets—notably the often-shared story of the two managers who shared an apartment on Lindell Boulevard because they were never there at the same time.

In the Sportsman's stands for the series was Major Billy Southworth Jr., the debonair, mustached son of the Cardinals skipper, Billy Southworth Sr. Having played in the bigs before, Junior was in a different uniform while watching the World Series. And with the series at 2–2, Mort Cooper pitched the game of his life—a World Series shutout with 12 strikeouts. The next day Mort and his brother were champions again.

Pass the biscuits.

Musial went into the service in '45. Slaughter was serving, too. And Southworth Sr. managed to manage that season, though he did so in mourning. In February of '45, Major Southworth died in a plane crash. The '45 Cards won 95 games, which is incredible considering who wasn't on the '45 Cards, but they finished in second place.

In 1946 Musial was back and so was "Country" Slaughter. And, good golly, the Cards had St. Louis agog. The Birds won the pennant, earning the right to face the Boston Red Sox for the first of four Fall Classics, a quartet played over generations.

Slaughter's Game 7 "Mad Dash," of course, proved to be the series-deciding play. "Mirandy" slide-whistle player Harry Walker smacked a single, and, running with the pitch, Slaughter just kept on running—all the way until his famous slide at home.

But the star of the 1946 series, which the Cards won in that seventh game, was "the Cat."

He was born in Broken Bow, Oklahoma. Harry Brecheen (pronounced Breh-keen) was one of the greatest lefties to ever play for the Cardinals. His concoction of a pitch called the screwball kept hitters flummoxed. "The Cat" was, indeed, quick. And slender. And splendid. From 1943 to 1949, his ERA for the Cards was 2.74. And against the Red Sox in the '46 World Series, he allowed just one run in three starts. All were wins, including Game 7—on one day's rest! "You're going to rest all winter, who cares?" Brecheen told the *Tulsa World* in 2001. "Tired arm? You're playing for all the marbles."

And all the biscuits.

33

THE 1985 WORLD SERIES

Here's all you need to know about high society St. Louis; it had rival cotillions. "There was Fortnightly, and there was League," Joe Buck said of these social and etiquette education programs, which much to the chagrin of many private school boys, provided dance instruction. League was about as classy as it got. It was held at the prestigious St. Louis Country Club and it was essentially a feeder program for St. Louis' debutante balls.

And so, on the Saturday night of October 26, 1985, the son of the Cardinals broadcaster couldn't watch Game 6 of the World Series because he had to go to this dance thing. "First of all, I was the guy pasted against the wall, not wanting to dance with anybody anyway," Buck said over beers at Lester's, a sports bar in Ladue, Missouri, approximately four minutes from St. Louis Country Club, site of the cotillion conundrum. "And they're having it on the night of Game 6 of the friggin' World Series? And not only do I not want to go to the dance—and I'm not going to dance with anybody—but this is taking up time during the game. I should be planted in front of the television!" And so, 16-year-old Buck sneaked out with other non-dancers and discovered that the guy at the front desk at the country club "had a little transistor TV. And that's literally where I was. You don't forget where you were when that happened."

Together these strangers peered at the tiny screen and saw perhaps the worst call in sports history. The St. Louis Cardinals of 1985, one of the most talented assemblages of Cardinals ever, led the World Series three games to two. And in that Game 6 of the I-70 series, the Cards led 1–0, heading into the bottom of the ninth. Three outs—with their lights-out closer on the mound—and St. Louis would win the World Series.

The Kansas City Royals' Jorge Orta led off against Todd Worrell. From a radio booth at Royals Stadium in Kansas City, Joe's dad did the national CBS radio broadcast, along with Sparky Anderson.

Jack Buck: "Orta leading off, swings, and hits it to the right side, and the pitcher has to cover. He is *safe*? Safe and we'll have an argument. Sparky, I think he was out."

Sparky Anderson: "I can't tell if his foot was on the bag or not, Jack."

Jack Buck: "He was *all over* the base as he took the throw from Clark and covered. The first-base umpire called him safe, and the tying run is on. That first-base umpire is Don Denkinger and he's in the middle of it, and Whitey Herzog is arguing with him. We'll watch a replay of it—a slow roller to the right side...Clark got it and shoveled it to the pitcher with his foot smack on the base while Orta was a step away! Another angle is seen, and he is *undoubtedly* out, but he is safe, and the tying run is on. Am I right?"

Sparky Anderson: "Well, he was on the base, no doubt about it."

Jack Buck: "Well, he had the base and he had the ball, man, what else? That's the rule."

He was so out. But Denkinger, of course, called him safe. "You saw the replay and you're sick," Joe Buck recalled. "His foot was there way before his—28 miles away."

Before your face could turn to a regular color, the bases were loaded. Dane Friggin' Iorg was up. One out, 1–0 game, bottom of the ninth. Iorg drives two in. See ya tomorrow night. "So that was not a good dance night for me," Joe Buck deadpanned.

I was five years old in '85 and have no memories of the World Series. But listening to Jack's call, I'm getting mad right here at my laptop. Now, yes, of course, the Royals still had to win another game. And you can blame the Cardinals for not being mentally tough enough—for bringing Game 6, if you will, into Game 7. But just like the 2011 Rangers, or the 1986 Red Sox, the Game 6 heartbreak broke this team for Game 7.

And having Denkinger as the damn home-plate umpire that game didn't help. And having superstar Bret Saberhagen pitching Game 7 for Kansas City didn't help. The Cardinals melted down. Starter John Tudor allowed five runs in 2⅓ innings. Then he punched a stationary electric fan. In relief, Joaquin Andujar lost it on the mound, having to be restrained multiple times. In the clubhouse, Andujar broke a toilet with a baseball bat. Three outs from a championship, the Cardinals proceeded to lose Game 6 and then Game 7. Saberhagen pitched an 11–0 shutout, and pandemonium ensued at Royals Stadium. One of the fans in the crowd hoisted a huge sign that read: "THE HEAT IS GONE."

* * *

By 1984 the German musician named Harold Faltermeyer had become the Brahms of the synthesizer. Faltermeyer previously produced numerous hits by Donna Summer while infusing pop music with the quintessential 1980s synthesizer sound. Faltermeyer was asked to score the soundtrack to a new cop comedy and he maestro'd a pair of masterworks. The first was "Axel F," the theme to the film, *Beverly Hills Cop*, starring Eddie Murphy as the street-smart Axel Foley. The synth-pop song, fittingly in F Minor, remains internationally recognizable to this day.

The second song Faltermeyer wrote for the soundtrack was a little more poppy. It had a synthesizer, sure, but also featured a potent sax sound, as well as guitar and a drumbeat. The song was titled "The Heat Is On," and it was glorious. "Oh-wo-ho, oh-wo-ho. Tell me can you feel it, tell me can you feel it, tell me can you feeeeel it? The heat is on!" Performed by Glenn Frey, formerly of The Eagles, the song reached No. 2 on Billboard in March of 1985 (trailing only "Can't Fight This Feeling" by REO Speedwagon). The timing coincided with the start of the baseball season, and it became the unofficial anthem of the St. Louis Cardinals.

The song perfectly complemented the "Runnin' Redbirds," whose fiery style ignited a brand of baseball never seen before. Sure, teams ran, even some Cards teams—Lou Brock, after all, retired with the most steals ever. But the '85 Cards put more heat on more catchers than any team ever had. And when it was over, the Cards finished with the fitting number—314, the St. Louis area code—of stolen bases. It was the most stolen bases by a team since 1920. "Why was the '85 team so good?" Andy Van Slyke, the outfielder who raised his family in St. Louis after retirement, asked in 2017. "Well, every night was a track meet, and some nights a baseball game was played. When you hit less than 70 home runs as a team, you wouldn't expect to get to the World Series. So we had to do things differently. Walk, get on base, steal, regardless of what the score was. It's a team record that'll never be broken again in baseball."

Vincent Maurice Coleman, who once moonlighted as a college football kicker at Florida A&M, was selected by St. Louis in the 10th round in 1982. The following year for Single A Macon, Georgia, Coleman stole 145 bases in only 113 games. That's not a typo. During this preposterous season, Coleman hit .350 with an on-base percentage of .431. Finally, a Cards rookie in '85, Coleman stole two bases in his first game. Three games later, he stole three in the game. He finished the year with 110 stolen bases, the same amount stolen by the Pittsburgh Pirates.

DANNY COX

My favorite story from 1985 has got to be about Danny Cox. The 6'4", 230-pound pitcher won the October 3 game against the New York Mets. The Cards had three to play for the regular season, and those Mets were two back.

This is an actual news article from United Press International:

ST. LOUIS — Right-hander Danny Cox of the St. Louis Cardinals took time out from a pennant race to travel to Georgia and punch his former brother-in-law in the mouth.

"I started it. I finished it," Cox said Saturday. "It only took two punches."

Cox, the winning pitcher in a 4—3 victory over the New York Mets Thursday night, punched Richard Diebold, his former brother-in-law, on Friday. He said Diebold had been threatening his sister, Maxine, and his parents, who live in Warner Robins, Ga.

"I think anybody in that situation would have done the same thing," said Cox. "If you wouldn't have, then you're not a man and you don't love your family. You've only got one family."

The incident occurred at Robins Air Force Base, about 60 miles from Atlanta. Cox returned to St. Louis Friday night for the game between the Cardinals and the Chicago Cubs.

ST. LOUIS CARDINALS

Coleman even made a steal at Uncle Leonard's. In the low-budget local TV commercial, he spoke about the steal he made on the new Panasonic big-screen TV, later sharing screen time with store proprietor "Uncle" Leonard Lewis, who excitedly told viewers: "You don't need to be Vince Coleman to get a major league deal on a big-screen TV!"

Later captured on the VHS titled: *Heck of a Year*, the '85 team had a heck of a year indeed. Coleman would win the Rookie of the Year, while Willie McGee would earn the MVP, hitting .353. Tommy Herr, like Coleman, also put up the number 110. That was his RBI total, an astounding amount considering he only hit eight home runs. "We scored a lot of runs and we just did it in an unconventional way," Herr said. "We had virtually everyone in the lineup who could steal a base except for Jack Clark. And Terry and Ozzie on the left side of the infield—that's as good as it gets, any era, any time in the history of baseball."

Okay, that's maybe a stretch, but consider this: from a sabermetric standpoint, '85 was Ozzie Smith's second best defensive season with St. Louis, per the rating on fangraphs.com, and Terry Pendleton had his best defensive season ever. "Defensively, we caught the ball better than any team I ever played on. We covered more ground," said Van Slyke, who played on playoff teams with the Pirates, too. "Ozzie Smith moved his body in a way I'd never seen anyone before. I'll put it this way: if Ozzie Smith decided at 5 he wanted to be a gymnast, he would've won a gold medal in the Olympics."

But the best player on the team was a pitcher. Tudor, who was once cut from his high school baseball team, came to the Cards for the 1985 season. He was just okay. Through May his ERA was 3.74. And then with a change-up that changed the course of his career, Tudor finished the rest of the season with a 1.37 ERA. Beginning in June, he went 20–1. And he tallied 10 total shutouts, the most in a baseball season since 1975—and the most since, too. After May, opponents hit .199 against him. It was as if every batter who faced him had a batting average under The Mendoza Line.

* * *

I still can't get over the fact that Tom Niedenfuer later joined the Cardinals.

It was always so weird to me. Here was the guy who allowed two of the most famous homers in Cardinals history (and in back-to-back games) and then he became a Cardinal? But there he was—teammates with Ozzie and Willie on the 1990 club.

Five years prior, Niedenfuer was a key right-handed reliever for Tommy Lasorda's Los Angeles Dodgers, who won the National League West. They took on the Cards, who'd won 101, in the 1985 National League Championship Series. The underdog Dodgers won the first two games at home. Thanks to a strong start by Danny Cox—and a stolen base by Coleman—the Cards won Game 3 back at Busch. Before Game 4 the most inexplicable injury occurred: Coleman somehow got his foot caught in the rising automatic tarp before the game. The injury ended his postseason. But his replacement, the wonderfully named Tito Landrum, tallied four hits, and the Cards won Game 4.

In Game 5 Ozzie homered off Niedenfuer, and St. Louis went crazy. In Game 6 Jack Clark silenced a stadium back in L.A. The Ripper's three-run homer with two outs in the top of the ninth inning also came off Niedenfuer. It was suddenly 7–5 Cards. In left field, Pedro Guerrero threw his glove to the ground. The Dodgers couldn't score in the ninth, losing the game and losing the series. Looking back, Lasorda could've walked Clark to load the bases, but Niedenfuer had struck out Clark earlier in the game, so Lasorda left him in. That's a chance you take when the heat's on you.

And so, the Cardinals went back to Missouri for the World Series... and never left the state. And just like in the NLCS, the Cardinals led three games to two going into Game 6, which would be played on October 26, 1985, the Saturday night Joe Buck had to go to that dance.

34

THE 2004 CARDINALS

It had been so long since the Cardinals made the World Series that the last time they did Ozzie Smith was their shortstop. And, sure enough, they were on the cusp—Game 7 of the 2004 National League Championship Series—and die-hard fan Mark McCarthy had to fly to his cousin's wedding. "The plane lands, so I run over to the FOX Sports bar in the Phoenix airport," said Mark, who had to wait for his parents' arrival on a different flight. "And I find myself face to face with many Astros fans. So I decided to stand outside of the bar to watch."

Roger Clemens was pitching for the Houston Astros. Jeff Suppan, who turned into Roger Clemens each October, was pitching for the Cards. Mark spotted someone else standing outside the bar, watching the game intently on the TVs. But it couldn't be. "I walk over to him and say, 'Are you...'" Mark said. "And he turns and faces me, and I realize it's him. It's 'The Wizard.' I'm stunned. I say, 'I was born the year you guys won the '82 series. You are the guy I've grown up idolizing!' He shakes my hand and asked what my name was. We talk for about 20 minutes! My phone rings, my parents have landed, and my dad wants to know the score. I told him we were losing, but he would never believe who I was with. They walk over, and Ozzie, in true fashion, introduces himself to my parents. He tells them that, 'Mark and I have been watching the game together.' We finally asked him: 'Why aren't you in St. Louis at the game?' He had an event in San Diego that he promised to be at, but if he knew it would've taken seven games to get to the World Series, he wouldn't have gone. We stood there maybe five to 10 more minutes, talking baseball with one of the greatest players ever. Finally, his flight gets called. He turns and says, 'Mark, it was great watching the game with you. Tom and Missy, it was nice to meet you. Go Cardinals!' And, of course, I had him sign the Cardinals hat I was wearing."

And then the Cards came back and won the game. For the first time in 17 years—since Mark was 5 and Ozzie was 32—their St. Louis Cardinals were heading to the World Series.

* * *

This insane team from 2004 won 105 games. It's tricky to rank a franchise's greatest teams because with baseball's small sample size of a postseason does the best team always win?

And even if it's *your* franchise's greatest team, perhaps you're facing another franchise's greatest team—like Boston's 2004 Red Sox. And this might sound uncouth, but can your franchise's greatest team possibly be one that didn't win it all? If so, the '04 Cardinals—not with the MVP but with the "MV3"—are in the conversation for greatest Cards team. Also in the conversation are the '85 Cards, the '67 Cards, any number of the '40s Cards, and, to be sure, the World Champion '31 Cards with Jim Bottomley, Chick Hafey, and the MVP, Frankie Frisch.

Of the Tony La Russa teams, "'04, to me, that was the best club," broadcaster Al Hrabosky said. "It's such a shame because they just didn't show up in the World Series. That first game in Boston, I think if they would've won that game, the *Cardinals* might've swept."

Indeed, the '04 Cards pitchers had a baseball-best ERA (3.75), throwing first strikes and inducing ground balls as if they were simply puppets to the marionette Dave Duncan.

St. Louis led the National League in batting average (.278) and slugging percentage (.460) and had three Gold Glove winners—catcher Mike Matheny, center fielder Jim "Jimmy Ballgame" or "Jimmy Baseball" Edmonds, and third baseman Scott Rolen. "I loved Scott Rolen," said St. Louisan Joan Niesen, a high school student in 2004 who became a *Sports Illustrated* writer. "I bought a Rolen shirt that season and I still have it...I wore it so many times it's now pink rather than red."

A fun trivia tidbit is that Rolen, not Albert Pujols or Edmonds, had the highest wins-above-replacement (WAR) on the team in '04. If you add up Rolen's 9.2 WAR, Pujols' 8.5, and Edmonds' 7.2, you get 24.9—better than *19 teams* that year. Their stats were so similar, but their styles were so different. The showman Edmonds drove a Ferarri, the Hoosier Rolen drove a pickup truck, and the machine Pujols drove perfectly placed pitches to faraway places that balls don't often go. "Pujols aims for distance in nearly every aspect of his life," wrote Lee Jenkins, then of *The New York Times*, in August of '04. "He broods before games and preens during them. A portrait of precocity, Pujols got married when he was 19 to a woman who has a daughter with Down syndrome, replaced Mark McGwire in the lineup when he was 21, and this week became the first player to hit 30 or more home runs in each of his first four seasons. Asked about the feat, he sounded like Barry Bonds, minus the sense of humor. 'I don't care,' Pujols said, puffing his chest. 'I can do it every year.'"

And at least for his Cardinals career, he did. All 11 seasons. And sure enough, on August 6, 2004, the same day the MV3 article ran in *The Times*, the Cardinals made it "MV4." Larry Walker—the hockey-loving Canadian, who was, alas, better at line drives than slap shots—was a preeminent ballplayer of his era. Once in 1995 he played in a playoff round. He hadn't before and hadn't since, but, suddenly, the former Montreal Expo and Colorado Rockie was traded to the best team in the National League. Walker, who hailed from the too-good-to-be-true town of Maple Ridge in the province of British Columbia, was once again bruising baseballs, albeit during an injury-plagued '04.

Walker was a slugger, but Walker was also a walker. He sometimes even walked more than he struck out, a seemingly preposterous preponderance, and in 44 games with the '04 Cards he had a .393 on-base percentage. Oh, and Walker walloped 11 homers. And in October he hit two homers per playoff series, finishing with a 1.086 on-base-plus-slugging percentage (OPS).

Now, in Cardinals history, just like, well, any team's history, there are postseason what-ifs. What if Curt Flood, a perennial Gold Glove winner, hadn't misjudged a ball in Game 7 of the '68 World Series? What if in '85 it didn't start to rain that day the tarp ate Vince Coleman…and if Don Denkinger didn't "Denkinger" the Game 6 call? What if Jack Clark was healthy against the Twins in '87? And what if ace Chris Carpenter, who'd lost just five times all of 2004, didn't miss the '04 playoffs with a shoulder injury?

ST. LOUIS CARDINALS

* * *

Twelve lucky high school boys were invited to the Halloween dance at the all-girls Visitation Academy. Twelve unlucky high school boys each had to dress as a crayon. "We made these amazing costumes. Everyone got a pair of tights in his or her color with coordinating Soffe shorts and T-shirts that we'd written 'Crayola' on," Joan Niesen recalled. "Oh, and we painted party hats for everyone to wear on their heads as the tip of the crayon. We were so proud of ourselves, and I remember one of my friends getting really excited about getting to be the red crayon for the Cardinals."

The dance, as they sometimes seem to be, was scheduled for the night of Game 1 of the 2004 World Series. And so, the Crayola set was one short, as the periwinkle crayon "parked my butt in front of the TV in the lobby," said Niesen, who was born in November of 1987. "I'd never seen the Cardinals in the World Series before. I'm pretty sure I lasted three innings out there and, by the time the Red Sox scored their seventh run, I decided it was time to go dance, but I was so depressed the entire time."

While Niesen was in the dance, the Cards made a valiant comeback. It was 9–9! But in came Julian Tavarez. All season the Cards took the good and the bad from this livewire of a righty. He had a sterling 2.38 ERA out of the bullpen that season; he also had been suspended for using a foreign substance. He logged some strong postseason appearances; he also lost his mind and punched a bullpen phone in the NLCS, breaking his non-throwing hand. (Never punch with your pitching hand, Crash Davis famously told Nuke LaLoosh.)

And in the eighth inning at Fenway, Taverez allowed a two-run homer to Mark Bellhorn, one of the few non-stars on that loaded 2004 Red Sox team. Boston became a buzz saw. MV3 was MV0, and the Cardinals were swept. The '04 Red Sox broke the curse. They're forever remembered for beating the New York Yankees in the American League Championship Series, but I don't think the country remembers how good of a team they beat in the World Series.

35

THE BRAD LIDGE HOME RUN

He smoked back then. His girlfriend at the time was asleep. He was alone in many senses of that cold word, as the final inning began. "The first eight innings, I was staring at my television and pacing and grousing," said the author Will Leitch, who was based in New York in 2005, the same year he started the site Deadspin. "I just got frustrated. *They're losing this, nobody hits Lidge, we're done.* So I went outside to smoke on the street, right outside by The Dakota, where John Lennon was shot. I'm about to call my dad because the season is about to be over. And there's a bar, and I see when I'm smoking that Eckstein has gotten a single."

After getting swept in the 2004 World Series, the singular mission was getting to the 2005 World Series. The Cardinals tallied a triple-digit win total—again. But here they were, just like against the Boston Red Sox, reduced to being participants in a formality. This time it was to make three outs in the top of the ninth and get out of the way, so the Houston Astros could celebrate their first ever World Series berth.

Brad Lidge earned the save in Game 2. And Game 3. And Game 4. And here he was in Game 5, leading 4–2 in the ninth inning. With two outs. Sure, that scrappy David Eckstein was on first. But just get a Jim Edmonds ground ball and put on the goggles. "But then Edmonds got on," Leitch recalled. "So, like all superstitious people, I'm like, *Okay, well I can't move now.* They're starting a rally while I'm on the street corner, watching it through a window of New York City bar, like watching it from far away. I could tell Eckstein's hit was a single, but I couldn't tell a lot. I'm on the sidewalk, and this is not like a sports bar. It's just like a grungy Irish bar. And I'm also not going to go in because I don't have any money at the time—Deadspin paid like $5 a day in the early days. And I can't go inside because I'm now *here*. They started to rally when I'd gotten disgusted with them and went out *here* to smoke. So I'm basically watching it through this clouded window on a pretty cold October night in New York City. And I couldn't quite tell what exactly was happening until Pujols hit his home run, and then it was quite obvious. I started screaming. Oh yeah, I started screaming. To be fair, it's New York, so someone is usually doing that on the street anyways."

The best part about the homer is everything. Albert Pujols walking toward first base, bat in his left hand, gazing at his Houston launch. The FOX camera person losing track of the ball and jerking the camera, trying to spot the ricochet. In the dugout Houston's Andy Pettitte mouths: "Oh my gawsh."

Brad Thompson was in the bullpen. "I will never forget—neeeeever forget—the moment when this ball was hit," said the former Cards pitcher. "That place was so loud, annoying-loud, and in the bullpen especially it was because it was all concrete there, and everything just reverberates. You couldn't even hear your own conversations. And Lidge hangs this slider, and then the only thing you heard were our screams in the bullpen."

On KMOX Radio Mike Shannon had the call: "Well, here's Albert Pujols at the plate right now. And I could tell you this: it couldn't come down to a better situation than this. And 1-for-8 lifetime is Albert against Lidge. And tonight Albert has popped to third, he struck out, he's grounded out to the third baseman twice. He's 0-for-4. And that doesn't happen very often either. He hit 41 homers during the regular season. Good speed on the bases. Eckstein at second, Edmonds at first. Two on, two out, Houston leads 4–2. Ninth-inning action. The pitch to Albert—swing and a miss! He went after the curve and he was fooled...Albert digs back in. Open stance, deep in the box, bends at the knees. Lidge is ready. With two on and two out, here's the 0–1 pitch...Swing and a long one! There it is, baby! The Cardinals take the lead as Albert Pujols comes through in the pinch, and the Redbirds lead this baby 5–4! What did I tell ya, folks? David Eckstein, The Man. This could be a *crushing blow, a crushing blow* to this Houston club! Albert Pujols, you talk about a Most Valuable Player, how is that, baby? Woooo! That thing left the ballpark in a hurry. A three-run home run and the Cardinals lead 5–4!"

An engineer named Greg Rybarczyk parlayed his expertise into sports, licensing his technology to ESPN. He now runs ESPN Home

Cardinals slugger Albert Pujols and Houston Astros closer Brad Lidge gaze in awe at Pujols' titanic three-run, ninth-inning home run in Game 5 of the 2005 National League Championship Series.

Run Tracker. He analyzes homers in real time, as well as numerous famous home runs from yesteryear, including the three-run homer by Pujols from October 17, 2005. Rybarczyk estimated that the exit velocity of the ball off Albert's bat was 116.9 miles per hour. For perspective, in the entire 2017 season, only eight batted balls had a faster exit velocity. "Had the ball continued uninterrupted back to field level," Rybarczyk shared via ESPN, "it would have carried 468 feet, a truly monumental blast."

And how about this comparison. Per Rybarczyk, the exit velocity of the Mark McGwire '98 homer—the one that prompted the Cardinals to put a Band-Aid on the broken *Post-Dispatch* sign—had a 115 mph exit velocity. "For the rest of my life, I will always remember being in that Houston stadium, where the press box is rather low, so you can really see and hear what's going on," said Frank Cusumano, the longtime sports broadcaster for Channel 5 in St. Louis. "And to see the Pujols homer against Lidge and to see that stadium turn into the world's largest morgue, I've never seen anything like it. It was like somebody pressed the mute button on the remote—complete silence. All you could hear was just a few claps...I've always loved *The Natural*. I thought for a second I was watching a movie. The only thing we needed was to slow it down and have music in the background."

Jason Isringhausen, the closer from Brighton, Illinois, still had to close. But if Izzy missed a spot and an Astro somehow got on? With the pennant-winning run at the plate, Thompson would've had trouble hearing in that bullpen again. But Isringhausen, the Cards' all-time save leader in an All-Star season, shut down the Astros 1-2-3. "So Pujols' homer not only kept the Cardinals from being eliminated," Leitch said, "but it gave everybody one last game at Busch. It ultimately ended up being a futile homer. Roy Oswalt shut them down in the last game of old Busch. But for me, I was away from home. I was not ready to say good-bye to this place yet. I wasn't quite ready for this stadium where I grew up to be torn down...It was a miserable game, but at least they got one more."

30

THE 1996 SEASON

I'll meet people and they say I was lucky, getting to grow up in a great baseball town such as St. Louis. But the reality is 1987, when I was seven years old, was my first year following the team. So after that World Series from seven until age 16—basically, my childhood—the Cards never made the playoffs. My youth was marred with lackluster play on tacky artificial grass.

And then after the 1995 season, like 73 things happened.

- **New manager**—The Cards hired Tony La Russa, who went to three World Series with the Oakland A's.
- **New ownership**—The passionate Bill DeWitt Jr., who as the bat boy for the St. Louis Browns loaned his uniform to Eddie Gaedel.
- **New grass**—Actual grass was installed at Busch.
- **New stadium renovations**—Busch added Homer's Landing in left, a retro scoreboard in center field, and green outfield walls. (Why were they blue to begin with?)
- **New players**—So many new players came aboard, such as Ron Gant, Andy Benes, Dennis Eckersley, Gary Gaetti, Todd Stottlemyre...and one new old player—Willie Dean McGee, home again.
- **New ad campaign**—It was: "Baseball like it oughta be."

A pair of fellows named James Palumbo and Kip Monroe came up with it, and the Cards poured $50,000 into the multifaceted campaign. On March 10, 1996, a full-page ad appeared in the *St. Louis Post-Dispatch*:

It oughta make you forget about work.

It oughta be real grass.

It outghta be steppin' on peanut shells.

It oughta be diggin' for second.

It oughta be something you can talk about with your girlfriend's dad.

It oughta be cold beer.

It oughta be autographing a kid's glove.

It oughta be fun.

St. Louis Cardinals.

Baseball like it oughta be.

Coming April 8.

"I believe in high goals," La Russa said at his introductory press conference. "I believe in big dreams."

Goddamn, where had this been?

The '96 Cards rejuvenated my love for my first crush—and rejuvenated the city's love affair with baseball. The outfield featured the coolest guy in town, Brian Jordan, our lite version of Bo Jackson. The muscular former NFL safety was a joy to watch, and you could tell the game was a joy for him to play. And man, he had some swagger.

The Cards had trouble meshing early. That was not a surprise, considering all these new guys were playing under new rules with a new boss. And there was dissent due to the way La Russa handled the shortstop position, starting Royce Clayton over the aging Ozzie Smith. So the veterans talked to La Russa. The team had players-only meetings. (Seemingly, no team in sports history has had a players-only meeting and *hasn't* started winning again.) And on July 12, the team had a breakout game at Wrigley Field, winning 13–3 thanks to seven St. Louis homers.

And that was right in the middle of Jordan's surge. From June 24 to July 24, Jordan had 43 RBIs. In those 28 games, he hit eight homers, stole 11 bases, and had a .429 on-base percentage. He was making baseball cool in St. Louis. Jordan played right, Gant played left. And in between was Ray Lay.

With that fluid, swooping swing, Ray Lankford was a spectacle in the left-handed batter's box, the best No. 16 on the Cards since Sixto Lezcano. Lankford's most famous highlight, of course, was when he body-slammed catcher Darren Daulton for a game-winning run. But he also hit the most homers ever at old Busch. And he was a 20 homer/20 steal guy five times, including in '96. He wasn't as good as

Ted Simmons, but he was the Ted Simmons of the 1990s, a great run producer overshadowed (more often than not) by losing baseball. This all made '96 that much more special. Some of the long-suffering guys—Lankford, Tom Pagnozzi, even Smith because he hadn't seen October since '87—were getting to experience important baseball again.

And who could've anticipated that the "baseball like it oughta be" ads *wouldn't* be the best ads of the season?

Even after winning Rookie of the Year, the World Series, the MVP, and batting title twice, Willie McGee was...still just so shy. "It's his humility," Smith told me. "He's never changed. The people love him here." McGee and Smith starred in a Cards commercial that was pretty epic. They dressed up as old men "Henry and Walter" and reminisced about the old Cardinals players, such as the acrobatic shortstop "The Lizard." "It was just something to do, some fun, just having some fun," McGee recalled. "For me to come out of character like that was like, wow, I couldn't believe that I did it, you know? It was all in fun. They took the video and showed it in the locker room, and nobody knew who it was. We had to tell them! I was like, 'Okay, we did a good job!'"

But even though Ozzie and Willie were graying like Henry and Walter, they still found ways to contribute to the '96 team. McGee was actually stupendous that season, hitting .307. And for all that was made about Clayton, both he and Smith finished with the same wins-above-replacement (WAR) of 1.5. And this particular '96 Ozzie-Willie collaboration, on September 2, was something out of '86. The Cards were one-and-a-half games out of first. They trailed the Houston Astros, their opponent that day at Busch. At one point the Astros led the game 7–3. But the Cards sent it to extras. And McGee's chopper up the middle scored a soaring Smith from second, as Smith slid home and beat the tag for the game-winning run.

A few weeks later, the Cards won the division. *The Cards actually won the division!*

It was such a strange, foreign feeling around the halls of Clayton High School. Our team was good! Jordan was the hero in the National League Division Series, making a Superman catch in the clinching game.

And the Cards led the National League Championship Series two games to one. My uncle, Lenny, took me to Game 4. It was a sports energy I had never felt. The stadium pumped the song of the season, "We're Gonna Win," an underrated anthem that infiltrated your bones.

And young Dmitri Young came to the plate in the seventh. He had 29 at-bats all season. But he was a lefty, the pitcher was a righty, and he ripped the baseball to left field. As it bounced off the wall, it had the same "roll" as the David Freese triple would in 2011. (Freese, wouldn't you know it, was a 13-year-old fan in the stands for the Dmitri Young Game.) Young's triple cut the lead to 3–2. Two batters later Royce Clayton drove in Young to tie the game. Watching the replay of the triple for this book, 21 years after it happened, I couldn't stop smiling. I was 16 again.

And then in the eighth inning, of all the people, Jordan hit a home run, and the Cards led the NLCS three games to one! I wish I could stop this chapter right here. Alas, the Atlanta Braves won the next three, Smith's final at-bat ever was a paltry pinch-hit pop-up, and the Cardinals wouldn't make the World Series until 2004. But baseball was reinvigorated in St. Louis—like it oughta be.

37

JIM EDMONDS

This particular millennium wasn't going as well for him as the previous one. Just three months into 2000, Joe Buck was recovering from back surgery. Sprawled out at home in St. Louis, he received a call from his dad, who was in Florida. "Tony La Russa wants to tell you something," Jack Buck told Joe Buck.

And the Hall of Fame broadcaster passed the phone to the Hall of Fame manager. "We just got you a center fielder," La Russa told Joe, who forever followed his hometown team, even into adulthood. "Jim Edmonds might be the best I've ever seen."

"And," Joe Buck said, recalling the call, "he wasn't wrong."

Kent Bottenfield. They got him for Kent Bottenfield. Well, Kent Bottenfield and Adam Kennedy (who was unproven at the time but turned into an excellent fielding second baseman and a playoff hero but still basically for just Kent Bottenfield). The portly pitcher had about a 4.00 ERA in 1999, but he won 18 games—and was an All-Star—and so, the win total wooed the Anaheim Angels.

Wins, as we've learned in recent years, are a terrible way to gauge greatness. Even some scouts were on to Bottenfield at the time. Per an article in the *Los Angeles Times*, an anonymous scout shared that Bottenfield's sinker/slider repertoire in March of 2000, "was being timed in the unsettling 84-to-86 mph range in Florida this spring. And that he had all the earmarks of a Willie Blair, who turned a 16–8 career year with the Detroit Tigers in 1997 into a major contract with the Arizona Diamondbacks, only to go 4–15 in '98 and virtually disappear from the baseball landscape." Similarly, Bottenfield was out of baseball before 2002 began.

Again, Kennedy did pan out for the Angels, but Edmonds is a Cardinals Hall of Famer. "One of the best athletes I've ever seen, raw athlete," Joe Buck said. "He can do anything. He picked up golf and became an 8-handicap in a summer. He's annoyingly gifted. I remember a spring training rain delay, and he and Edgar Renteria were playing soccer with one another in the clubhouse at Roger Dean Stadium. Edmonds was playing goal, and Renteria was doing his tricks. He came from Colombia, you know, flipping the ball around and doing fake kicks and then shooting, and Edmonds was diving all over the place, making saves. And then they switched, and Edmonds was better at it than Renteria."

Edmonds is remembered for his defense, which is fair since he played center field pretty much the way Spiderman would, but even if he was just a pretty good fielder, his offensive numbers would've still made him a star. Outfielder Tommy Pham, who led the Cards in batting average for much of 2017, said: "I don't care about batting average. I think that's an overrated stat. It doesn't truly measure a hitter's offensive profile...Offensively speaking, OPS (on-base-plus-slugging percentage) truly measures a hitter because it's telling you if a guy can get on base—and if the guy can drive the ball. I feel like .850—you're pretty solid, regular. At .900 you're All-Star. At .950 you're pretty much in your own league."

Well, Edmonds played 17 seasons in the major leagues. His career OPS was .903. His *career* OPS was All-Star level. And really, that's weighed down a little by some good-not-great seasons before coming to St. Louis. So let's try this again: Edmonds played eight seasons with the Cardinals. His OPS was .947. Per Pham's explanation, Edmonds' entire Cardinals career was pretty much in his "own league."

Of course, it's possible Edmonds will be most remembered for something with the Angels. On June 10, 1997, the Angels were at the Kansas City Royals. You've seen it. The center fielder ran full speed with his back to the infield, leapt forward toward the warning track, arms out, like a superhero flying. In midair, he caught the ball and belly-flopped onto the warning track. There were two on and two out

An eight-time Gold Glover, Jim Edmonds makes one of his—spectacular, though typical—diving catches during a July 2005 contest.

in the fifth. The game was tied at the time. Even the partisan Kansas City fans gave him an ovation. Calm professional ballplayers lost their damn minds. For instance, eight-year vet Luis Alicea, watching his Angels teammate from second base, threw his glove into the air in ecstasy. Forty feet high, it was estimated. "I'm sorry," Angels utility man Tony Phillips told reporters after, "but Willie Mays don't do stuff like that."

With the Cards, No. 15 made innumerable catches worthy of gazing and gawking. Two in particular have left jaws forever strained. On July 16, 2004, the Cards were visiting the Cincinnati Reds. Ninth inning, Reds down two. Cincy's Jason LaRue drilled a deep fly. This thing was gone. Nonetheless, a defiant Edmonds sprinted toward dead center and looked over his left shoulder. But he didn't see it. So Edmonds kept sprinting and spotted it over his *right* shoulder as he approached the warning track. Still sprinting, he jumped at an angle at the wall, extending his arm as far over as seemingly possible and caught it! He landed on the ground. His mouth agape. Even the Reds announcers went nuts.

And the second catch? Of course, Game 7 of the National League Championship Series on October 21, 2004. A lot of cities have "The Catch." Dwight Clark in San Francisco. David Tyree in New York. Julian Edelman in Boston. But "The Catch" in St. Louis took place in *baseball*.

The Cards trailed 1–0 in the second inning. Two were on, and Houston Astros catcher Brad Ausmus drilled a liner toward left-center field. This one was destined to clear the bases, maybe even to put the game away. But Edmonds tracked it down, diving diagonally. "There's no way he catches this ball," FOX commentator Steve Lyons said on the broadcast during the replay. "Look at where he is, look at the ground he's making up and the full dive and extension."

The Cards went on to win the pennant that night. Talking with Joe Buck, who has covered many a football game over the years, I suggested that Edmonds would've made a great safety. "Yeah, a great anything," Buck said. "Those guys can see things that the rest of us can't see, and they probably don't know they see it. Now it's a little twitch or little something that's telling him this guy's trying to pull the ball—*And he's a right-handed batter, so I'm going to take two steps to my right, and if he cranks one out there, I'm going to have the best chance to have it be an out.* I never saw Curt Flood. But Edmonds' first step was always right, and that gave him the opportunity to go make those catches. Balls that looked like they have no chance of being caught, all of a sudden, there he is. He put that athletic ability into somebody who's already pretty baseball smart."

While "The Catch" was his greatest defensive moment for the Cardinals, Edmonds' greatest offensive moment came about 20 hours prior. Across St. Louis—on slow-pitch softball fields at Shaw Park and at the batting cages at Tower Tee and during backyard games in Wildwood—Cardinals fans reenact Edmonds' double-fist clench from Game 6.

Down three games to two in the NLCS, Edmonds skied a Game 6 walk-off winner. "I mean," Joe Buck said, "that ball is the definition of the 'launch.' Like when they talk about launch angle today, it was a chin-high pitch that he hit up. I was doing the ALCS broadcast that year and I remember seeing that highlight...Oh my God, that ball was murdered."

And to think, after all the gifts he gave St. Louis, Edmonds then accidentally gave us one of the greatest of all. On December 14, 2007, in one of his first moves as general manager, John Mozeliak traded Jim Edmonds to the San Diego Padres—for David Freese.

38

THAT ONE GUY

At Busch Stadium, he's like Norm Peterson from *Cheers*. Everybody knows his name. Except nobody knows his name. "Hey, it's...that one guy," said seemingly every St. Louisan ever. Since 1996 Todd Thomas has been "That One Guy." Literally, that's what it says on the back of his Cardinals jersey, which naturally has uniform No. 1.

He's the in-game emcee for the St. Louis Cardinals, which is his dream gig. And he's marketed his identity on not having one. "Early on, at old Busch Stadium, I'm running with my microphone, trying to catch an elevator," said Thomas on a 2017 day at a St. Louis Bread Co. "The doors were shutting, and Ozzie Smith is in there. He says, 'That one guy! We got to hold the door for him.' *Ozzie Smith just called me That One Guy!* This job is my passion, and you're doing it for one of the top fanbases in all of sports...It's one of those things I said I'd do until it's not fun anymore, and at 47 I'm still having a blast."

Incidentally, St. Louis Bread Co. is actually Panera Bread. But it started in St. Louis in 1981, so in St. Louis, Panera is never Panera; it's "Bread Co." I've lived in and visited many cities as a journalist, but few cities love their own stuff more than St. Louis does. That goes from gooey butter cake to Nelly to Becky "The Queen of Carpets," who would wear a sash, crown, and gown while flying on a carpet in commercials. We get a kick out of the people or things who represent us. Especially for those who move away, these links to back home matter. And so, when I flew home for the 2005 National League Championship Series and spotted That One Guy at Paddy O's by the ballpark, I excitedly got my picture with him on the disposable camera I'd brought...even though I didn't even know his real name.

Between innings are Thomas' innings. They cut to him on the big screen at Busch, and he plays sponsored games with fans, spearheads dance competitions, or dances while playing the sponsored games with fans. He oozes exuberance.

He was born and raised in Bement, Illinois. "It's a real small town between Champaign and Decatur," he said. "There are 1,600 people in my town. I had 32 in my high school class. My wife—she's a South City girl—had more in her high school than I had in my town. And I grew up right on that line that's 50/50, Cards/Cubs."

Back in 1981 Thomas was in middle school. His dad managed a grain elevator in their tiny town. "And he was also the president of our town's drug awareness program," Thomas said. "They got a big grant and so they had all these speakers come. The very first speaker was Cards catcher Darrell Porter. He had just come from Kansas City to St. Louis and had had drug problems. Part of his way back in, he was doing these talks. He spoke at our school to our whole student body in the morning and he was speaking to the parents at night. So he needed a place to hang out."

So Thomas came home from school that day, and there was the Cardinals catcher. "A Major League Baseball player in my house!" He recalled. "He ate dinner with us. We have a picture of him in between me and my brother. And that's it. That's all I needed to become a Cardinal fan. And then that following year was '82. The Cards win the World Series, he was the MVP, and I'm like, *Holy cow, how great is this?*"

At Busch, Thomas admitted, he was "that one guy" even before he was That One Guy. As he tells old stories, Thomas' body sort of gyrates with the emotions involved in them. He gets into it. "This is the year before I got the job with the Cardinals," he said of his 20s, "and 'The Macarena' was a popular song. I was in bad seats, kind of nosebleed seats, but this kind of shows you why I have the job that I have. I have always been that kind of guy. I had been the mascot at SIU-Carbondale for a while, the Saluki. I've always had a lot of spirit.

Well, I kept doing the dance, 'da-da-da-da-da-da, hey Mac-a-re-na!' People around me were getting tired of it. I would do it every inning. Finally, I started getting people to buy in. It was sort of like the wave. I had my whole section doing it! And then the next inning, they played 'The Macarena' over the PA, and everybody's like, 'You did it!' And I'm thinking, *It was bound to happen. It's like the most popular song out there.*

"So my first season with the Cardinals, they just wanted me to do one promotion at the game. And I don't know if you remember it, but..."

"Of course I remember it!" I interjected, as if he was David Freese saying, "I don't know if you remember it, but this one time I hit a walk-off homer in the World Series."

Thomas' first promotion was famously known to fans as "The Southwest Airlines Family of the Game." Here's how it went. He would be in the Southwest Airlines box with, yes, the family of the game. He'd introduce them and then offer up some sort of adequate prize—say, a Tom Pagnozzi autographed picture—but everyone knew what was coming next. On the big screen, there were three locker doors, and each had a prize behind it. At least one of the prizes was friggin' awesome. So, he'd ask the guy if he wants to keep the original prize or choose behind a door. The guy would always say he wants to go for the doors, and then Thomas would scream to the stadium: "HE WANTS TO GO FOR THE DOOOOOORS, EVERYBODY!" "There's almost a cult following for it," Thomas recalled. "I'm also a DJ. I did a wedding, and the groom came up to me and said, 'At some point I want you to say, 'He wants to go for the doors, everybody!' I want to get it on video!'"

As a teenager in the mid-1990s, I recall a game when Thomas offered the Pagnozzi picture and then the big doors option, and the guy chose the picture. Thomas was just so used to doing the doors line, he goes: "HE WANTS TO...um, keep the picture?"

"Back at old Busch, our room was just by the old clubhouse," Thomas said. "Jim Edmonds came by one time and said, 'What's the good door tonight?' What he was doing was getting feedback and then saying, 'I bet the best prize is behind door No. 3.' I remember one time he gave me a thumbs-up afterward! Who would've thought anyone gave a crap what's behind the doors for the 'Southwest Airlines Family of the Game' promotion?"

The job does have its perks. That One Guy has done bits with numerous celebrities visiting Busch over the years, including John Goodman, Andy Cohen, even Tony Orlando, the '70s singer who was promoting his new show in Branson, Missouri. "It's a Saturday morning, and we were orchestrating the introduction, so I'm supposed to meet him beforehand," That One Guy explained. "Hi, Tony, nice to meet you, I'm Todd."

"Hi Todd, how are you?"

"Well I'm a little tired, I've been tying yellow ribbons around oak trees all morning!"

Looking back, Todd called his joke about Orlando's yellow ribbon song the "dumbest thing ever...And it was crickets. He looked at me and didn't say anything, which was even worse. I felt like Chris Farley—'What did I do? I'm so stupid!'"

That One Guy also emcees pregame and postgame parties at ballpark bars. The aforementioned Paddy O's is a gleeful spot by the ballpark on the other side of Highway 40. It's now expanded into a spacious sports bar in a clichéd kind of way, but it used to be an older bar with character and characters. "I will share with you a story that happened at Paddy O's," Thomas said. "The Mullet Man story. So there was this guy I pointed out who had a mullet, and I brought him on stage. Now, a lot of what I would do is poke some fun that didn't humiliate them and then give them a beer, and everyone would salute them. 'Mul-let Man! Mul-let Man!' So he became kind of a little celebrity. People were buying him drinks and stuff. I mean, it was a really bad mullet. This was before Game 7 NLCS in 2004, and I said something on stage: if he'd let me cut his mullet on stage, I would give him tickets to the World Series *if* the Cards won. But he didn't want to do it. So that was before the game. Now it's postgame. We won; he's drunk. He comes up and says he wants me to cut his mullet for World Series tickets. But it was no longer an 'if'; it's a 'when.' And I said, 'No, no, that's not on the table anymore. I can get you tickets for a game next season though, but not World Series.' He comes back 15 minutes later and says, 'I'll do it.'

"And I say, 'You'll do what?' You know, to confirm.

"He goes, 'You can cut my mullet for tickets for next year.'

"I said, 'You understand right? Next year, not World Series.'

"So I bring him up on stage. 'Hey I got Mullet Man here! And he's gonna let me cut the mullet!' And it's like we won the game again! And so I cut it. It's all hacked up, I throw the mullet, the place is going crazy. Crazy! So I gave him my business card. The next day I get a call.

"'Hey, I'm whatever-his-name, you cut my hair last night. I want World Series tickets.'

"And I said, 'We had an agreement: tickets for next year.'

"He said, 'No, that's not the way I remember it.'

"'That's not the deal.'

"And he said, 'Well I'm going to call 'Contact 2'.'

"Now, Contact 2 is a news segment on St. Louis' Channel 2, in which a journalist follows up on the complaints of regular people, exposing some injustice in their life. It's a big hit with viewers.

"And I'm thinking, *Please call Contact 2!* This would be the greatest story ever! I can see it, serious TV journalist Elliott Davis: 'Did you cut his mullet on stage?'

"'Yes I did.

"'Did you promise World Series tickets?'

"'No I didn't!'

"But I was nervous. Mullet Man had my business card with my address and he was kind of making threats. So after the weekend, he calls me back. And my wife knew about this, and she was nervous, too. And he says, 'Hey, I want to apologize. I got really drunk when we won the NLCS. I woke up and was hungover, so I started drinking tequila. I didn't go into work, I looked into mirror, and I was pissed. So that's when I called you. But after the weekend, I went into work. And *everybody* is saying how great my hair looks! I'm actually thankful you cut the hair!'

"And now this guy is the hit of the shop," That One Guy said with a smile. "I changed this guy's life!"

THE CARDINALS' FIRST EVER WORLD SERIES CHAMPIONSHIP

I'm trying to think of the modern equivalent. Down two, late in Game 7 of the NBA Finals...and LeBron attempts a half-court shot? It's hard to come up with a comparison. The play was unique. Ninth inning, Game 7, 1926 World Series. The Cards led the New York Yankees by a run.

Babe Ruth walked. There were two outs. Again, it was Babe Ruth, who, even in good shape, was a portly gent. And he attempted to steal second.

That's it. That's how the Cardinals won their first World Series—throwing out Ruth trying to steal. "I'll never know why the guy did it," pitcher Grover Cleveland Alexander said, "one of the grandest sights of my life."

Yet the guy who threw Ruth out didn't even become famous for his World Series-winning play. In fact, I didn't even know the catcher's name. Do you? It's Bob O'Farrell. And he even won the Most Valuable Player award—not of the World Series, but the actual season!

Instead, when most people talk about the '26 Cardinals, they talk about Grover Cleveland Alexander, the epileptic, alcoholic has-been who saved the season. His story lived on. St. Louisans for generations heard of the hungover Alexander coming out of the Yankee Stadium bullpen. They even made a movie about him. It starred Ronald Reagan.

But what about O'Farrell? And what about the poor sap who was at bat? He represented the potential World Series-winning run and he didn't even get to swing.

* * *

Elba, Nebraska. Its population dipped into the high 100s in the 1990 census, but since then the population has stayed steady—right above 200. It's the home of Grover Cleveland Alexander, who is also referred to in history, in no particular order, as "Old Pete," "Dode," "Alex," "Alec," "Alexander the Great," and the occasional "Grover." He was one of the best there ever was. He pitched hard and lived hard, battling demons, physical issues, and poverty, too. "The Hall of Fame is fine," Alexander said after his Cooperstown induction in 1938, "but it doesn't mean bread and butter."

With his face weathered, worn like it was leather, most pictures of him as a player make him appear more like a manager. And he, of course, wore out the leather of his catchers, starting as a rook in 1911 through the Roaring '20s and into the Depression. In fact, for five consecutive full seasons, he led the league in ERA. Each time he was under 2.00.

Playing for the Philadelphia Phillies, Chicago Cubs, and Cards, "Old Pete" finished his 20-year career with 373 wins—third most ever—but is most remembered for a save.

The Cardinals became known as the Cardinals in 1900 after years of previous names. They were the Brown Stockings, Browns, and, for a lone season of 1899, the Perfectos, whose star player was Cy Young. In 1899, sure enough, Cy Young had a Cy Young-type season, posting a 2.58 ERA with a league-high 40 complete games for the St. Louis Perfectos-but-soon-to-be-Cardinals.

Entering 1926, the best the Cards had finished in the 20th century was third place. But the '26 team, featuring player/manager Rogers Hornsby, finished with 89 wins and the pennant. In what seemed more like penance, though, the Cards had to face the damn Yankees. New York had been to the World Series in three of the past five seasons. And they'd go the next two seasons, too.

In this Fall Classic of 1926, the Cardinals faced a rejuvenated Ruth, who dealt with health issues in an ill-fated 1925 season. That offseason, according to Ruth historian Bill Jenkinson, Ruth hired a personal trainer, the most-renowned physical fitness coach of the time. His name was Artie McGovern, the former flyweight who later penned a book titled *The Secret of Keeping Fit*.

Ruth's 1926 season was, well, Ruthian. And in Game 4 of the World Series at St. Louis, he had arguably the greatest World Series game ever. He went 3-for-3 with three home runs. The other two times up, he walked. And he scored four total times. On his second homer, off of a fellow named Flint Rhem, the sultan's swat broke a plate glass window at Wells Chevrolet Company across Grand Avenue in St. Louis. There's an old picture of the Babe and the window.

After a Game 5 win, New York led the series 3–2, and the series headed back to New York. This, of course, set up the legendary story of Grover Cleveland "Old Pete" Alexander, who would turn 40 in four months and, with the season on the line, pitched a complete game in Game 6. It was something out of Hollywood. Hall of Famers Ruth, Lou Gehrig, and Tony Lazzeri went a combined 1-for-11 on the day. Really, the only uplifting player for New York was "Long" Bob Meusel, who doubled, tripled, and walked against Alexander. So the series went to a Game 7.

* * *

On October 10, 1926, Ruth homered in the third inning. But by the bottom of the seventh, the Yankees trailed 3–2. They loaded the bases. Two outs. Lazzeri was up. And the player/manager Hornsby motioned to the bullpen for Ronald Reagan. As depicted in the 1952 film, *The Winning Team*, the actor was slouched on the bullpen bench, hungover following a raucous night after his Game 6 win.

Reagan slowly walked onto the field. At the mound he met Hornsby, who was played by the actor Frank Lovejoy, kind of a less-talented Bob Hope lookalike. "Now, remember what Bill Killefer said," Lovejoy told Reagan. "He said, 'As long as Alex can stand on his two feet, he's still the pitcher I'd want to have in there when we're in a tough spot.'" (Killefer was Alexander's favorite catching target in their Philadelphia days. He was also a Cards coach in 1926.)

"Well," Lovejoy continued as Hornsby, "you can see how things are. What do you think you can do with Lazzeri?"

"Well," said Reagan, wringing the ball in his hands, "there don't seem to be any room on the bases left for him."

So "Old Pete" struck him out.

Maybe the best line about the strikeout wasn't even in the movie. Years later, the catcher, O'Farrell, told the writer Bob Broeg: "I'd say that was the most famous strikeout other than 'Casey at the Bat.'" On Alexander's Hall of Fame plaque, it reads: "WON 1926 WORLD CHAMPIONSHIP FOR CARDINALS BY STRIKING OUT LAZERRI WITH BASES FULL IN FINAL CRISIS AT YANKEE STADIUM."

But there were two more innings to go. Now, the movie had its own ending. In the ninth inning, the pitcher Reagan—encouraged by a blown kiss from Doris Day in the stands—struck out the final batter for the '26 title.

But here's how it actually happened. Alexander walked a batter—Babe Ruth—with two outs in the bottom of the ninth. So here was the greatest player in the sport, standing on first base as the tying run. "Long" Bob Meusel was at the plate. Gehrig was on deck.

Meusel had finished the regular season hitting just .154 in his final 59 at-bats and was lousy for most of the series, too. But he already had a hit in Game 7. He had the big personal offensive breakout in Game 6, and for the entire regular season, his batting average was .315. "I wondered why Babe tried to steal second then," O'Farrell said in *The Glory Of Their Times*, the classic baseball history book. "A year or so later, I went on a barnstorming trip with the Babe, and I asked him. Ruth said he thought Alex had forgotten he was [on first]. Also that the way Alex was pitching, they'd never get two hits in a row off him, so he better get in position to score if they got one. Well, maybe that was good thinking and maybe not. In any case, I had him out a mile at second."

In a way, you can make a case for the steal: the Babe was larger than life. The Babe *was* baseball, bigger than the rest of the Yankees. So he took it upon himself to create the win *for* the Yankees. But instead, the World Series ended in the weirdest way ever, as the big-boned Babe was thrown out by O'Farrell. At second, Ruth simply popped up and shook the hand of player/manager Hornsby, the man who applied the tag. "He probably figured it would catch us by surprise," Alexander said in *The Baseball Chronicles*. "I caught the blur of Ruth starting for second as I pitched, and then came the whistle of the ball as O'Farrell rifled it to second. I wheeled around, and there was one of the grandest sights in my life. Hornsby—his foot anchored on the bag and his gloved hand outstretched—was waiting for Ruth to come in. There was the series. That was my second big thrill of the day (the first being the Lazerri strikeout in the seventh). The third came when Judge Landis mailed out the winners' checks for $5,584.51."

And so, Robert Arthur O'Farrell of Waukegan, Illinois, forever walked around with a right arm that ended a World Series. Back then, the esteemed baseball award voters met after the postseason to elect the MVP of the season. And the voting wasn't necessarily solely numbers-based. O'Farrell did hit .293 in 1926 (and actually had a sturdy .371 on-base percentage, though that probably wasn't brought up in the meeting). But it was his valiant catching that season—capped off by the greatest caught-stealing play in history—that earned O'Farrell the hardware.

The next year, too, was a big one for O'Farrell strikes. He opened a bowling alley back home in Waukegan. As years went by, Alexander and Hornsby became the names associated with the Cardinals' first ever World Series championship. Bob O'Farrell is a name we don't know but should. And poor "Long" Bob Meusel had a chance to be a Game 7 World Series hero but never even got to swing.

LOCALS AT THE HOT CORNER

Ken Oberkfell grew up in Maryville, Illinois, 16 miles from Busch Stadium. Ken Boyer grew up in Cardinal Country (Alba, Missouri) and, though fans would've loved Boyer if he was from Micronesia, it only added to his legend that he was from Missouri. So on one lucky day, little Ken met big Ken, the great third baseman Boyer, the 1964 MVP, World Series hero, and Oberkfell's idol. "I was probably about nine," Ken Oberkfell said. "He was at a car place, signing autographs. Dad took me and my brother."

So cool, right? So now try to fathom what happened next. Oberkfell became a Cardinal, and his manager...was Boyer. "It was like a dream for me," Oberkfell said.

And then, when Whitey Herzog took over in 1980, he wanted to move Oberkfell to third base. Whitey brought back Boyer to tutor a fellow Ken. "I'm like a little kid," recalled Oberkfell, who, of course, also won a Cardinals World Series at third base. "Yeah, it was very special. Ken Boyer helped me a little bit make that transition to learn the position, so that was even extra special. One of my all-time favorite Cardinals was helping me learn *his* position."

Third base for the St. Louis Cardinals has almost become a local heirloom passed down from one fortuitous fan to another. Consider that the past *five* third basemen to start for a Cardinals World Series winner were all from the area. David Freese of the 2011 Cardinals grew up in the suburbs of Wildwood, Missouri, about a half-hour from Busch Stadium. Scott Rolen, 2006 third baseman, grew up in Jasper, Indiana, about three hours from

Busch, where he sometimes road-tripped for games with his parents. Oberkfell started at third in 1982. Mike Shannon, 1967 third baseman, grew up in St. Louis on Winona Avenue, eight miles from Busch.

And Boyer, of course, was there in '64.

Two other Cardinal third basemen, both former All-Stars, grew up Cardinals fans. Scott Cooper went to Pattonville High School in suburban St. Louis, while Gary Gaetti hailed from Centralia, Illinois, just an hour or so from Busch. In a sport in which most teams don't even have one player from the area, consider the peculiarity of all these local kids playing for the Cards—and all playing third base.

Young Rolen sprouted into a 6'4" stud...on the basketball court. He considered college hoops offers. But, of course, he could hit, too. Scouts scouring the Midwest discovered this big kid on the diamond, but they worried the Hoosier would choose hoops. A Philadelphia Phillies scout named Scott Trcka, whose family was apparently skimpy with vowels, kept showing up to ballgames. Trcka would chat with Rolen's friends in the stands and a got the sense that Rolen just liked baseball more. The Phillies drafted Rolen in the second round, hoping he'd sign. They even took him, of all places, to St. Louis. The Phillies were playing the Cards that day in 1993 and, per an article in *The Philadelphia Inquirer*, the team gave Rolen a uniform and a chance to take some pregame grounders at third.

Except that the starting third baseman, David Hollins, wasn't happy about this draft pick patrolling his turf. "Get lost," Hollins told him.

"He scared me good," Rolen recalled. "He wasn't rude, but he made it very clear he didn't want me around. Here I was on cloud nine, ready to have a great time, and that happened."

Ultimately, Rolen still signed. He won the Rookie of the Year in 1997. And in 2002 he was back at third base at Busch—this time as a Cardinal. It was the trade of a lifetime for the Jasper kid. He became one of the "MV3," along with Albert Pujols and Jim Edmonds. From 2003 to 2006, the Cardinals third baseman was an All-Star all four years. On June 1, 2003, a total of 46,103 fans arrived to Busch Stadium for Scott Rolen Bobblehead Day. The fan favorite got on base three times, including via a double. And he made a leaping, late-inning catch, preserving a one-run win. Word was that as many as eight busloads of folks from Jasper made the trip to the game.

KMOX Radio carries and crackles into Indiana, and Shannon's voice would narrate and marinate the state. Shannon broadcasted Rolen's games as the kid defended third base like a soccer goalie. And it was Shannon, himself, who stood at third with the birds on the bat, nearly 40 years prior. Shannon's unselfish decision to become a third baseman—thus opening up an outfield spot for the newly acquired Roger Maris—was vital for the '67 Cardinals, who, of course, went on to win it all. Shannon manned third the next year, too, finishing seventh in the '68 MVP voting. "I've got to know Mike Shannon pretty well. We're on a first-name basis," Twins third baseman Gary Gaetti told the *St. Louis Post-Dispatch* in 1987. "The Cardinals were all my heroes growing up."

Gaetti was an Orphan. Note the capital O. That was the nickname and mascot of Centralia High School. They say they're the Orphans because—generations before—writers said their teams looked so ragtag that they looked like orphans. Today, the cheering section at Centralia games is called "The Orphanage." The town is hard-scrabbled. Hard-lucked, too, due to numerous economic hits over the years. Gaetti was born in 1958, which means he was just the right age to fall for the Cards during the 1960s heyday. A *Minneapolis Star-Tribune* reporter asked Gaetti if he was the best ballplayer as a boy in Centralia. "I don't know. That's a tough question to answer," Gaetti said before pausing. "I know this: there was nobody that wanted to be the best more than I did."

He went to Lake Land Junior College in Mattoon, Illinois, the hometown of great writer Will Leitch. Sure enough, the St. Louis Cardinals drafted Gaetti. But he wouldn't end up a Cardinal for 18 more years. Gaetti continued to develop as a college ballplayer, crossing state lines to play at Northwest Missouri State University. The following year, he was drafted 11th overall by the Minnesota Twins. (The Cards had the 12th pick, so they chose pitcher Ralph Citarella, who only started two games ever, but one of them was the famous "Sandberg Game" in 1984. That day Willie McGee hit for the cycle, but Ryne Sandberg homered off Bruce Sutter in both the ninth *and* 10th innings, and the Cubs won in the 11th. During the broadcast they called the starting pitcher "The Citarella Story.")

Gaetti and the Twins made the World Series in '87, of course facing Gaetti's favorite team from childhood. In Game 7 Gaetti plowed into Cards catcher Steve Lake, who somehow held on to an outfield throw for an out. But the Twins did win, and Gaetti was locked into lore in the Land of 10,000 Lakes.

Finally, in 1996 he came home. Then 36, Gaetti provided some swat for the rejuvenated 1996 Cards, hitting 23 homers and 27 doubles. The Cards had a vacancy at third entering '96 because of the Cooper debacle. Born the very day after the Cards won it all in '67, Cooper became something of a local legend at St. Louis' Pattonville High. He became a two-time All-Star with the Red Sox. Cooper returned to St. Louis (a dream) in '95 and hit .230 (a nightmare).

So he went to Japan the next season.

Boyer. Shannon. Oberkfell. Gaetti. Cooper. Rolen. Incredible. But of course, unless some Stan Musial-Albert Pujols hybrid from Cardinal Country someday defends the hot corner in St. Louis, the epitome of the local legend playing third for the Birds will be Freese, the man who redefined dreaming.

With each story the hair grows a little longer, the rebellion seems a little fiercer, the badassery exudes a little badassier. Meet Ted Simmons, the rock star ballplayer. "He would wear ripped-up jeans on the plane, and manager Vern Rapp wanted to kill him, but he was a next-level thinker, brilliantly smart," said the famed broadcaster Joe Buck, Jack's son who was often around the team in the 1970s. "Really, really great guy. There's not anybody who played with him, who played against him, who doesn't respect how his mind worked. He's kind of a baseball savant."

Simmons spoke out publicly against the Vietnam War and the president. "Simba" played baseball tough. His first full season as the Cardinals catcher was 1971 and—until he was traded after the 1980 season—he played baseball with a lion's ferocity. But for fans of recent generations, he's gone unappreciated. "To me, he should be in the Hall of Fame," former Cards teammate Ken Oberkfell said. "Cooperstown. I mean, the guy put up numbers, knew how to play the game, knew how to teach the game."

As of early 2018, Ted Simmons was not in the Baseball Hall of Fame. It's possible that the Modern Baseball Era Committee could get Ted in. But in one of the more peculiar cases, the catcher didn't even come close in his first ballot—only 3.7 percent of the writers voted for him in 1995. "Simmons was overshadowed by Johnny Bench," said Art Holliday, the longtime St. Louis sportscaster. "He was arguably the best offensive catcher of his generation. Bench had more power, but Simmons was a more consistent hitter, but he played on a crappy team. And Johnny Bench became an icon. So Simmons suffered by comparison."

But Ted Simmons did have a Hall of Fame career. Baseball historian Jay Jaffe authored *The Cooperstown Casebook*, which makes meticulous explanations for players unfairly deemed unworthy. Jaffe said Simmons, an eight-time All-Star, should be in. Through his (JAWS)

Jaffe **W**ins Above Replacement **S**core, he determined that Ted Simmons was the 10th best catcher—ever. And as of 2017, there were 15 catchers in the Hall of Fame.

Simmons, who played from 1968 to 1988, finished with 2,472 hits and 248 homers while hitting for a career average of .285 with a .348 on-base percentage. The 2,472 hits are the second most of any player who played mostly catcher (behind Ivan Rodriguez). And when Simmons retired, the 2,472 hits were the fourth most ever by a switch hitter. He tallied 1,908 hits strictly as a catcher, and even that is the fourth most hits for a catcher.

But Jaffe zeroed in on Simmons' era—notably the 1971–80 seasons in which Simmons was the Cardinals' starting catcher. (After that era he feuded with new boss Whitey Herzog and was shipped to the Milwaukee Brewers.) But during those 10 full seasons, Simmons hit .301 with a .367 on-base percentage. That is really, really good for a catcher. That is really, really good for anyone. His 44.6 Wins Above Replacement (WAR) in that era was 11th best in the majors. When adjusted for his home ballpark, his 131 on-base-plus-slugging percentage (OPS+) was 16th best in the majors.

And when you look at the slash stats—batting average, on-base percentage, and slugging percentage—Simmons finished in the top 10 of those a combined 15 times. Johnny Bench only did that six times, Gary Carter only did it four times, and Carlton Fisk only did it nine times. All three are in Cooperstown. It is *incomprehensible* that he only got 3.7 percent of the writers' votes for the Hall of Fame. "I just remember, like, holy shit, this guy's really good," Buck said. "He's one of those guys—there's a long list in baseball of really good power hitters that have nobody hitting behind them, no protection. Ralph Kiner had no protection. Simmons was it. He was all they had."

Now, his defense was good not great. That became the narrative. But modern advanced stats show that he wasn't as bad as earmarked. Yes, they stole on him a lot late, and he dealt with passed ball issues early on in his career. But he was also valiant back there. Ron Fimrite captured the essence of Simmons in a 1978 *Sports Illustrated* profile. God, Fimrite could write. He had one of my favorite lines in a profile on Harry Caray: "Cabdrivers stall traffic to hail him." On Simmons,

Fimrite wrote of the thoughtful, radical, hair-flailing, hair-raising ballplayer who also read classics and collected antique furniture. In that piece Fimrite quoted Tim McCarver, the ex-Card who had joined the Philadelphia Phillies: "Sometimes I think the Cardinals are trying to kill him, catching him in all those games in that St. Louis heat. If they caught him 130 games instead of 150, he'd hit .360. What can you say about a man who switch-hits and has no weaknesses at the plate? He can wait on the curveball and he's quick enough to get around on the fastball. If he played in Cincinnati, where the ball really carries, he'd hit from 30 to 35 home runs, the way Bench does. He plays in Death Valley and still hits more than 20."

Simmons was valuable but volatile. He once reportedly got in a fight in the hall by the dugout…with a teammate. And Simmons clashed with Rapp, who was unapologetically old school, while Simmons was unapologetically Simmons. "He was kind of a rebel," Buck said. "Vern Rapp lost the team, and part of that was these really strict rules of what to adhere to—cut your hair, no facial hair, kind of militaristic, and it was during the '70s. These guys were like— 'Screw you, old man. I'm not listening to you.'"

One of the neater things about Simmons is he loves St. Louis. He raised his family there and still lives there. As Fimrite wrote, Simmons became a trustee of the St. Louis Art Museum in 1978. I'm not sure how many current Cardinals know that there even is an art museum.

Frank Cusumano, a St. Louis native and sportscaster, has his own special connection with Simmons. "I absolutely loved the fact that Ted Simmons had long hair and would march to the beat of a different drummer," Cusumano said. "And even on a 99-degree day, when the Cardinals were 16 games under .500, he'd go 2-for-4. I've gotten to know him a little bit, and it still freaks me out when I see Ted Simmons now and he says, 'Hey Frank.' He knows my name—that's Ted Simmons! He actually went to one of our basketball games at DeSmet in high school during our 63-game winning streak. For some reason [star player Steve] Stiponovich could not shoot because he was double-teamed, and they weren't going to guard the rest of us stiffs, so Steve kicked it out to me with about 30 seconds left, and I got lucky and hit a shot. Ted Simmons was at the game because everybody wanted to come see Steve. And he came to Kemoll's like two days later and he wrote on a menu for my dad: 'Frankie, nice shot against CBC, keep up the good work.' I hold it with more importance than my marriage certificate."

42

CHRIS CARPENTER

He was a Cub. I mean, he'd been with the Cleveland Indians for the 2009 season, but in the eyes of Chris Carpenter, Mark DeRosa was a Cub. See, the infielder had played and played well for Chicago in 2007 and 2008, and both years the Cubs topped the Cards for the division title. In June of 2009, DeRosa was traded by Cleveland to the Cardinals, and "Chris Carpenter met me at the door and was very hesitant to let me come in," DeRosa shared. "He said, 'I need to know your head's right, and you're a Cardinal. And you're going to walk in this door as a Cardinal or else you're not allowed in.'"

That was Carp, unabashedly loyal, unwaveringly competitive. "Carpenter," Deadspin founder Will Leitch told me, "is basically the New Hampshire redneck version of Gibson. He was mean, he was nasty, and he was absolutely your least favorite guy to face—but your favorite player if he was on your team. I'll never forget him screaming at Brendan Ryan for being the weird guy that Brendan Ryan was. He's like a slightly less-asshole John Lackey but a ton better pitcher. I still think he's gonna come back years later and throw 250 innings."

The first time I met Carp, it was by accident. I was sitting with Tony La Russa, interviewing him for this very book. We were in a room at Busch Stadium with members of the Cardinals' Hall of Fame wearing their famous red Brooks Brothers blazers. My back was to the room as I asked La Russa about Carp's bulldog mentality. La Russa was looking past me at something and then he said, "He just gave me a dirty look!"

In his own red blazer, Carp was sitting a couple tables away and heard his name. "We're talking about you!" La Russa playfully yelled to the great retired pitcher. "Don't give me a dirty look!"

"I did?" Carpenter replied. "I think it's just my face."

Besieged by injuries over his career, the 6'6" Carp completed six full seasons with the Cards during his St. Louis tenure. Five times he finished in the National League's top 10 in win-loss percentage. Five times he finished in the NL's top 10 in strikeout-to-walk ratio. Four times he finished in the NL's top 10 in innings pitched and walks-and-hits-per-innings-pitched (WHIP). Three times he finished in the NL's top 10 in ERA.

He was a bulldog. "He checks all the boxes," La Russa said. "Every box. A true No. 1 who's going to take the game and want to be out there. And if it isn't good enough, 'I screwed it up, and it wasn't about my teammates.' And if it is good enough, 'It's about my team that got the runs.' He works. And he cheerleads in the dugout—'Hey, you guys bullshittin'? Come on, if you're a pitcher, you'd want us to pay attention, so get your ass on the top step.' And he had a code of ethics about respect...I saw one guy say, 'I'm sorry, Mr. Carpenter. I won't do it again.'"

How important was Carp to Cards lore? Consider that he won a Cy Young Award, but he won't even be remembered for that. And he hurled eight innings of three-hit ball in a 2006 World Series win, but he won't be remembered for that. What he'll be remembered for is a span of five moments in 65 days—from August 25, 2011 to October 28, 2011—when the emboldened ballplayer embodied the St. Louis Cardinals.

Moment No. 1: The Meeting

On August 25 the Cardinals—as so many fans recall and talk about to this day—were 10½ games out. They had a 1.3 percent chance of making the postseason. So Carp and some vets held a players-only meeting. He spoke of accountability. Or, as Jason Motte described it, "He said that we pretty much just needed to play our butts off for the next month or so."

And for the next month or so, they played their butts off. It was incredible. And on the last day of the season, they were tied with the

Atlanta Braves for the wild-card—back when there was only one wild-card team per league.

Moment No. 2: Game 162

Carp started for St. Louis at Houston. A win against the Astros would guarantee at worst a "Game 163" playoff with Atlanta. A loss? Carp and the Cards would have to hope the Braves lost, too. Well, Carp pitched a two-hit shutout. He won the must-win. And, as the fairytale goes, the Braves blew it in the 13th inning, and the Cardinals were in the tournament.

Moment No. 3: Game 5

On the phone with Motte, the closer that postseason, I asked about Carp. And in three minutes and six seconds, Motte said the word "compete" or "competitor" nine times. *Nine times*. "I played in St. Louis long enough that I had other guys come over, like a Lance Berkman, Carlos Beltran, who had played against him for years," Motte recalled. "And once they got there, they're like—'Man, I hated you.' And he's like, 'Good! I'm not there for you to like me.' He was out there to compete. And one of the most-famous games would be Game 5 of the 2011 National League Division Series, us versus Philly, him versus Roy Halladay."

It came to this: the deciding game of the National League Division Series would be on the road against a 102-win team, which was throwing its ace. "They're boys, they're good friends from a long time ago," Motte recalled just two months before Halladay died in a 2017 plane crash. "And they go on offseason vacations together and hang out. And you've got 'Doc' versus 'Carp,' two great pitchers just competing their faces off. We ended up winning 1–0 after two hits in the game. There was a triple and a double, and then it was crickets the rest of the game. And just watching those two guys who are, yes, friends off the field, but on the field, they're trying to help their team win. And that's what it's all about. He was out there to win the ballgame."

When Carpenter indeed won the ballgame—a three-hit, 1–0 shutout—Yadier Molina and the infielders came at him from all sides,

Chris Carpenter throws during Game 5 of the 2011 National League Division Series when he outdueled Philadelphia Phillies ace Roy Halladay.

and Carp unleashed a primal scream, as his mouth opened impossibly wide. The headline the next day in the *St. Louis Post-Dispatch* read: "PHILLIE-BUSTER." "Obviously, the defining image of the Cardinals' insane 2011 playoff run is David Freese's homer, his finger in the air, though I still like the triple more," Leitch said. "But none of that happens without Carpenter being such a monster against the Phillies."

Moment No. 4: The Dive

The play that best encapsulated Carpenter the pitcher wasn't even a pitch. It was in the first inning of Game 1 of the 2011 World Series. A chopper was struck between first and second. First baseman Albert Pujols backhanded the ball with the glove on his left hand. And with his body falling back—almost like a second baseman turning a double play—Albert tossed the ball toward first base. But it was about five feet in front of first base. Like a football wide receiver, a sprinting Carp dove headfirst, catching the ball in midair, and momentum just carried Carp full speed across the base for the out.

Again, *across* the base.

Carpenter's timing was perfect. And it was also a crazy, dangerous play, as the sprinting batter stepped on the base just inches from Carp's pitching hand, and Carp's body slid across. A 3–1 putout had never been this incredible.

Moment No. 5: Game 7

Carpenter pitched his butt off in Game 5 of the World Series, but the Cards' pen lost it. The Texas Rangers were a win from winning it all. There was one scheduled day off between Game 5 in Texas and Game 6 in St. Louis. But rain postponed Game 6. So there were *two* days between Game 5 and Game 6.

The day with the redcoat Hall of Famers, I asked Tony when he knew Carp would start Game 7 of the 2011 World Series. "He was the pitcher. The only question was—without the rainout—would he have pitched on two days rest?" La Russa admitted.

Can you imagine that? No rainout, Cards win Game 6...and Carp starts Game 7 on two days' rest? Of course, the rainout made it three days' rest for the Cardinals' ace. "You had to win Game 6 first, and the worst thing you can do is even start hinting, and word gets around that you're talking about Game 7," La Russa recalled of those days leading up to Game 6. "We had to win Game 6. So when it was over, we said, 'Carp, we'll let you know.' The way the story goes, I called [pitching coach Dave] Duncan and said, 'Who do you think should pitch Game 7?' And he hung up on me. But that never happened. Truth was, as soon we went to Game 7, we knew it was Carp."

And so, 36-year-old Carpenter, who led the league with 237⅓ innings pitched in the regular season and then battled through three rounds of the postseason, would start the biggest game of his life on just three days' rest. He went six and got the win.

It was inspiring. Insane. He allowed two runs in the first, and that was it. Carp pitched through the sixth, and the score at that point was 5–2. The Cards tacked on one more run. Motte got the final out. "Carp's a gamer," Motte said. "He reminds me of the movie *Major League*, when Bob Uecker said, 'This guy threw at his own son in a father-son game!' Carp was one of those guys from a pitching standpoint, where I'm pretty sure Carp would throw at his own son at a father-son game if it meant intimidating someone. He was out there to win. We're not out there just getting participation trophies. So Carp went out there with one thing in mind—I'm going to do everything I can do to win this ballgame. And I think that rubbed off on a lot of us."

43

BEST FANS IN BASEBALL

Before Pam found Jim, she found Ozzie. Growing up in St. Louis in the 1980s, long before her Emmy-nominated role as Pam on *The Office*, Jenna Fischer would go to Cardinals games at Busch Stadium, which on the inside looked as drab as an office, but then? "There's nothing quite like walking through those tunnels in a ballpark, and then as you emerge, seeing that bright green field," Fischer said by phone. "It has a really peaceful but also magical quality to it. And I love the pace of baseball. The breeze, especially at a night game. Summer time in St. Louis. I just have a lot of really fond memories of going to Busch Stadium with my family. The St. Louis baseball fans are very loyal and very enthusiastic. They're not fair-weather fans; they're all-weather fans. But I think also that they're fun fans. I've never experienced Cardinals fans to be weirdly aggressive or uncool. They're just there to have fun and love their baseball team with all their hearts, and it's a really cool energy. The whole city gets behind it. It's in the bones of the city."

They call them the "Best Fans In Baseball." Whether that's a compliment or an insult, well, it depends on who you ask. Some say that Cards fans aren't as much adorable as they are obnoxious. At first, the narrative was that St. Louis fans are special. They appreciate their history and cherish the nuances of the game. To honor the hurler's endurance, they applaud if a manager sends his starting pitcher to bat late. They'll also applaud if an opponent makes an amazing play because acknowledging greatness doesn't cancel out the competitive aspect of fandom. They just get it. "Probably the most knowledgeable fans I played in front of in my nine years," said David Howard, who played two years for the Cards in the late 1990s.

But then, the narrative became that St. Louis fans *think* they're special, which is different than if others point it out. "BFIBs," pronounced "bee-fibs," has become a sarcastic nickname for the Cards fans who come off as entitled, snobby, or whiny. So yeah, perhaps there's an arrogance to some Cardinals fans, but at least it's agreed upon that Cardinals fans, if anything, are categorically a passionate fanbase. "It's amazing the feeling playing here. It really is," said pitcher Brad Thompson, who was on the World Series winners of 2006. "There's an expectation of winning but also a crazy amount of support, which is nuts. I always found it fascinating when a guy like me would go to the mall, and somebody knows who you are, the last reliever sitting out in the bullpen. That does not happen in other places. It's a different place here."

The Cardinals fanbase is tethered together by red lacing. And that connects generations, all of whom have experienced Fall Classics. Consider that starting in 1926, the longest the Cards went without a World Series appearance was 18 years (1946–64). And the 17-year drought from 1987–2004, though painful for stretches, was at least peppered with playoff appearances in '96, '00, '01, and '02.

Of course, you hear about how KMOX Radio and its powerful signal grew Cardinals fans on the farms of Illinois and Iowa and, really, all over the nation. So in the years before cable television, the fanbase became as strong as the signal. "We are to baseball as what city to what sport?" asked Tom Ackerman, sports director for KMOX. "Green Bay to football? Pittsburgh to football? Detroit to hockey? We almost relate more to Alabama football, a college team. That's why I connected to Indiana basketball like I did as a college student. It reminded me of the Cardinals fan experience. They get frustrated easily, there's a lot of history, they respect the game, they know the game. We need the Cardinals, and the Cardinals need us."

It was perhaps best illustrated in 1987, their third pennant-winning season in the previous six. At that time only three MLB cities ever had three million fans come in a season—New York, Los Angeles, and (in 1987) St. Louis. Los Angeles had a metro area of 10 million people. New York, split with two franchises, had 18 million. St. Louis had a metro area of 2.5 million people.

And now, they get three million annually at Busch. "St. Louis is such a devoted sports town, and Cardinals fans are the most loyal fans that you will ever meet," said Ellie Kemper, another Emmy-nominated actress from St. Louis. "I think the enthusiasm for the Cards comes from the amazing stadiums the city built for them—both past and present—and also the fact that these guys are incredible baseball players."

There's a bond. St. Louis claims its Cardinals. When a former player returns to town, the fans give a loud ovation for his first at-bat back even if it's Shane Robinson, who had a .231 batting average in his five years with the Cardinals. (That ovation actually occurred.) "When I got to St. Louis, it just felt right," said former Cardinal Andy Van Slyke, who later raised his family in St. Louis. "It just felt like this is where I wanted to be, needed to be. The way fans embrace St. Louis Cardinals baseball players is unique to any other city in the country. It's almost like it becomes your alma mater. It's your high school team, your college team, all wrapped up in one."

And in death the Cardinals fans mourn with the families and with their baseball family. When Stan "The Man" died in 2013, here's how *St. Louis Post-Dispatch* scribe Joe Strauss captured the scene: "An unforgiving cold ripped down Lindell Boulevard on Thursday afternoon, but it didn't matter. Husband and wife, mother and child, brother and brother steeled themselves in a line that snaked from the front doors of the St. Louis Cathedral Basilica toward the street and hundreds of yards west. Young and old, black and white, dressed in business attire or sporting Cardinal red, all had come to see their friend, their hero—yes, their example—one final time. Stan Musial rested inside, surrounded by a Navy honor guard and watched over by family. The line of hundreds that waited patiently in the freeze quietly wound its way through the cathedral's aisles to glimpse The Man in his Cardinal-red sport coat lying in a flag-draped casket. No organ music played. Only the sound of shuffling feet filled the cavernous place of worship."

Strauss passed away in 2015. He'd written about the Cards for more than a decade. Numerous team executives attended his funeral. And the next season, there was a moment of silence for Joe on Opening Day.

In June of 2002, the voice of the Cardinals went silent. Jack Buck died on the 18th, and thousands of mourners attended an on-field visitation—some in black, some in red. Four days later I got a call from my dad. He sounded solemn. Darryl Kile, a popular pitcher, had died unexpectedly due to blockage in two coronary arteries. Kile was 33 and the father of three. Kile's last start was on the afternoon before Buck died. Kile got the win, pitching a strong seven-plus innings—vintage D.K. During the eighth inning, Tony La Russa took out his workhorse. St. Louis fans, naturally, gave Kile a standing ovation.

44

THE FRESHEST MAN ON EARTH
AND OTHER GREATS

Perhaps my favorite nickname of all the Cardinals nicknames belonged to a fellow named Arlie Latham, the third baseman of the 1880s teams who was "The Freshest Man on Earth." I consider this an obvious precursor to both "The Fresh Prince of Bel-Air" and "The Most Interesting Man in the World." As explained in *Baseball Anecdotes*, the smooth-talking Latham "loved to clown around and persisted in shouting and gesticulating throughout every game he played. Unofficially, he was the father of 'chatter,' the baseball tradition."

Arlie's mustached mug would be sculpted onto the Mount Rushmore of Cardinals Nicknames, alongside "Ice Box" Chamberlain, "Vinegar Bend" Mizell, and "Pickles" Dillhoefer, whose name was both playful and a play on words. Similar to most franchises, the Cardinals have had their share of Slims, Spuds, and Spikes. Every Joe is Smokey; every Rhodes is Dusty. But St. Louis has been especially mellifluous; some of the most harmonic monikers wore the birds on the bat. And beyond the mainstreams—"The Man" and "The Mad Hungarian"—some of the lesser-known names had the best "nicks."

"Vinegar Bend" Mizell was actually born in Leakesville, Mississippi, but the town was pretty close to Vinegar Bend, Alabama. "Vinegar Bend"—the southpaw, not the southern town—was an All-Star for the Cards in 1959 before being traded the next year to the Pittsburgh Pirates. It was a win-win. He got a 1960 World Series ring, and the Cardinals got a second baseman—Julian Javier, a key cog on the World Series teams later in the decade—out

of the trade. And the man who was born in Mississippi and nicknamed after a town from Alabama, Wilmer David Mizell, later became a U.S. Congressman...for North Carolina.

Nineteenth century St. Louis hurler Gus Weyhing actually had three great nicknames: "Cannonball," "Rubber Arm Gun," and "Rubber-Winged Gus." Perhaps the best kind of nicknames are the ones that somehow lost the "nick" and just became the name. For instance, on baseball-reference.com, George Aloys Fisher is literally listed as Showboat Fisher—no quotation marks necessary. Fourteen years prior to Showboat Fisher, the 1916 Cards had Steamboat Williams. Around the turn of the century, the Cardinals also had Cupid Childs, Cowboy Jones, Stuffy Stewart, and Peanuts Lowrey. Ossee Schrecongost sounds like a nickname, or a made-up name, but that was the old catcher's actual name.

Numerous nicknames came from physical descriptions, some obvious one like "Shorty" Fuller (he was 5'6") and "Bones" Ely (6'1" but 155 pounds), while others were more nuanced, such as "Pebbly" Jack Glasscock. George Washington McGinnis was "Jumbo," while Thomas Jefferson Sullivan was "Old Iron Hands." Those who looked down upon Arnold Hauser couldn't make up their minds. Some called him "Pee-wee"; others called him "Stub." And plopped behind the plate was catcher Vern Clemons aka "Tubby."

Other nicknames featured a player's hometown or nationality like "Frenchy" Bordagaray or Herbert Perdue of Gallatin, Tennessee, who was called "The Gallatin Squash." Lon Warnake was "The Arkansas Hummingbird." A fellow Arkansan was pitcher "Pea Ridge" Day, and according to the SABR website, "If sportswriters loved to type 'Pea Ridge,' they were absolutely enamored with printing descriptions of the 'Hog Calling Pitcher.' After strikeouts or other advantageous events on the diamond, Day would strike a pose on the mound and bellow out a prolonged hog call or other such screeches."

I particularly like the "The" nicknames, be it Pepper Martin ("The Wild Horse of The Osage"), Roger Bresnahan ("The Duke of Tralee"), or Edward Burlton Heusser ("The Wild Elk of The Wasatch"). Charlie Grimm probably liked his nickname ("Jolly Cholly"), while the same can't be said for Frank "Creepy" Crespi. There was "Tacky" Tom

Parrott, "Spittin'" Bill Doak, "Buttermilk" Tommy Dowd, and "Fidgety" Phil Collins. And in more recent generations, there were Delino "Bop" DeShields, Jack "The Ripper" Clark, Rex "Hurricane" Hudler, and Mike "Spanky" LaValliere. At third base in the 1970s was Ken Reitz, "The Zamboni." In 1974 Arnold Ray "Bake" McBride, or sometimes "Shake N Bake," won the National League Rookie of the Year. And the closer in 2016 was Seung-Hwan Oh, aka "Stone Buddha" aka "The Final Boss," while his closing contemporary, Trevor Rosenthal, was "Closenthal."

While the Cardinals are a team for ornothogists, felinologists are also fond of the Birds because the team has had its pick of the litter in this cat-egory: Andres "Big Cat" Galarraga, Johnny "Big Cat" Mize, Harry "The Cat" Brecheen, Harvey "Kitten" Haddix, and Jim "Kitty" Kaat. One pal suggested I include J.D. Drew's derogatory cat nickname. Other animated animal nicknames include "Possum" Whitehead, Stan "Happy Rabbit" Rojek, Emil "Antelope" Verban, and the long-armed shortstop Marty Marion, aka "The Octopus." And naturally, Frank Dodo's nickname was "Bird."

Perhaps the most creative baseball-y nickname was accidental. In 1935 the Cards had a player named Lyle Judy. At the time there was a famous puppet show called *Punch & Judy*, so Lyle naturally earned the nickname "Punch." But in later years, the phrase "Punch and Judy" hitter became popular in baseball when referencing a guy who doesn't hit the ball hard and instead gently scatters his hits. But we'll never know if Lyle "Punch" Judy was a "Punch and Judy" hitter because in his 11 big league at-bats he never got one hit.

There was probably some cognomen confusion in the dugout in 1903, when the Cards had both "Sunset" Jimmy Burke and "Sunny" Jim Hackett. And in '45 the Cards had George "Lefty" Dockins and Gene "Lefty" Crumling. However "Lefty" Crumling was a misnomer mystery since he batted and threw right-handed. As a rook in 1889, Charlie Dufee hit 16 home runs, earning him the nickname "Home Run" Dufee. But he only hit three the next year. Joseph "Speed" Walker played two games and got two hits but never stole a base. Perhaps the most sobering sobriquet news is that Clarence Beers *didn't* have a nickname.

Some of the best players in baseball with some of the best nicknames in baseball made cameos as Cardinals before blossoming somewhere else. For instance, Hall of Famer "Rabbit" Maranville and "Dazzy" Vance wore the birds on the bat as did All-Stars "Preacher" Roe and Sal "The Barber" Maglie. Ex-Cardinals player Mordecai "Three Finger" Brown actually had "four and a half fingers on his pitching hand," per the SABR website. "Because of childhood curiosity, Mordecai lost most of his right index finger in a piece of farming equipment. Not long after, he fell while chasing a rabbit and broke his other fingers. The result was a bent middle finger, a paralyzed little finger, and a stump where the index finger used to be." Brown was a St. Louis rookie in 1903, went 9–13, and was then dealt to the Chicago Cubs.

In a way, this trade was Brock-for-Broglio before Brock-for-Broglio. Consider that St. Louis sent "Three Finger" and Jack O'Neill to Chicago for Jack Taylor and Larry McLean. You've never heard of those final three humans. However, Brown is in the Hall of Fame. In the Cubs' World Series-winning seasons of 1907 and, of course, 1908, Brown produced a 49–15 record and a 1.44 ERA. He was even mentioned by Mr. Burns in a classic episode of *The Simpsons* called "Homer at the Bat."

And finally, there was the 1953 Cards pitcher who went by "Preacher" Jack Fasholtz—and somehow avoided a different nickname.

45

CLOSERS

During the 1982 season, a baby was born. That fall the bearded Cardinals closer, Bruce Sutter, threw the final pitch of the postseason—a swinging strike three, which earned the Cardinals the championship. The baby grew up to become a bearded Cardinals closer himself.

And in the fall of 2011, Jason Motte threw the final pitch of the postseason—a fly out to left, which earned the Cardinals the championship. Sure enough, Sutter actually became Motte's mentor. "I got to know him a little bit better just through the World Series stuff," Motte told me by phone. "And really since then, it's been someone I've called to talk to, and we'll also text back and forth. A good friendship was born there in St. Louis."

So when Motte's first son was born in 2016, Jason and Caitlin named the baby: Sutter Motte. "Baseball-wise, obviously he was a great player and stuff like that," Jason said of Bruce, "but just the person I got to know from all my years there—and the person everyone around said he was—was just a very kind individual. A good friend and a good friendship formed over the years, and we were just happy to do that. He was honored. He said, 'You know, you're going to make this old man cry!'"

From Sutter to Motte to—who knows, maybe Sutter Motte himself in the future—the Cardinals closer has always been a time-honored position in St. Louis. Some of the best to ever do it have done it at Busch, including Dennis Eckersley, Lee Smith, and Jason Isringhausen (who leads the franchise with 217 saves). There's been a closer who won the Rookie of the Year. There have been rookie closers who were suddenly closing out playoff games. And there have been a litany of others who have nailed down the ninth in their own way; 361 men have saved at least one game for the Cardinals—from Bill Smith to Bob Smith (but not Bryn Smith or Bud Smith), from Anthony Reyes to Alex Reyes (and also Dennys Reyes), Bill Kline to Steve Kline, Tracy

Stallard to Tom Niedenfeur, Andy Benes (but not Alan Benes) to Cris Carpenter (but not Chris Carpenter).

But Sutter was the best of them all. "It's a great feeling when Sutter stepped on the mound," said Ken Oberkfell, the third baseman on the '82 team, "because it meant the game was over. He put it away. Guys like him, Goose Gossage, Jeff Reardon, these guys were legitimate closers. I mean they would close and not just one inning. Nowadays, if a pitcher throws one inning as a closer, he ain't going back out usually, which I've never understood, but that's not my place."

The Cards actually got this Hall of Famer from the Chicago Cubs, too, but it wasn't a lopsided trade like Brock-for-Broglio. On December 9, 1980—the day after John Lennon was killed—the Cardinals acquired Sutter for Leon Durham, who would make two All-Star teams for the Cubs. Chicago also nabbed Ken "The Zamboni" Reitz and a player to be named later, who later became Ty Waller, a player who later no one could name.

Sutter was a stud. In four seasons with St. Louis, he led the league in saves three times. In 1984 he saved 45 games, a National League record, while notching a 1.54 ERA in an astounding 122⅔ innings out of the pen. But he'll always be remembered for '82 and the night Jack Buck announced: "That's a winner! A Worrrrrrld Series winner for the Cardinals!"

* * *

I saw Lee Smith once at The Galleria. After shopping for CDs at Camelot Music and big-head sports T-shirts at Superstars, I went down to the mall food court with Michael Slonim, my best friend from growing up. Seeing a Cardinal outside of Busch Stadium was a lot like seeing a teacher outside of school. It's weird. My biggest takeaway, though, from this day was that "Big" Lee Smith was indeed big. As if there were children, and then there were grown-ups, and then there was Lee Smith. The great closer autographed the only thing I had to sign—a liner sheet from my tray at the food court.

But that wasn't my only brush with Smith in 1991. Eleven-year-old me got to see Smith up close on perhaps the biggest day of his whole dang career. On October 1, 1991, the Montreal Expos *hosted* the Cardinals at Busch Stadium. The Expos had to play some late-season home games on the road due to some crazy structural damage that autumn to Montreal's Olympic Stadium.

Since these games weren't supposed to be in St. Louis—and since St. Louis was out of the division race—Slonim's dad got us seats right behind home plate. And that night we witnessed "Big" Lee set the National League record for saves in a season. He notched his 46th of the season, eclipsing, yup, Sutter's 45 from 1984.

Later that year, Slonim and I were pleased to spot ourselves in the background of the highlight while watching the year-long recap VHS produced by the folks from *This Week In Baseball*. Smith saved the game for rookie starter Omar Olivares, whose biggest claim to Cardinals fame was that, for a while, his uniform number was his initials—OO.

* * *

By 1993 Big Lee would finish his St. Louis career with 160 saves, at the time passing Todd Worrell for most ever by a Cardinals reliever. "Worrell," Joe Buck said, "was like—*whoa*. He was in good shape, he was young, he had that cheesy mustache, but he could just blow it. And that was the first time I remember a scenario like, 'Oh, let's bring in the guy who can throw a million.' It was cool."

In 1982 the Cards drafted the 6'5" Worrell out of a place called Biola University, which is in a place called La Mirada, California. It proved to be one of the best first-round picks in franchise history. "We called him 'Tiny,'" pitcher Joe Magrane said. "How he came to be was in the minors. He could always throw hard, but in the second time through the lineup, he started getting touched up. Jim Fregosi was our manager in Triple A; Todd was our No. 1 pitching product. And Jim said, 'I think we should make a closer out of this guy. He'd be of more value to us.' So he turned him into a closer and he was just blowing everybody up. He gets called up in September and he's doing the same thing right through the postseason in '85."

Worrell scorched that September, becoming the closer on what was already one of the finer clubs in Cardinals history. On September

Part of a legacy of great bearded Cardinals closers, Jason Motte (left) calls Bruce Sutter (right) a mentor and a friend. (USA TODAY Sports Images)

28, 1985, Worrell's 25th birthday, he pitched a combined three scoreless innings in both games of a doubleheader. About a month later, he picked up a save in the '85 World Series. And he was in line for another one, pitching the ninth of the ill-fated Game 6. At least no one will forget who the pitcher was during the Don Denkinger Play since Worrell is in the photo on bar walls across St. Louis.

After all that, the next year was when he was officially a rookie and he won the Rookie of the Year, saving 36 ballgames. "Any time you faced a pitcher who was really tall, there was an intimidation factor," second baseman Tommy Herr said. "Their release point because of their wingspan was a little bit closer to the hitter. It's a matter of inches, but when you're throwing that hard, a matter of inches means it's either by you or not by you. Obviously, Todd being a big, strong, hard-throwing guy, he was an intimidator out there. But a thing that was special about him was—his command was very good. He wasn't just a hard thrower who didn't know where it was going. He could throw hard in, hard away, and backed it up with a pretty good slider."

Magrane, a rookie in '87, remembers the sound 30 years later. He'd be on the mound, grinding through a start. "You're feeling tired, but you can hear the mitt popping—Todd warming up—and it was a very reassuring feeling," Magrane recalled. "Because you knew if you could get through it, he could come in and immediately dominate."

* * *

There are regular human two-digit pitches, and then there are the superhuman three-digit pitches. Trevor Jordan Rosenthal, aka Closenthal, could hit the century mark of speed. Unlike Worrell, an earmarked first rounder, Rosenthal was nabbed in the 21st round in 2009, coming out of Cowley County Community College in Kansas.

In fact, Rosenthal had just begun pitching for Cowley County, when a Cardinals scout spotted him. They took a chance on the big arm, and during development that arm began to hit triple digits. Sure enough, in October of 2013, Rosenthal saved at least one game in the National League Division Series, National League Championship Series, and World Series. "He can do 99 to 100. It is effortless and it's in the zone and...it just looks different," manager Mike Matheny said in 2017. "It's sneaky and it jumps on guys, and he's got some good downhill plane. He's in a real nice spot, and then you never know when he's going to pull out the change-up."

When Rosenthal's 2016 ended prematurely due to injury, the Cards' new closer became Seung Hwan Oh, the 34-year-old rookie. The Korean had pitched professionally in both Korea and Japan but came to the states in '16 with the reputation as a nasty reliever. He had not one but two nicknames—"The Stone Buddha" and "The Final Boss." He had dated a famous Korean pop star. And because of the language barrier, the Cards provided him with a translator, Eugene Koo.

Oh starred in his first St. Louis season, saving 19 games with a 1.92 ERA. And in baseball-mad St. Louis, Koo began to get a cult following of fans. Koo was a sweet man who had essentially won a sports fan's lottery—he got to *be* a St. Louis Cardinal (just without the playing part). He went everywhere Oh did, he had a locker in the clubhouse, and he'd stand next to Matheny during Oh's innings...and go out for any mound visit with the Korean closer. The "Best Fans In Baseball" gave Koo the nickname the "Best Translator In Baseball."

And on Opening Day of 2017, Koo did the coolest thing ever. After they announced the Cardinals Hall of Famers and non-starters, they announced the on-field staff (and then, finally, the starting lineup). So guys such as the trainer and strength coach ran onto the field, jogged down the line, shaking every man's hand. Sure enough, next up was translator Eugene Koo. And he was carrying his cellphone in his left hand, recording the moment as he shook hands with his right. It was awesome. There was Gibby and Ozzie and Whitey, who turned to Ozzie and said, "Hey, it's my translator!" And then Koo scurried past each current player, receiving a high five or handshake from each one—except from the playful Rosenthal, who jokingly tapped Koo below the belt.

46

BRUMMER STEALS HOME

On a summer day 35 days later, Ken Oberkfell tried explaining the unexplainable. "I was standing next to Whitey, and all of a sudden, here comes Brummer, heading for home plate," Oberkfell recalled. "And Whitey's like: 'What the...*yes!*'"

Glenn Brummer, the third-string catcher, attempted to steal home with two out in the bottom of the 12th inning. And he was safe. "To me, that is the most hard-to-think-of ending," said author Will Leitch, who is actually from Matoon, Illinois, the same small hometown as Brummer. "It's hard to remember a play that's less likely than that. It's the most bizarre possible way. There's no other Glenn Brummer moment in Cardinal history. There's no reason he should've had the self-confidence or even the status on the team to try that. Imagine if he gets thrown out? I'm sure Whitey Herzog would say, 'Our idiot third-string catcher is never getting on the field again!'"

Brummer, of course, decided to steal home on his own that day. It was August 22, 1982. It was a championship season, but the regular season would come down to the final days. So yeah, a guy who finished the season with a 0.0 wins-above-replacement (WAR) won a key game for the Cards with a walk-off stolen base. "I mean, that was Brummer's claim to fame!" Oberkfell said. "He very seldom played, but boy, he did that day—and it was something."

Glenn Edward Brummer loved farming so much that his teammates called him "Tractorhead." During his playing career, he lived on a dairy farm in Mountain Grove, Missouri. Bullpens weren't as vast back then, so the Cards were able to carry a third catcher, and Brummer's main responsibility was actually catching in the bullpen for the relievers they did have. (The other two Cards catchers that year both ended up being World Series MVPs. Backup Gene Tenace won it in '72 with the Oakland A's while Darrell Porter would win it that fall.) "It's exciting being in a pennant battle, not knowing from day to day what's going to happen, but honestly, a bullpen catcher's job is kind of boring," Brummer told *The New York Times* in 1982. "Sometimes pitchers don't have a lot of time. They're going into the game after one hitter. So you can't be sloppy. You have to make sure you catch the ball and you have to make good, sharp throws back to them."

Brummer's first big league hit came in 1981 off of Philadelphia Phillies pitcher Nino Espinosa. Brummer finished with six hits that year and he had only 15 in '82, but one of them was a 12th inning single that zany August day. The San Francisco Giants were in town and were wearing those garish orange jerseys that clashed horribly with the green of the Astroturf. They trotted out a lineup with some familiar characters in Cards history, including future St. Louis first baseman Jack Clark and future St. Louis Public Enemy No. 1 Jeffrey Leonard.

This afternoon the Cards were down to their last out. But in the bottom of the ninth inning, Oberkfell ripped an RBI double, resuscitating the team. And in the 12th inning, the bases were loaded for David Green, who seemed like a good guy to have at the place; he was hitting .339 at that point. But the pitcher, Gary Lavelle, was a lefty. Pitching from the stretch, he paid no attention to that third-string catcher over on third. "I could've been sitting in the upper deck for all he knew," Brummer told *The Times*.

Brummer began to creep down the line with each pitch. The count was one ball and two strikes. In the KMOX booth, Mike Shannon narrated the action to the folks at home: "Brummer's the big runner. He's at third. Two down, sacks jammed, Lavelle at the belt, *Brummer's stealing home! he is saaaafe!* And the Cardinals win! Brummer stole home! Their dugout comes out, and they congratulate him. You wouldn't believe it! Glenn Brummer steals home. And now the Giants are out arguing the call. The umpire never called the two-strike pitch!"

That's the funny thing about Brummer's inexplicable steal; some would argue it shouldn't have happened. I mean, we can *all* argue that the third-string catcher shouldn't have tried to steal home. But it shouldn't have happened because the pitch Lavelle threw was strike three. Right down central. But the ump, so caught off guard by the stealing Brummer diving headfirst into home, called it a ball.

Everything about it was categorically bonkers. From the dugout Oberkfell recalled, "Whitey just started shaking his head. So someone had asked him, 'Whitey, did you give Brummer the steal sign there?' And Whitey said, 'If I were to give Brummer the steal sign there, they should fire me right on the spot!'"

After Brummer stole home, they stole home plate for Brummer. The team autographed it. And they had the famous artist, Amadee Wohlschlaeger, draw a "WANTED" poster of the "thief" Brummer right there on the front of the plate. Brummer ended up donating it to the Cardinals Hall of Fame, where it's on display today across the street from Busch Stadium.

And for a younger generation, the legend of the Brummer Steal became sort of a cult classic kind of like the Mike Laga Foul Ball, the 1986 foul that literally sailed out of old Busch Stadium. It was the only ball to ever leave the confines, and the crowd gave him a bizarre ovation. As for Brummer's steal, "This is when it was *all* on the radio," said Leitch, who was six years old at the time. "Unless you were there at the stadium or it was Tony Kubek and Bob Costas on the *Saturday Game of the Week*, there was just no way to watch these things. So the Brummer play because it has this, of course, incredible call almost became the notion of legend for years and years and years...It was such a strange, bizarre thing. Unless you had the newspaper or were actually there, you couldn't have imagined it. I remember being so excited—someone in the early days of MLB.com, who had to have been the same age as me, went and found footage of that play! It's so unusual, so strange. I was pleased the MLB.com guy found the definitive proof of it because it was one of those things that you just wonder—I know it was from my childhood and I feel like I remember it, but it can't possibly be true."

But it can indeed be proven. Years later, I was at a sports memorabilia shop in Illinois. Sure enough, there was a black-and-white, blown-up photo for sale of Brummer sliding over home plate. It was autographed and only $20. I had to buy it. It was signed: "Glenn Brummer—I WAS SAFE!"

47

SEAT CUSHION NIGHT

Ladies love Toms. It's as if you come out of the womb as a Thomas preordained to become prom king. Tom Cruise. Tom Brady Tom Selleck. Tom Ford. Tom Jones.

And if you ask a certain generation of St. Louis ladies or men—the 1980s generation that hung out at Balaban's in the Central West End—Tom Herr was the Tom of Toms. Herr played second base, but they all dreamed of getting farther than that.

Thomas Mitchell Herr, the former Blue Hen from the University of Delaware, came to St. Louis in 1979. He patrolled his patch of Astroturf until 1988, when he was traded to—of all teams—the Minnesota Twins, who had beaten the Cards in the World Series the previous October. Alas, for the ladies of the 1980s, Herr was a married man. Kim Herr was his high school sweetheart from up in Lancaster, Pennsylvania (where they pronounced it LANK-us-ter as opposed to Lan-cas-ter). One of my prized possessions is *Cooking With the Cardinals*, the 1985 cookbook prepared by the players' wives. Kim Herr's big contribution was her Derby Pie, which she wrote is "destined to be the hit of the day!"

¼ cup margarine
1 cup sugar
3 eggs
¾ cup light corn syrup
¼ teaspoon salt
1 teaspoon vanilla
½ cup chocolate chips
½ cup black walnuts, diced
2 tablespoons bourbon whiskey
1 8-inch or 9-inch unbaked pie shell
(Cream margarine, and pour in sugar gradually. Add beaten eggs, salt, syrup, and vanilla. Include nuts, chocolate chips, bourbon. Stir. Pour into shell. Cook 40-50 minutes at 375 degrees. Garnish with whipped cream before serving.)

ST. LOUIS CARDINALS

Her husband treated fans to his greatest St. Louis season in 1985, when he had some preposterous stats that popped off the back of his Topps card—eight home runs and 110 RBIs. Let those numbers sink in. Herr slugged just .416 that year, but in an era when counting stats were king, his RBIs earned him a fifth-place finish in the '85 MVP voting. (Actually, how amazing is this? In 1985 five of the top 11 MVP vote-getters were on the Cardinals, including Willie McGee, who won the hardware.)

As for Herr, No. 28 only hit 28 homers in his 13-year career, but he'll be forever remembered for his extra-innings, walk-off grand slam in the pennant-winning season of 1987. The fan giveaway that day was a white Cardinals seat cushion.

Sure, the Cards faced the New York Mets in the playoffs in 2000 and 2006, but the rivalry was hottest in the summers of the mid-1980s. From 1985 to 1988, the National League East division winners rotated: Cards, Mets, Cards, Mets. There were some amazing moments, too. Darryl Strawberry once hit the Busch Stadium scoreboard clock on an 11th-inning, 11th-hour homer. And Mets catcher Barry Lyons, chasing a pop-up, once barreled into the Cards' dugout, breaking the leg of star starting pitcher John Tudor, who wasn't even playing that day.

The Mets were pond scum. Or at least that's what they were called in St. Louis in the mid-80s. It was a delightfully disgusting insult popularized by St. Louis radio disc jockey JC Corcoran. "The Mets Are Pond Scum" T-shirts were similarly popular in St. Louis as "I Heart NY" T-shirts were in Queens. Even David Letterman once did a breakdown of the Mets versus Pond Scum, determining that while one Met is named Mookie every Pond Scum is named Mookie.

Actually, during a different Mets-Cards game in 1987, Herr was at bat when he suddenly called time. There was a commotion above. The fans were going bananas. It was because a little airplane flew by with a banner that read: "JC SAYS THE METS ARE POND SCUM!"

On April 18, 1987, Ron Darling faced Danny Cox in front of 41,942 inevitably comfortably seated fans. On their complimentary cushions, Cards fans watched a game featuring 17 All-Stars and three MVPs. But

THE METS ARE POND SCUM

In 2000, when the Cards finally met the New York Mets in a postseason, JC Corcoran reprinted the famous T-shirts from the 1980s. It was a big year for him as his book also came out. Since I was at college, my mother, Josette Hochman, dotingly went down to the station to get me a "Mets Are Pond Scum" T-shirt. She loved Corcoran and was actually going to his book signing that weekend. Sure enough, she ran into the man himself at the station.

Mom excitedly explained that she and two friends planned to attend the book-signing.

"I have an idea," Mom said. "When I walk up to you, can you say my name? They'll think that you and I actually know each other and they'll be impressed!"

"Um, sure, okay," he said. "What's your name?"

"It's Josette."

"Josette?"

"Yeah, Jo-sette."

"Jo-sette. Okay, yeah, got it. Jo-sette."

Sure enough, that weekend, my mom and her two friends stood in line at the bookstore to meet Corcoran. Mom anxiously waited and waited—could this line move any slower?—when finally they made it to the front. JC looked up, realized this was the lady from the other day, racked his brain...and joyfully said: "Joselle!"

no one saw this coming, not the meteorologists nor the Metropolitans. Doppler radar was deceived by this downfall doppelganger. Because suddenly and stunningly, it rained cushions. They still talk about it around St. Louis.

And what a game, too. St. Louis trailed 5–0 in the top of the fourth inning and tied it with five in the bottom. In the bottom of the ninth, Ozzie Smith scored on a wild throw. In the bottom of the 10th inning, the Cards needed to tie it again—and did so via the first major league hit by Tom Pagnozzi. Three batters later, tie game, the bases were loaded. And Herr walloped a Jesse Orosco high fastball. "I was hoping," Orosco told the *St. Louis Post-Dispatch*, "it would hit a bird or something."

As soon as Herr's homer sailed over the Montreal Expos logo on the left-field wall, Busch Stadium fans flung their seat cushions onto the field. "Being in the 300 level, I got good air on the throw," recalled St. Louisan Sean Connors, who was 10 at the time. "I remember my dad driving home, listening to KMOX, and hearing [the replay of] Jack Buck's call. [It] gave me goose bumps."

And as Herr scored, the seat cushions soared. Herr even picked one up at home and gleefully tossed it into the air. And while on the air, Buck joked that the Cards could have another seat cushion giveaway the next day—since the fans had thrown them all back. "I was there," said fan Bill Goodfriend, who moved to St. Louis in 1985. "As a native New Yorker, it became part of my indoctrination and eventual embrace of Cardinal Nation."

For 29 years after, no Cardinals player hit an extra-innings, walk-off grand slam—until 30 Aprils later. Just like Herr, another 31-year-old Cardinals infielder did it. With his socks high, his shoulders back, his hands bare, his beard black, Matt Carpenter came to bat against the Toronto Blue Jays on April 27, 2017, in the 11th inning. Game tied, bases loaded.

From the dugout, teammate Greg Garcia spotted the stats on the Busch Stadium scoreboard. With the bases loaded, Carpenter had a career .566 average with 51 RBIs. "So he does this a lot and he's real good at it, so we like our chances with Carp up there," Garcia said. "But we noticed the big goose egg under home runs. So we're like, *This'll be a good time for his first*, and he didn't disappoint."

Carp swatted a hanging pitch over the right-field wall for a walk-off, extra-inning grand slam. Cardinals 8, Blue Jays 4. The next day, manager Mike Matheny recalled the Herr-like at-bat, explaining that some "get in the box, put themselves in a pressure situation. Others get in that exact same spot and see that the pressure is on the other guy. And then they go huntin'. I think Carpenter does that as well as anyone in the game."

As for seat cushions, the tradition continued. The encore was during another pennant-winning season in 2006. The Cards had lost eight straight. And sure enough, they trailed in the ninth inning 4–3 against the Cleveland Indians. But Cleveland botched two plays. The second was a throwing error by future Cardinals infielder Jhonny Peralta. And as Aaron Miles scored the winning run, the fans frisbee'd their white seat cushions onto the field, a time-honored tradition in these parts.

48

TATIS, WHITEN, AND HOME RUN FEATS

It was his freshman year of college. He was just trying to fit amidst a new dorm, new people, new laundry responsibilities. Tom Ackerman, a nice young lad from St. Louis, lived in McNutt Residence Center at Indiana University. His roommate was also from back home. On September 7, 1993, they were casually watching *SportsCenter*, when the show went live to the Cardinals-Reds game. Turned out that Mark Whiten, the St. Louis outfielder, had hit three home runs in the game. And he was up. "So we're watching the at-bat when he hit it. We just went *nuts*!" Ackerman said. "We're running up and down the hallway, high-fiving. If they ever wondered how big of Cardinals fans we were, they figured it out quickly."

"Hard Hittin'" Mark Whiten. Four homers in a game. At the time, it had only been done nine times in baseball history. And Whiten's 12 RBIs was also tied for the most ever in a game.

"I remember later getting to hear Jack Buck's call. I think it was one of his best calls actually," said Ackerman, who ultimately became the sports director at KMOX Radio. "At the end he says, 'What a blast that was! What a blast this is!' It's just cool."

Over the centuries the Cards have had a few surreal homer accomplishments. Some of them, like Whiten's, might've been matched over time. Other Major League Baseball players have since hit four homers in a game. The Cardinals themselves allowed one, sure enough, to a player on the Cincinnati Reds, Scooter Gennett in 2017.

But one surely won't be matched. It's too bonkers. On April 23, 1999, Fernando Tatis hit two grand slams...in the same inning...*off the same pitcher*.

How did this happen? I mean, as of 2017, only 13 players have ever even hit two grand slams in the same game. Tatis was the only one to do it in the same inning and the only guy to do it off the same pitcher. The Cards were in Los Angeles that day. My best friend from growing up was actually at the game. He'd been to dozens of Cardinals games at Busch. Sure enough, the first Cardinals game he goes to in L.A. has the rarest of feats. "It was the second semester of my freshman year at USC," Michael Slonim recalled. "The series against the Cardinals had been on my calendar since the schedule had been announced. I was wearing my Cards navy blue road hat. I stood and cheered when the Cards scored. Other fans gave me a bit of a hard time after the first grand slam."

Entering that historic third inning, the Cardinals trailed 2–0. Dodgers pitcher Chan Ho Park promptly loaded the bases, and Tatis' first slam drove in the trio of Darren Bragg, Edgar Renteria, and Mark McGwire. Some zaniness ensued during the spin around the lineup. The Cards scored a bunch but made a base-running blunder. The Dodgers' manager, Davey Johnson, was ejected during the inning. And Los Angeles tallied an error that made six of the runs unearned, including the final four of the inning. Those, of course, were courtesy of Tatis' second grand slam of his career—and of the inning. "After the second," Slonim said, "I was yelled at in Spanish, and people threw peanuts at me. I still have the ticket stub from that game. A few years later, I was talking to a friend, when he brought up that game as a bit of trivia. I told him that I was there. Amazed, he told me that he had at one point looked in a baseball record book, something that was printed in those pre-Internet days, and under the record for 'Most Grand Slams in One Inning,' the list said: Fernando Tatis—2. Many Others—1."

Another implausible tale, that of Keith McDonald, who never got a hit that wasn't a homer, is kind of like a warped "Moonlight Graham" in *Field of Dreams*. McDonald got his brief chance in the bigs, had the most success possible...and then never really got a chance again. A career minor leaguer, McDonald finally got the call in 2000. And on the Fourth of July, fireworks ensued. In his MLB debut, the pinch-hitting McDonald hit a homer in his first at-bat.

Two days later, he pinch-hit again. And homered again.

McDonald became just the second player *ever* to homer in his first two at-bats. The other fellow played in St. Louis as well. Former Browns outfielder Bob Nieman homered in his first two at-bats, and both of them were in the same game at Fenway Park on September

TRIVIA TIDBITS

Mark Whiten's Four-Homer Game
- Mark Whiten was batting sixth that night. (Bernard Gilkey hit third, Todd Zeile hit cleanup, and Gerald Perry hit fifth.)
- Whiten's fourth homer was off Rob Dibble.
- The game was the second of a doubleheader. The Cards lost the first 14–13 and won the second 15–2. So St. Louis scored 28 runs in one day.
- Geronimo Pena also homered for the Cardinals.

Fernando Tatis' Two Grand Slam Inning
- The Cardinals won 12–5, and Jose Jimenez was the winning pitcher.
- Eight years later Tatis and Chan Ho Park were actually teammates for the Triple A New Orleans Zephyrs.
- Born in 1975, Tatis was a New Year's Day baby.
- The 1999 season was clearly Tatis' best in the bigs. He finished with 34 homers, 107 RBIs, and 21 stolen bases while hitting .298 with a .404 on-base percentage and .553 slugging percentage.
- Of the 13 men to hit grand slams in the same game, only one guy never hit a grand slam before or after. Remarkably, it was a pitcher. On July 3, 1966, Tony Cloninger hit the only two grand slams of his career.
- Cloninger's final season in the bigs (1972) was with the Cards. He had a 5.19 ERA in 17 games.
- St. Louis native Bill Mueller, who hit two grand slams in a 2003 game for the Boston Red Sox, was the only player to hit one from each side of the plate.

Keith McDonald's First Three Hits Go for Home Runs
- Before 2000 only two Cardinals had ever homered in the first at-bat (Eddie Morgan in 1936 and Wally Moon is 1954). Then, two Cardinals did it in July of 2000 (McDonald and then Chris Richard on July 17).
- After that, five more Cards would homer in their first Major League Baseball at-bat. Three were pitchers (Gene Stechschulte, Mark Worrell, and Adam Wainwright), and the other two were Hector Luna and Paul DeJong.

Stan Musial's Five Home Run Doubleheader
- Musial finished the season with 36 homers, his most since he hit 38 in 1948.
- Former Cardinals foe, Keith Moreland, the Chicago Cubs infielder, was born on this May 2, 1954, day.
- In April of 1954, Tom Alston became the first African American to play for the Cardinals. The first game of the May 2 doubleheader was the only four-hit game of his career. Alston went 4-for-4 with a homer and a walk.

14, 1951. So that alone made the Cards catcher, McDonald, part of history. McDonald had seven more plate appearances in the 2000 season. He only tallied one more hit, and that was yet another homer. Three hits, three homers.

Alas, they sent McDonald back down to the minors that July. He would return as a September call-up...but not until the following year. In 2001 he had just two September plate appearances. Both were outs, and that was it. He'd bounce around the minors for a while more but never returned to the bigs. And so, Keith McDonald hit 78 homers in 3,585 minor league plate appearances. And Keith McDonald hit three homers in 11 major league plate appearances.

Perhaps the most storied of the zany Cardinals home-run feats came from their most storied player. On a single day, Stan Musial hit five home runs. Of course, the catch was that it was in a doubleheader. But it's still crazy to think that he woke up the morning of May 2, 1954, with three home runs hit that year. He went to bed that night with eight home runs hit that year. "Musial, by the way, had never hit three home runs in a game in the majors," the Hall of Fame scribe Bob Broeg wrote. "He did it once in 1941 at White City Park in Springfield, Missouri, where—to her great annoyance—his No. 1 fan, wife Lil, was diapering infant son Dick in the restroom every time Musial homered."

In the first game of that famed 1954 day, Musial hit three homers, and his third was a three-run homer. It broke a 6–6 tie in the eighth, and the Cardinals went on to defeat the New York Giants. St. Louis actually lost the second game 9–7, but Musial hit a pair of homers both off Hall of Famer Hoyt Wilhelm. "And perhaps his best swing of the day," Broeg wrote, "was a 420-foot shot collared by Willie Mays at the center-field fence—another homer if the wind had been blowing from left field instead of right."

The five homers were a seemingly unmatchable record, and in the stands to see it happen was an eight-year-old named Nate Colbert. He ended up going to Sumner High in St. Louis and ultimately made the big leagues, too.

And in 1972 the San Diego Padres' Colbert hit five home runs in a doubleheader. Only two men ever did it, and the second was in the ballpark to see the first.

49

JULIAN JAVIER
AND HIS HAT

I always said if I ever met Julian Javier, the first thing I'd ask would be about the World Series hat. During the 1967 Fall Classic, the Cards were on the Fenway Park field, celebrating their World Series win. Bob Gibson struck out George Scott, and a mob of Cardinals bobbed in place—when an umpire scurried by and yanked the red hat off Javier's head.

Wait, what?

Sure enough, the 80-year-old Javier, the second base stalwart on those 1960s teams, showed up in St. Louis from his Dominican Republic home. It was the summer of 2017—50 years after the Cards beat the Boston Red Sox for the title—and the old ballplayers united at the new Busch Stadium. I had to know: was the umpire's grabbing of the hat discussed beforehand? "No, no, it was a surprise," Javier told me. "He got my hat, so I figured, keep goin'! We won the last game and [I thought] I don't care about [the hat] because I can get another one."

In the video footage, Javier smiled at the umpire, Augie Donatelli, who then disappeared out of the frame. So I had to ask Javier: did he have any idea what happened to that hat? "About 35 years ago, I went to see family in Tampa, St. Petersburg, Naples," Javier said. "Augie Donatelli had a bar there, and I said, 'Augie! Where's my hat?' And he said, 'Right there! On top of the bar!' And he got it right down."

So for a *St. Louis Post-Dispatch* column, I began making calls, trying to find Javier's hat.

* * *

The bar, fittingly, was called El Cap. And I soon learned about an American hero, the ump who got his first gig at a Prisoner of War camp. Parachuting out of a B-17 bomber over Berlin during a World War II air raid gone awry, Sergeant Donatelli landed in a tree. With a broken ankle, he was soon captured by German guards. "He was one of five brothers. All went in the war," Augie's son, Patrick, said. "The only exercise in the camp was soccer and softball. And my dad played minor league ball. But he couldn't play [because of his ankle], so he became the umpire." And that's how it happened. Augie learned to ump as a POW.

August Joseph Donatelli was born in August in the Western Pennsylvania town of Heilwood, back in 1914. Heilwood is 79 miles from the town of Donora, home of the Musial family.

After being liberated by Russians in 1945, Donatelli returned to the states and, sure enough, became an ump. Known for his energy, he cracked the majors and became a staple for decades. Young fans remembered his mellifluous, fun name. And there was Donatelli in 1954, umpiring the doubleheader when Stan Musial hit five home runs. And on the cover of the first ever issue of *Sports Illustrated* that same year. And in the face of New York Mets manager Yogi Berra—*and* Mets outfielder Willie Mays—arguing a controversial 10th-inning call in the 1973 World Series. "He had quite a life," Patrick said.

In 1963 Augie and his half-brother, Steve, flew a little twin engine plane south to Florida, a galaxy away from the coal-mining country of Western Pennsylvania. They bought a bar. "The cheeseburgers pay for my racehorses," the bar manager told me.

I called El Cap in St. Petersburg and met Mary Jean Bonfili, a jubilant lady who ol' Augie used to call "Jeeeeena!" Augie had opened the bar with his half-brother all those years ago. Steve's son married Mary Jean. All three men have since passed. The old ump died in 1990, and his storied life even made the obituary pages of *The New York Times*.

But Mary Jean is still at El Cap, working like a horse, and when she's not, she's breeding one. She owns both thoroughbreds and greyhounds that race, and two years back, her horse Benny Is a Jet, a 12-to-1 shot, won at Saratoga. Mary Jean excitedly explained to me that El Cap has numerous connections to St. Louis. On the front window of the St. Petersburg bar, there's a neon sign of a Cardinal perched atop the word BUSCH. And perched at the bar is a Cardinals fan. She promptly put me on the phone with Rob Stuart, the fan who grew up in St. Louis. "If you didn't know you were in Florida," he said, "you'd feel like this was a St. Louis bar."

Since numerous teams would come to Florida for camp and with all of Augie's baseball connections, "this bar was the original sports bar in St. Petersburg. It truly was," Mary Jean said. "The Cardinals spring trained here, we used to get all those wonderful people from St. Louis, and they were the best fans in the world. And they were the nicest people, I might add. The city has grown a lot. But El Cap is where the ballplayers hung out. The Yankees, the Mets. Bruce Sutter's been in here. He taught one of my bartenders how to throw the split-fingered fastball."

Good lord, this was perfect. Of all the bars to serve as an accidental museum for a piece of Cardinals history, it was a St. Petersburg bar with a St. Louis vibe that appreciates St. Louis tradition. *So, Mary Jean, where is Javier's hat?* "I have no idea," she said. "It could be in a box, but that box was in the attic. But we had bugs, so I got rid of the bugs and got rid of the junk!"

Mary Jean then laughed like Javier had. She admitted that if she had known that an old hat had value, "I would've protected that. But I didn't know that and I don't think my husband knew that."

Patrick said that "it disappeared into the black hole of the El Cap memorabilia. I have a feeling that sucker is long gone. It's been 50 years. If you had been on top of this a little earlier, maybe you would've had a shot at it!"

So I reached out to Patrick's brother, David Donatelli. He was known as "Lil' Augie." Donatelli's elder son got that nickname as a kid, and some friends still call him that. On the phone from Florida, David told me a cool tidbit: Major League Baseball gives out rings to the umpires chosen to work each World Series. "And I have the 1967 World Series ring," he said.

"Very cool! Where do you keep it?" I asked.

"On my finger."

David was 65 in 2017. The ring from the Cardinals-Red Sox World Series "hasn't left my finger since he gave it to me when I was 25," he said. "When I pass on, I'll will it to my stepson. I'm very proud of my father and his achievements. The fact that he came from being a coal miner to a big league umpire? How can you not be proud? The guy barely got out of high school and came back from the war and said, 'I'm going to go to umpire school on the GI Bill.'"

Both David and Patrick remember when their dad returned from the famous 1967 World Series. He'd enter the house with his gigantic fiberglass umpire cases and "just unfurl his bags," Patrick recalled. On the road their dad would normally grab some baseballs for the boys. In October of 1967, he also grabbed a hat. But Augie didn't swipe it because it's valuable; he swiped it because it's sentimental. Augie had a fun and big personality and he wanted to bring a little bit of the World Series home to his sons. "And my recollection of the hat," Patrick said, "is that when I was 11 I wore it religiously. It was like I was sleeping with the hat. It was Javier's hat! A Cardinal hat! And it was a hat that Dad brought for me. It stayed with the family for quite a while. And the smell of the hat was a very distinct, kind-of-baseball aroma."

But soon, young Patrick stopped wearing it. So Dad took the cap to El Cap. All these years later, the El Cap remains, but the cap is gone. I tried to find the thing, but so it seems, under Augie Donatelli's watch was one final strikeout.

50

ADAM
WAINWRIGHT

He was a no-name pitcher suddenly thrust into a high-leverage role. Adam Wainwright was on a back field about to throw his first live batting practice of 2016, but the ace had forgotten his cleats. "So I ran into the clubhouse," Matt Bowman recalled of his first Cardinals spring training. "I brought them back and at the time I thought: *That was the most important thing I would ever do for the Cardinals, getting Adam Wainwright his cleats!*"

Bowman chuckled while sharing the story. He did become a name, finishing second in the National League in games pitched in '17. But he forever remembers the spring of '16 when he was a no-name, and Wainwright was the biggest name. "Adam was particularly—almost remarkably—helpful to me, considering my odds of making the team looked slim," Bowman said. "But he was still there as a sounding board, even as a mentor. I was certainly struck by how willing he was to help everyone out, including someone in my position."

The cool guy in class isn't also supposed to be the nice one. But such was the case with Wainwright, such *is* the case with Wainwright, and one suspects such will be the case even when No. 50 is 50, visiting Busch and spending an inordinate amount of time talking curveball grips with some rookie born the year that Wainwright was one. In the tradition of Stan Musial, Jack Buck, and Ozzie Smith, Wainwright is just a good human who happened to, along the way, become a St. Louis baseball legend. His charity work is at the level of an Albert Pujols or Jason Motte or others who dedicated their time and soul to making the less fortunate feel fortunate.

And Wainwright is just, if I may, charming. Disgustingly charming. He shares self-deprecating stories, actually enjoys public speaking, loves being a father, paints his face for big U.S. soccer games, gardens, disproportionately adores Chick-fil-A, and is comfortable being a baseball goofball with the caveat, the understanding, that when he's pitching—he's the baddest motherfucker in town. "He wants the ball in every big spot and he stepped into that role, just like Chris Carpenter or the pitchers before him," said former Cardinals outfielder Jason Heyward, now a rival with the Chicago Cubs. "He's funny every day—except for the day he's pitching."

He famously started as a reliever, closing out the 2006 National League Championship Series and World Series. And Waino actually missed the historic 2011 season due to Tommy John surgery but, of course, made a memorable speech to teammates and fans at The Knights of the Cauliflower Ear dinner. So his elite five-season span was actually within the years of 2008 to 2014. Wainwright finished second in the Cy Young voting twice...and third in the Cy Young voting twice. And his record was 103–53 with a 2.87 ERA. He struck out 1,098 batters. He walked just 293. He was stupendous. "As he got better and better, we really had twin aces with him and Carpenter," manager Tony La Russa said. "The cruel irony was in January of 2011 we had an Opening Day decision. Dave [Duncan] and I were going to reward Wainwright, and he stepped forward and said, 'No, you can't do that. Carp's the man.' That's just the real-ness of him. Adam had this burning desire to not just be a great player but be a great teammate and a great leader, and that's exactly what he became."

Wainwright had this running gag. He'd be hanging with relievers Motte and Trevor Rosenthal, "And then Waino," Motte recalled, "would be like: 'Hey Motte, remember that time I closed out a World Series and you closed out a World Series? That was pretty cool, huh? Not anybody can do that.' And I was like, 'Yeah, that was pretty cool.' And he's like, 'You're right, man, that was pretty cool.' Him just being Waino, the only way Waino could be."

Rosenthal, who became a Cards closer himself, grew close to the tall goofball. They'd talk about families, fastballs, and fantasy football. What impressed Rosenthal was how others—and how many others—also grew so close to Wainwright. "He's just a really cool person, a guy who relates to, really, anybody," Rosenthal said. "He's friends with all different people from different walks of life. You watch batting practice, and he goes out in the outfield to shag baseballs, and people are just attracted to him. Guys come over, and they just want to talk to him, be around him. He's definitely a fun guy."

Adam Wainwright rejoices after finishing off his complete-game victory in Game 5 of the 2013 National League Division Series.

If other guys, for instance, got into gardening, it might seem silly. But Waino makes even horticulture seem cool. "He really knows how to take care of the soil," Rosenthal confessed. "He's into tomatoes. He's got some nice sweet peppers. He's really getting into the agriculture. And he makes some *really* good pickles."

"They're very pickle-y," shared Cardinals first baseman Luke Voit. "Honestly, it tasted like they were from a restaurant or something. And it's nice that they're not factory made. They're very fresh."

In 2014 Wainwright manufactured the lowest ERA of his career, 2.38. He got MVP votes. He was at the top of his game, which made it even more maddening that he had to miss another season. This one was 2015—the 100-win season—and then when Waino returned, he battled more injuries and inconsistencies into the following seasons.

Always a craftsman, though, he got crafty. During spring training of 2017, for instance, Wainwright rediscovered his curveball by watching an instructional pitching video starring...Adam Wainwright. "A big part of why my curveball was so bad [in 2016] was that my grip changed without me really knowing," he shared. "I was sitting on my couch last week after a game and was going, *Where is this thing? Why is it not the same?* And I remembered I did a curveball video with Al Leiter out on the bullpen mounds over here from 2012 or '13. I looked it up on [MLB.com], 'Adam Wainwright teaching a curveball' and I realized my grip was off.

"I needed to just twist the ball a little bit more, which made the seams fit on my fingers better. It created a couple levers for me to pull off the seams. I told my wife, 'Hey, I think I just figured something out.' I went and got a ball from the bedroom and came back and said, 'Go stand about 10 feet away.' I just flipped it to her and said, 'Yeah!' I knew right away. As soon as I felt the seams coming off my fingers, I knew it was going to be better."

It was, and he cobbled together some nice starts in '17, though some other starts fell apart. He was 36, not 26. Warming up for a particular start that August, Wainwright felt discomfort in his throwing arm. He told Yadier Molina: "Stay with me. We're going to do some crazy stuff out there today." What happened next Wainwright compared to a "science fair experiment." Since he didn't have much of a fastball, he threw curveballs at a preposterous velocity—one at only 61.8 miles per hour, another that went 59. But he kept the Atlanta Braves off-balance in his five innings, earning the win (and surely a blue ribbon from the science teachers). Atlanta's manager that day, Brian Snitker, was Wainwright's manager in the minors back when they were both big league dreamers.

Growing up in Georgia, Wainwright was fixin' to be a Brave. He had three idols growing up: John Smoltz, Tom Glavine, and, of course, Greg Maddux, the best of the trio, and that's saying something, considering all three are in the Hall of Fame. Wainwright was 10 when Glavine won the Cy Young in 1991, starting an eight-year period in which those men combined for seven Cys. They made baseballs dance. Wainwright, of Brunswick, Georgia, yearned to be like them. And then, of all the teams, the Braves drafted Wainwright, a high school senior, with the 29th overall pick in 2000.

All of this, of course, makes it all the more poignant to know that the Braves organization then traded him away three years later. And of all days. On December 13, 2003, he was speaking with his girlfriend's father. The minor league pitcher had gone over there to ask if he could marry the man's daughter. A phone call interrupted Adam. He thought that day would change his life—but this?

Married and maturing, humbled and hungry, it was September 11, 2005, when Wainwright made his major league debut, pitching for the Cardinals. His first game was against the New York Mets. Thirteen months later, he faced the Mets again, throwing his famous curveball to Carlos Beltran.

[Acknowledgments]

Thank you to my wife, Angela (LaRocca) Hochman, for being my teammate and soulmate. Pretty Baby, you motivated me throughout the marathon that was this writing process. You ignite me and energize me.

Thank you to my dad, Jere Hochman, for raising me in my childhood home—Section 244, Row 5, Seats 1 and 2 of old Busch Stadium.

Thank you to my mom, Josette Hochman, for teaching me about the passion of writing and the emotional power of storytelling.

Thank you to both my parents for instilling a work ethic within me and showing me how to live life right.

Thank you to my sister, Emily Hochman, who leads the league in awesome. You have such a big heart and perfect sense of humor. I'm proud to be your brother.

Thank you to Jeff Fedotin, Josh Williams, Noah Amstadter, and all the other talented folks at Triumph Books. I sincerely appreciate your dedication and desire.

Thank you to the *St. Louis Post-Dispatch* sports editor, Roger Hensley, for allowing me to write this book—and for all the support over the years in St. Louis.

Thank you to all the journalism teachers and mentors over the years, from St. Louis' Clayton High to Mizzou to New Orleans to Denver to St. Louis, home again.

Thanks you to all the *Sports Illustrated* wordsmiths who have inspired me for decades—Steve Rushin, Rick Reilly, Gary Smith, Lee Jenkins, Austin Murphy, Tom Verducci, S.L. Price, Chris Ballard, and, of course, the late, great Frank Deford.

Thank you to all the ballplayers and managers and journalists and St. Louisans who shared their stories with me.

Finally, thank you to baseball for just being so baseball.

.

[Bibliography]

Books

Bissinger, Buzz. *3 Nights in August.* Houghton Mifflin (2005).

Broeg, Bob. *100 Greatest Moments in St. Louis Sports.* Missouri Historical Society Press (2000).

Broeg, Bob. *Redbirds: A Century of Cardinals' Baseball.* RiverCity Publishers (1988).

Eisenbath, Mike. *The Cardinals Encyclopedia.* Temple University Press (1999).

Feldmann, Doug. *St. Louis Cardinals Past & Present.* MBI Publishing (2008).

Goold, Derrick. *100 Things Cardinals Fans Should Know & Do Before They Die.* Triumph Books (2010).

Golenbock, Peter. *The Spirit of St. Louis.* Avon (2010).

Harbach, Chad. *The Art of Fielding.* Little, Brown and Co. (2011).

Halberstam, David. *October 1964.* Random House (1994).

Hornsby, Rogers. *My War with Baseball.* Coward-McCann (1962).

Jaffe, Jay. *The Cooperstown Casebook.* St. Martins (2017).

Kodner, Gary and Kodner, Oliver. *St. Louis Cardinals Uniforms & Logos—An Illustrated History.* Cardinals Hall Of Fame Productions (2016).

La Russa, Tony and Hummel, Rick. *One Last Strike.* HarperCollins (2012).

Law, Keith. *Smart Baseball.* HarperCollins (2017).

Okrent, Daniel and Wulf, Steve. *Baseball Anecdotes.* Oxford University Press (1989).

Post-Dispatch staff. *Busch Stadium Moments. The St. Louis Post-Dispatch* (2005).

Post-Dispatch staff. *Stan Musial—Baseball's Perfect Knight. The St. Louis Post-Dispatch* (2013).

Post-Dispatch staff. *We Shocked The World. The St. Louis Post-Dispatch* (2006).

Videos
2011 World Series Champions
A City on Fire—The Story of the '68 Detroit Tigers
Bull Durham
Heck of a Year
St. Louis Cardinals—The Movie
That's a Winner

Periodicals
St. Louis Post-Dispatch
Sports Illustrated
The Denver Post
ESPN The Magazine
The New York Times
Los Angeles Times
Tulsa World

Websites
baseball-reference.com
fangraphs.com
espn.com
mlb.com
sabr.org/bio
si.com/vault
vivaelbirdos.com
youtube.com

[About the Author]

Benjamin Hochman, a St. Louis native, is a sports columnist for the *St. Louis Post-Dispatch*. Hochman studied journalism at Mizzou, graduating in 2002. From there, he became a sports reporter at *The Times-Picayune* and *The Denver Post*, becoming a columnist for *The Post* in 2013. In 2015 he was offered his dream job—sports columnist at his hometown paper.

Over the years he has won numerous writing awards, notably the Associated Press Sports Editors' annual honors as both a beat writer and a columnist. Hochman previously wrote the book *Fourth-And-New Orleans,* which was published in 2007, about Hurricane Katrina and football. On July 1, 2017, Hochman married a St. Louis girl, Angela LaRocca. They live in Clayton, Missouri.